Contents

Red Letter Day	7
Obscure Individuals	17
Dear Oliver	29
How to Read a Letter	71
The Coming Out Letter	95
To Whom It May Concern	117
How to Write a Letter	129
The Business Letter	155
Polly	175
What's in a Name?	191
Local Hero	213
Dear Heroix	237
Silence Like a Bruise	259
The Failure of Language	291
Afterword	309
Acknowledgements, image credits, notes, about the author, Northe family tree	320

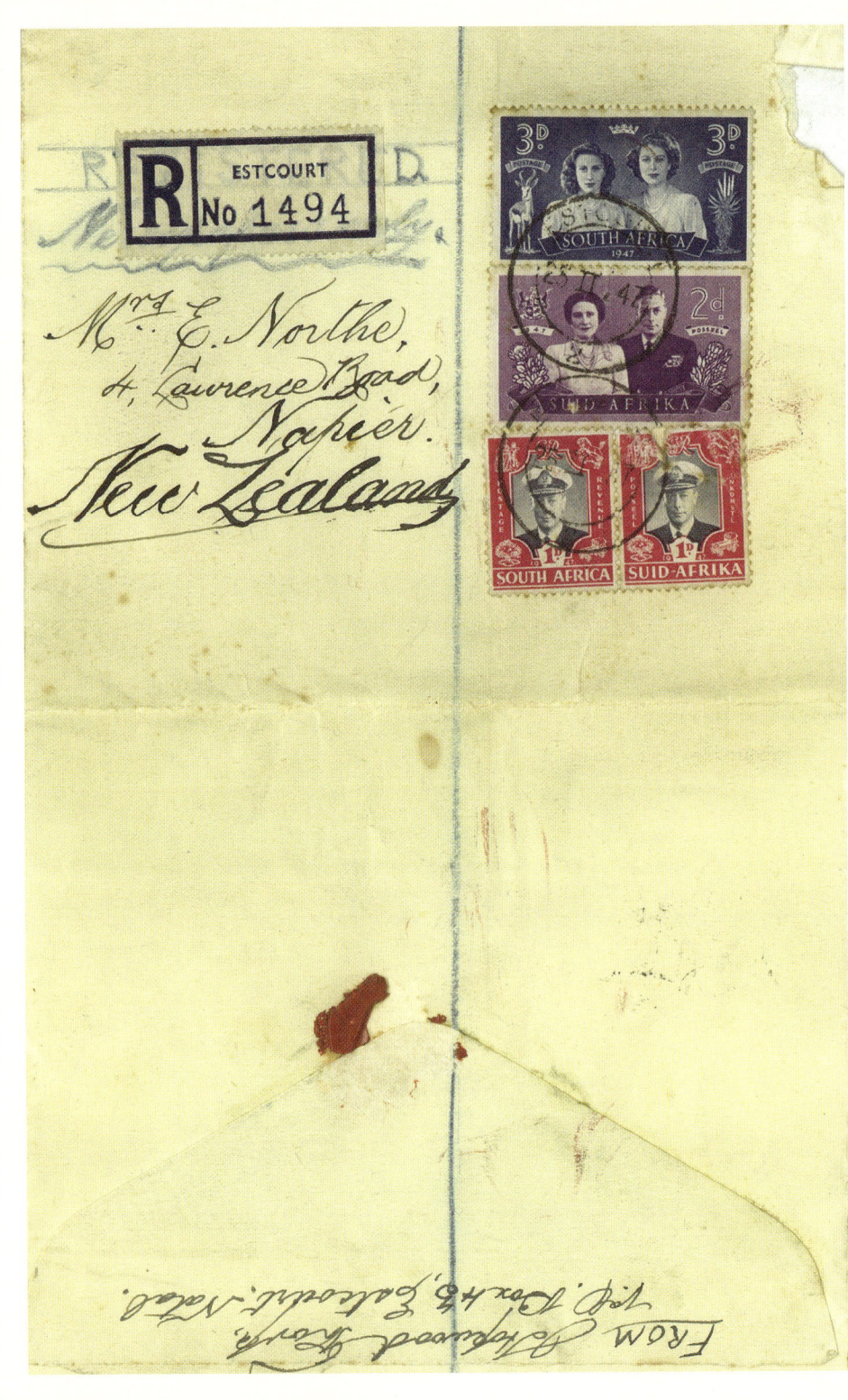

Dear Oliver

The magic holiday at Hicks Bay. Bess and her two sons Peter and Russell, 1960.

Uncovering a Pākehā history

PETER WELLS

MASSEY UNIVERSITY PRESS

...management of the Animals now Entrusted to you. Be very par[ticular] with regard to the monkeys. You had better make a contract with Hyde or some other Barber in Hastings, to come and dress the monkeys hair and Moustaches at regular days, and should they take cold and their Eyes become red put a Cabbage leaf poultice on their heads and see their finger & toe nails are not allowed to grow too long. And **Mind** they must not on any account have "Roast Turkey" for dinner. As regards the Crocodiles and Alligators, dont let them go to bed with wet skins. rub them dry; before they go to Roost amongst the willows and notice particular, if their Wing feathers are beginning to sh[ow] ... but out next month. You will have to Anchor them about ... will leave you. The Camels, Dromedady's, Kangaroos, and ... require careful attention. dont give them any Curie. And with ... Tigers, you must be particularly careful in your daily in... ...sh, and Talons. See that they are cleaned, washed and filed ... give them more than half a Picanniny a day Each, unless you can ... ...ip load of Picanninies from Africa, then you may give them a t... think of all the items necessary for your guidance in this great ... ...probably see you before you start with the Show up the Country. ...ake final rules and regulations. N.B. Keep down the Expenses. ...

Red Letter Day

OPPOSITE

A letter sent to my grandmother from South Africa in 1947: 'If you got a letter it was exciting.'

As with all change, you lose some things, you gain others. The digital present is full of marvels, but it isn't hard to think that something has been lost. Is it as basic as speed versus silence?

THE INTERCONNECTEDNESS HAS ALREADY BECOME indispensable, but its noise has rendered older media like cinema and books almost redundant. Almost. But not completely. Just as silence is powerful, so is reading a well-argued book of non-fiction or a vividly imagined novel — these have their own unique qualities.

But some things seem to have been left behind. The personal letter is one of them. So few people write letters anymore, a handwritten letter has become something really special. A gesture outside the norm. Instead we punch out illiterate emails and texts, no longer bothering to be grammatical, let alone witty and insightful. Speed is all. We all use the new technologies while tacitly accepting that data collection is screening or filtering what we write, collecting our likes and tastes so we can be better exploited and even, in a political sense, utilised when needed. In abandoning the letter, which was essentially private, we have lost something really important — a kind of freedom.

The derogatory term for letters is 'snail mail'. This is a wry comment on the slowness involved in writing a letter, but also on the fact that the writer had to take the stamped envelope to a letterbox, from where it was collected, sorted and then, some time later — it could be days, it could be weeks — it arrived in the letterbox of the addressee.

If you got a letter, it was exciting. Sometimes you even waited to open it, as if saving a surprise. If the letter was from a lover or a particular friend you could carry that letter around with you in your bag. Your fingers might touch it when you were feeling tense. You could get the letter out and find another meaning in a sentence. The very handwriting was the signature of a soul.

You can tell I'm a fan of the letter. In fact I still write letters to a friend, a fellow author, who is similarly committed to the humane qualities inherent in what one might call 'slow communication'. But then letters were always a part of my life. My mother's family — her mother and two sisters — lived in separate cities in New Zealand. Nobody ever called long-distance to chat in my childhood. Right up until the 1970s toll calls were for emergencies and sparked a rush of adrenalin: a toll call presaged a crisis of some kind. Letters, on the other hand, were cheap, and they were part of the currency of family life. Each week a letter from my grandmother in Napier, with its signature pale-blue Basildon Bond envelope (signalling 'quality'), dropped into our letterbox in Point Chevalier in Auckland. The address would be in my grandmother's flowing handwriting — she was born in 1883 and so it had the hint of copperplate about it. She used a fountain pen, and the ink was either radiant blue or the more sober blue-black. My grandmother died in 1967. She never used a ballpoint.

These letters provided a view of village life as detailed as Elizabeth Gaskell's *Cranford*, but they were such common currency that they were thrown out after a certain period of time. (The latest letter was usually saved so that you could refer back to it to see if there was anything you needed to answer.)

Just a handful survived. And when I had the onerous task of shifting my mother out of what passed, by then, for the family home, I found various letters dotted all over the house. An historian friend, knowing the pressure on the middle-aged 'child' clearing out a parent's house, advised me to get a box and throw anything into it that I might want to look at later. (You can get very easily carried away with 'cleansing the past'.)

I did this, saving, for whatever reason, the bunch of telegrams sent to my parents when they wed three months into the Second World War; childhood letters from a time when my brother's fingers — and mine — could hardly model the words; a wartime aerogramme from my mother to my father while he was fighting overseas; a letter from my sage grandfather in the final months before he died; and a delightful collection of letters written in highly ornate copperplate, in coloured inks, and sent to my eight-year-old grandmother by a grown man in the 1890s — a time when adult–child relations were viewed with less suspicion.

Years later I looked through them. It was then that this book occurred to me. I could see that the letters were part of an overall narrative, one that I knew implicitly: the story of an ordinary Pākehā family and how they made sense of their lives. I knew there were other, older letters, too, which a great-uncle had unearthed in the 1950s. These went back to the 1840s and traced that fracture line when my mother's family, the Northes, left Cornwall forever and made New Zealand their home. In this sense the letters traced an archetypal journey from the period of what has been called 'the Anglophone settler explosion', one of the great migratory patterns in history, when 20 million people left Britain and Ireland to create homes in other places and spaces.[1] It was a migration that changed the world.

I began to see the letters in a wider context. A letter was once part of how you experienced being human — how we saw, thought, imagined, expressed ourselves. Letters are history written as a part-time serial, with many key parts lost. But from what is left we can extrapolate and fill in, imagine, and set people and events in the context of time and place. This makes them sound very grand, but really the letters I'm talking about are just the haphazard communications of an ordinary Pākehā New Zealand family over time — the sort of detritus that remains when the past evaporates and leaves behind a certain number of exhibits, none of which make any claim to literary or historical greatness. I decided their very ordinariness was what made these letters interesting. They showed the history of a family not notable for anything in particular — except its quiet genius in being itself.

I began to form the idea of writing a book based on what these letters could tell us about the past. Part of living in digital time is that we've been robbed of a sense of chronology. There is simply the relevant now and the irrelevant past. Yet physically, psychologically, we are still subject to chronology — we are young, we grow old. And as you grow old, increasingly you look back. The past, which seemed at one time boring or incomprehensible, silently shifts into a shape that begins to make sense. You realise how you misunderstood things, how you didn't know vital pieces of information about your parents' lives, their childhoods, even their emotional states. The same goes for all the generations before. You are not only who you are — the unique genetic experiment that is a one-off — but you are also a composite of all the generations that went before. The past speaks through us.

I put the letters into some form of chronological order and decided I would write a book about my family. This is, I thought, what we do when, strictly speaking, we no longer have a family. We conjure one out of the past. This is not so strange. It's how the past is redefined, after all. We walk back into the past and recognise things we overlooked in our urgency to keep moving ahead.

THE JOURNEY OF MY ANCESTORS from Britain to New Zealand could be said to be the ur-journey of so many Pākehā New Zealanders. We are over-familiar with its shape — poverty in the homeland, struggle across the seas, the hard impact on landing. Scrabbling around for a way to survive. Gradually, some success as adaptation takes over, accompanied by a loss of memory about origins as the present obscures a now-distant past. Even the act of looking back — the search for genealogical origins — is a Pākehā cliché. Why do it?

Richard Holmes, author of *Footsteps: Adventures of a Romantic Biographer*, has defined the biographical enterprise as 'a handshake across time': 'It is an act of human solidarity, and in its own way an act of recognition and love.'[2] Pākehā on the whole do not love ourselves. We may laugh at ourselves. We rarely understand ourselves. There is a kind of numbness here, a mute silence. But it also has something to do with shame.

Pākehā stand in a strange and controversial relationship to history in Aotearoa. In my lifetime we have gone from being slightly unreal heroic 'pioneers' to villainous exploiters of Māori culture and thieves of Māori land. Today we live with the psychological displacement of being defined by what we are not: we are no longer 'pioneers', 'settlers' or 'colonists'; we have been stripped of identity and returned to the present simply as 'non-Māori'. This negative tautology expresses our predicament. Effectively it delivers us back to a psychological homelessness. We are no longer Pākehā with whom Māori had their first few centuries of contact, the outcome of which created the contemporary world in which we live. We're the shape of a silhouette without a face. Maybe it's my wish to paint this face in, to personalise a little of our Pākehā past, that has led me to write this book.

When later in life I turned out to be a writer, I asked myself where this strangely ambiguous gift had come from. Other writers had grandparents who told mythic stories from Ireland or the Māori world.

It took me a long time to recognise I had gotten my storytelling streak from my mother. It was not that she was so much a storyteller as a person who had an emphatic and — I realised as I got older — highly individual view of the world. Part of this view of the world was predicated on her family.

It's interesting what you don't know about yourself. Part of ageing is a kind of filling in of blanks, areas that you were not even aware existed, let alone understood, were highly influential on the way you saw life. My blank was this. I had not realised that my mother's constant reference to her family arose precisely because her family was no longer around her.

This needs explaining. My mother was born in Napier to a family who had made Napier their home in 1858. This family had hardly ventured further in all the subsequent years. In 1939, a few months into the war, she married my father, Gordon, who came from another small town to the north. Together they shifted to Auckland. My mother never came back, except for relatively fleeting visits. I grew up in an atmosphere saturated with stories about Napier, the dramas of the 1931 earthquake and her family's central role in Napier's development.

It was only when I came to live in Napier in 2007 — drawn back by the magnetic force of all her childhood stories — that I came to a different understanding. My mother's family was not, in fact, central to the development of the small town. They were simply one of any number of commercial families who had helped create its infrastructure, and had enriched themselves to varying degrees.

My understanding took another step when, after it became clear my mother could no longer look after herself, I brought her back to live in Napier. She was then ninety-two. I knew the change from being an independent woman in charge of her own life to living in a small studio in a retirement village, without a car, would be difficult. But what I had not factored in was something else entirely. I had not realised my mother regarded it as one of her achievements that she had managed to get away from the claustrophobic confines of a small town and create a flourishing social life in the biggest city in New Zealand. I had not understood that she actually rather despised the provincial town she had come from.

From childhood onwards, I had only been fed stories expressing her love of her family — and, seemingly indivisibly, of Napier. But the fact is her affection was predicated on distance, on missing close links, on her own position in a small society in which she had been known, her parents were known, her grandparents were known. (This is the fixative of small-town life. It is not always a charitable view.) I never knew this. I never sensed this.

As it was, I had come to the end of my own love affair with Napier. I had shifted here with my partner, Douglas Lloyd Jenkins, and I had integrated myself into the history of the town. It had given me the subject matter for two substantial books. But at the end of eight years there was a disillusioning event. Douglas was director of the museum and art gallery in Napier. After it was rebuilt, it became mired in a bitter dispute, as is not unusual in these cases, and I began to experience what Anthony Trollope so feelingly called 'the true hatred of provincial life'.[3]

Yet now I could not leave. My mother's presence necessitated my staying, or at least returning with the regularity of a good son. I would henceforth live in the town in the mood of someone recovering from a love affair: I looked about me ruefully, but with a glance made sharper by a sense of reality.

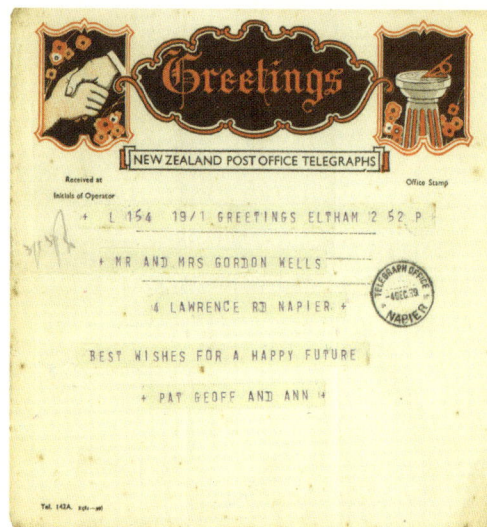

ABOVE
Bess as a baby, with her parents Ern and Jess and sisters Jean and Patti in 1916. They were a close, affectionate family, everyone with a nickname.

CENTRE
Wedding cables kept in a trunk.

BELOW
Visiting Bess at her retirement village for the ritual of tea.

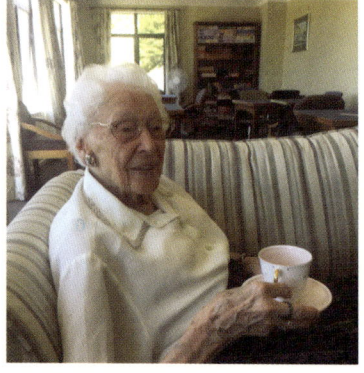

ABOVE

The R. Northe & Sons yard in Napier. Coal was a dirty but lucrative business.

CENTRE

Bess and Jess, her mother, thought alike.

BELOW

A rare photo of my family together on graduation day, Auckland, 1974.

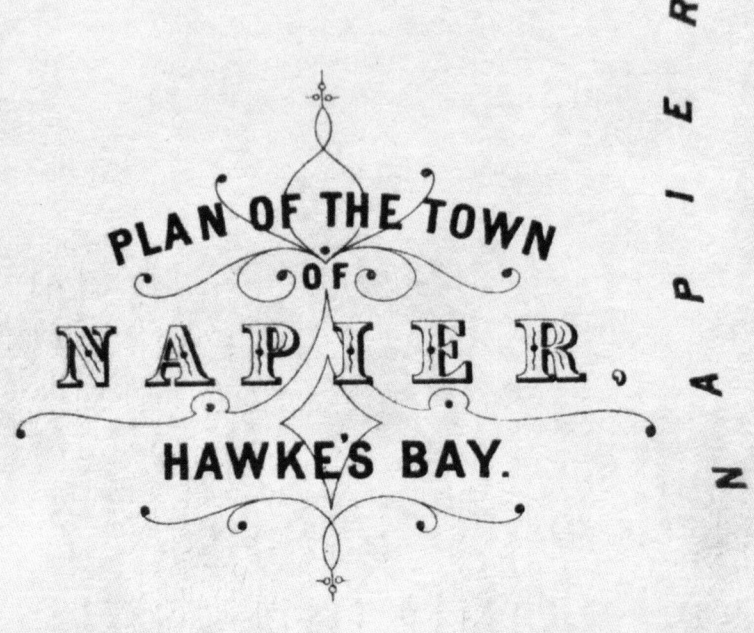

Obscure Individuals

OPPOSITE
Part of Alfred Domett's map of the new town of Napier: 'I had a wish to describe a world that was on the very point of vanishing.'

It began with a beautiful plan on paper, drawn up by a dreamer.[1] Alfred Domett was an English poet who drew the original map of Napier. But, like so many migrants to New Zealand, he was also a main-chancer. He had not gone to the ends of the earth without hoping he could upwardly mobilise. This did not quite happen in Napier.

MUCH LATER, AFTER HIS PLANS for a Hawke's Bay sheep run had come to nothing, he wrote to Superintendent Donald McLean: 'I trust you are by degrees "feathering your nest" — a process which Scotch birds are generally said to understand very well.' He could not get anything better in Hawke's Bay, he wrote, than 'a crow's nest of sticks or an ostrich's of scraped sand . . . Oh Moab is my washpot,' he bewailed.[2]

This mixture of dream and barren reality was typical of the experience of many who came to New Zealand. Domett was given the job of naming the central grid of Napier's streets (when really it was no more than a fantasy). He reached up to the top shelf of British writers he admired — Dickens, Tennyson, Browning. He did this to offset the possibility that his beautiful plan might be sullied by the names of local Pākehā — or, as he scoffingly called them, 'obscure individuals . . . (ruffians probably, and runaway convicts) whose names render the places themselves distasteful'.[3]

Since my family, the Northes, were among the 'obscure individuals' after whom a Napier street was eventually named, this is a fitting juncture at which to introduce the Northes within the wider world of Napier. (And when I introduce historical Napier itself, I am really remarking on it as a representative colonial space, utterly itself in its fixations and the geographic specificity of place — hill, swamp, ocean — but really just like one hundred thousand colonial towns scattered all over the empire.) The Northes, too, could be said to be representative of many ordinary migrants to New Zealand, landing with a thud and after a profound culture shock, awakening to financial opportunity in whatever form they could find it. They too began 'feathering their nests'.

NAMING CHANGES EVERYTHING. And since Domett was given the job of christening the new town, it was he who chose the name of Napier. This had a specific contemporary relevance. In 1857, the British Empire experienced a shocking moment, the Indian Mutiny, an uprising against British rule by Indian soldiers of the Bengal Army in which British men, women and children were hacked to death — a brutal reminder that the imperial overlords were made only of flesh. It caused a sense of panic. The British Empire, anyway, was a fragile construct, held together by a surprisingly small number of people. To say Napier was named after a moment of panic is, however, wrong. Napier, named after General Napier (and Clive and Havelock and Delhi Road and Scinde Island and all the other 'Indian' names of Hawke's Bay), celebrates not the shock so much as *the fight back*. The new names celebrated people — and battles and events — famous at the time for overcoming a dreadful moment of imperial self-doubt.

Yet the kernel was a moment of devastating terror. White fright lay behind the name; the thought that British men — but in particular British women and children, too — had been somehow trapped inside a dark and stinking room, while outside was an endless sea of infidels, people of a different colour, desperate to get inside that room and start hacking.[4]

Napier was fiercely isolated. In the 1850s it was virtually impossible to reach it overland. There were no roads, only foot tracks. Auckland was at best two or three days' sail away, as was Wellington to the south. The settlement looked out to sea or, if it looked inland, it was to country inhabited almost entirely by Māori.

When two local iwi prepared for inter-tribal war, the few whalers, storekeepers and Pākehā dribs and drabs who had arrived in Napier petitioned the government for protection. A resident part of the British Imperial Army, the 65th Regiment, arrived on 14 February 1858 and occupied the most brilliant strategic position on the top of Mataruahou, soon to be renamed Scinde Island, after the Battle of Scinde. The fort had an unparalleled 360-degree view of a landscape over which the soldiers had to be constantly on watch. Death by hacking was only a blink away.

Hence the new institutions of the town had, by the 1860s, a kind of guarded quality to them. They included not only Government Buildings for administration and court cases, but also the necessary corollary — a prison. The population was so small that this had to double as a lunatic asylum and as a debtors' prison. There was also the fort on the top of Scinde Island, a lookout — a place to which people could rush and hide when the hacking was about to begin. It is here that Sergeant John Northe, the lynchpin between Britain and New Zealand in our story, comes in. He was the fort's barrack sergeant, one of its miniature emperors, but also its sweeper and bar manager and landlord's representative: a deeply ambiguous position.

The Napier Barracks was made of battens of stout wood and uprights — the same practical, unbeautiful design as the prison. It was surrounded by an eight-foot barricade of rammed earth. For a while the officers lived nearby in houses made of raupō, while the ordinary ranks like John Northe, his wife and family of nine suffered under tents cut into the wedge of the hill itself, in the Onepoto Gully. It was provisional and basic. It looked like it could all vanish in a blink.

Down at the port, on the eastern side of the hill, was a wharf and, in time, pubs and brothels and a slaughter house. The port was the reason for the town's existence, and became a key stopping-off point between Auckland, the old capital, and Wellington, the new capital, commonly called the Empire City or, more derogatively, the Dusty City. It processed onto ships whatever the surrounding landscape could export: flax, wool, whale oil. It also took in everything the province needed: top hats, stoves, glacé leather high-heeled shoes, corrugated iron, books, valerian, cases of whiskey. And gradually a town grew up on diametrically the other side of 'Scinde Island' — basically on the only piece of flat land there was. (Domett's private view of Napier was that it was 'a hopeless spot for a town site . . . a precipitous island of barren, uninhabited ridges covered with fern and rough grass dissected by gorges and ravines, with a narrow strip of shingle skirting the cliffs, and joined by the mainland south by a five mile shingle bank'.)[5] Napier's streets were gradually filled with tiny wooden cottages; shops appeared, a theatre, a photography studio. Hotels proliferated, and altogether 'the beautiful plan' on paper started to have a dynamism all its own. What started out as a dream had by the 1870s become a reality.

IN 1871 NAPIER HAD A population of 2179, an increase of 352 since the census of 1867. (Some 165 births were registered in the calendar year 1870 alone.) There was an almost equal number of males (1164) and females (1015). To give some sense of scale, Wellington's population at the same time was 7890.

This increase overall was quite some accomplishment, since the years between 1867 and 1871 had been a harrowing period of war, insecurity and financial depression. When the East Cape was ravaged by the prophet-warrior Te Kooti Arikirangi, Napier was vulnerable. There were fears it would be sacked and burnt to the ground, its Pākehā population slaughtered. Ngāti Kahungunu, for reasons of self-interest as much as anything (they leased land to many settlers), provided a protective shell around the small, isolated settlement. The sense of paranoia faded.

Then in 1871 the price of wool began to rise with the beautiful ease of a dream, so Napier's wealth increased. By the end of 1871, for example, Napier's banks held one-quarter of the nation's savings. This financial x-ray gives us a sense of Napier's position in the hierarchy of towns in New Zealand, although photographs of the period tend to show the place as empty, and as provisional as a tent.

Maybe the sense of overwhelming isolation gave the town a febrility, a hyper-activity which led to the creation of a great many clubs and associations. If Richard Halkett Lord, the London-born editor of Napier's *Daily Telegraph* and friend of Charles Dickens, drawled that 'dullness reigns supreme in Napier', this was offset by the seemingly agitated tadpole swarm of activities created by energetic individuals who went out of their way to provide diversions.[6] The fact is a town with a population of 2716 had an astonishing *three* newspapers.

The level of alcohol consumption was remarkable, too. Napier, like every colonial outpost of the Empire, was saturated in alcohol. In 1871 three breweries turned out 180 barrels of beer per month, the equivalent of 12 gallons of beer for every man, woman and child in the province. In the same year 10,440 gallons of spirits were imported. You could say people drank for enjoyment, but I feel drinking helped people who were profoundly affected by loss. Every migrant loses his or her country, loses the tang of the air they knew, the individual rhythms of seasons, the comfort of known faces. Every migrant awakes to a new day with a sense of psychic dislocation. For some this would be bearable. But for others, caught in the long-term drudgery of colonial life, there was only alcohol to soften the pain.

The lure of alcohol was a dangerous one for the lost souls of colonial New Zealand — Pākehā *and* Māori. For the working classes it was especially ruinous. The difference between a man drinking and a man sober was often the difference between a modicum of prosperity or children scavenging for food and resorting to petty crime. Children themselves often started drinking at an early age. For many people, colonial New Zealand was less a mythic land of plenty than a cruel and unsparing universe.

EVERY FEW DAYS I VISIT my mother. Often as I walk into her room Bess raises her face, but I can tell she is not sure who I am. She waits till she hears my voice — at this point she recognises me. I watch the softening of the muscles on her face as she relaxes into a smile. The words we exchange go back to childhood. They could be the calls of birds in a tree. 'Hello, Pete,' she'll say, using the childhood version of my name. 'Hi there, Mum,' I'll say, with my own special lightness of intonation, and then I'll move forward and brush my lips across her raised face, just by her left cheekbone.

We'll settle then into a ritual that is as fixed in its way as a pavane. This involves 'having a cup of tea'. This deploys the archaic use of a teapot, tea leaves, two porcelain cups, a milk jug — and usually a plate for biscuits that come out of a biscuit tin. Occasionally my mother will comment on why, of all the cake tins she possessed, I selected 'such an old one' to take into the exile of her retirement village. I do not say that is precisely why I saved it. (It is a wartime cake tin and shows Santa Claus parachuting from a plane into a snowy fantasy English landscape.)

This hints at the nature of our relationship. I am the custodian of the past while my mother is freed from the clammy hold of all the old connections. Why have I kept myself as curator? It imprisons me as much as it defines me. You could say I hold on to all the threads of the past because they offer some comfort.

My mother's memory, at ninety-eight, has all but gone. That is, she recalls certain things but not necessarily in the right order. One day Bess said to me, 'What did Russell die of, Pete?' This was a reference to my elder brother, her only other child. I hesitated a moment before giving in to the gravity of truth.

'AIDS, Mum.'

'What?'

'AIDS. You know. HIV.'

It was almost certainly not the answer she wanted. Or expected.

After less than a minute, she repeated the question.

'What did Russell die of, Pete?'

I reflected for only a nanosecond on the fact that my brother's death — now almost a quarter of a century ago — was an event so tragic that my mother lost her reason. It broke her life in two as effectively as when a plate is smashed right down the middle. She had eventually gained wisdom and stature through the act of acceptance — accepting the unacceptable, I suppose you could say. But now it was being winnowed away by the scouring process of memory loss.

I repeated the statement about AIDS, aware that it seemed almost brutal. Once again she appeared to both accept the statement and, simultaneously, subsume it in the endless rollback of memory breaking apart. I was used to this. In some ways it exhausted me. My actions were, I knew, those of a man eternally rolling the Sisyphus wheel up the hill. The fact I was prepared to do this was perhaps a sign of my desperation. There was only my mother left — I had no children, no further family. But we were locked in a symbiotic relationship that I knew would soon enough have an endpoint. The very nearness of this endpoint — a year, two years, five years, eight years — meant I continued on with what some people might see as a pathetic charade.

Yet the reality was we still had a warm, close relationship that was not without its pleasures.

'Where is Jean?' she asked me one day. She was referring to her elder sister, who had at times deployed the haughty viewpoint of an older sibling who sees further because they have been alive longer.

'Aunty Jean died in 1984, Mum,' I said, thinking quickly. 'You were in the hospital with her the night she died. You were sleeping in the same room.'

I filled in details that were important to me, that had been handed over to me, much as important plans of a past military success might be handed over to provide useful intelligence in the future. (How to deal with death. How to behave in an emergency. How to go into the house of death and make yourself at home.)

'Really?' she said to me, not entirely convinced.

'Yes, it's almost thirty years ago now,' I said by way of fastening the date into a firm chronology.

'What year are we now?'

(I had my uses.)

'2014.'

'Well, it's no wonder I haven't had a letter from her lately,' Bess said. 'I was just thinking the other day, a letter from her is definitely overdue.'

I burst out laughing, and she, catching my lilt, laughed too.

In this shared pleasure lay the reason I still dropped in to visit my mother every few days. I did this to check on her, but I did it as much to try to keep her in some sort of chronological sequence. I knew she dreaded losing her studio apartment and being consigned to the hospital wing where you had your own room but were stripped of the last vestiges of independence.

Her doctor had told me in a matter-of-fact way that Bess was suffering

LEFT
Bess's sisters saw her as spoilt. 'I could do no wrong,' she told me.

CENTRE
Bess in her prime, when she was working as the receptionist at Napier's Masonic Hotel.

BELOW
Bess (right) with a friend at a children's party.

dementia. He said it was just luck whether she reacted to her dementia in a violent way, 'in which case there was a further place that she could be placed', or whether she accepted it calmly, in which case she could stay in the hospital wing.

This may have been another reason for my frequent visits. It was one of the last services I could do for her. But it was also something more. My mother has always been at the core of my understanding of the past. It was through her that I had entered the archway to the past and walked inside. This had been immensely productive — I had made films and books that were the product of my attempt to understand, synthesise, perhaps even mythologise the stories and the discrepancies within the stories she had told me.

So my visits to her were protective, but they were also a way of touching, almost superstitiously, the blarney stone of the past. I sensed it was all about to vanish. I would be left. And then I would be the repository of all the stories.

There was a further fact. I was now foreseeing my own death in the longer term. And, feeling the hour was late, I had begun to feel impatience with the stale stories of the past. I had come to understand how, if these stories had been a source of creativity, they had also — powerful as myths — confined me and even created distortions in my own personality. They had inhibited me and created aspects of my personality I had come to see as faults. I was almost spontaneously snobbish, or rather the way I saw people reflected some of the anxieties that arose from my mother's family's perspective on their origins. I lacked the broad strength of the uninhibited. I had had to fight my way towards understanding my own perspective across what now seemed a battlefield of redundant mores and out-of-date ideals.

I felt a curious mix of impatience, sorrow, regret, anger and a deeper sense that soon it was all going to vanish completely. All I could do to retain it was to fight to the close with the only weapon I possessed — my own intelligence deployed in the form that had become my closest friend and ally. Words.

WHEN I WAS WRESTLING WITH the problem of how to make this book speak to the future, I found myself writing a letter to the newest member of the extended family: a baby whose arrival is a delightful surprise. The letter to him is like a hand reaching into a future I will in time vacate. (That 'handshake with history'.)

I had a wish to describe a world on the very cusp of vanishing. I wanted to explain — explain a little about what had formed me, which in turn is an explanation of the way this world, or at least my understanding of it, was shaped. With this in mind, I began writing a letter to an eight-month-old child who may or may not ever read it.

Let me explain who this child is. His name is Oliver and he lives in San Francisco, and he came, with his two mothers, to Napier. His grandmother is my cousin. My mother is his great-aunt.

I wanted to explain to him this past which is slipping away — the past of his colonial New Zealand family, and even the life trajectory of someone like me who fought for human rights for gay men and women (as we once called the struggle). How life has changed beyond recognition, while accepting it will change again profoundly in his lifetime. In writing the letter I seemed to find a way of talking — explaining, making sense — that looked at the past but with an eye to how inexplicable it might be to the future.

So in a larger sense this is book about family letters, which neurologist Oliver Sacks correctly described as 'a corrective against the deceits of memory'.[7] It functions as biography and autobiography (and social history), but it also looks and meditates on an uneasy present. Some people say we are living through the Anthropocene Period, when the human impact on the ecosystem is so critical that extinction of the species is possible. Other people describe this as a time of 'acceleration', when changes are so fast and transformational that many people struggle to keep up, feel left behind. I am very aware of the fragility of the present. So if this book is about family letters set in a past on the point of vanishing, it is also, in the form of 'A Letter to Oliver', my letter to the future.

Dear Oliver

OPPOSITE
Bess with Pauline, her niece's daughter, and Pauline's son Oliver: 'Your ancestors had this quality of toughness.'

This is a letter to try to explain a world that is receding so fast it will have vanished entirely by the time you are a young man. I myself might even be dead. Certainly you will have trouble working out who I am. Let me explain.

YOUR GRANDMOTHER GERALDINE IS MY cousin. Geraldine and I had the same formidable grandmother. And the Northe family from which we are both descended on our mothers' side was a formative influence on Geraldine, me, and our other three cousins. You see, our family is small. It's like a compact family firm, one that appeared for a while to proliferate — my grandfather had seven brothers — then it contracted.

Part of this contraction was that my brother and I were gay. We grew up in a time when gay men and women did not have families. It was biologically impossible. If a gay man or woman wished to have a child they might instead assume a different persona, swallow their real self and pretend to be heterosexual. Then they could have children. And often those children grew up not knowing their father or mother was actually gay. Life is different now — better in many ways — and I am glad of it.

But take it from me, we are related — just.

I am telling you this story because I want to explain to you the New Zealand side of your family. Well, your mother is not New Zealand-born and your grandmother Geraldine, though born in New Zealand, has lived in Canada much longer than she ever lived here in New Zealand (which will probably be called Aotearoa by the time you read this). But Geraldine is very much a New Zealander. Her view of life was formed by her childhood, and by her early life in New Zealand.

Your grandfather Grant — who married Geraldine — was also born a New Zealander, so that this part of your past — so distant as to appear imaginary to you to whom the real world is everything — yet coursed through the memories of your grandparents, provided them with a moral basis to make decisions about the world. A country forms you whether you are aware of it or not. Its weather, the form of its landscape, the way people murmur, queue, clap, argue. But it's even more than that. Because on both your grandmother's and your grandfather's side of the family you are descended from colonists — people who now stand on the wrong side of history, who have no claim for sympathy or empathy, who stole land from indigenous people, crippled their souls, sold their treasures and most of all supplanted what was native to the landscape with a false identity, all based on the distant land from which these colonists came.

You will believe all this. It is the only story that can be told. Yet there is never one story. Life is made up of many contrasting stories, many of which conflict at certain points. And from these conflicting, raw edges comes a sense of the varied hues of truth. But this is getting too complicated. Let's simplify things by saying I will try to explain a little what it was like to be born into a colonial family, long after Aotearoa ceased to be a colony: yet this is a fact — a colony can remain inside your head, in the pinpoint of the pupil of your eyes. You could hear it in what your grandmother said without thinking. You observed it in the way things seemed so fixed. Then the world changed all around you to the extent that the past dropped away, fell off the edge of time and vanished to become some form of space junk. But this is getting too complicated also.

Let me just say this. The past lies inside me. (Just as the past lies inside you, although you will not be aware of this yet.) My grandmother Jessie Northe — she was born in the nineteenth century, in 1883 — is inside me as I sit here writing. This grandmother was a snob. You may not know what a snob is. A snob is a socially anxious person who is constantly on guard to cover over what they feel are their inferior origins. Snobs can be quite difficult people to be around, as they are judgmental and nearly always observant. This is because they are always minding what was called their p's and q's. (This means being overly polite, careful of what you say and do. In my childhood, repression was seen as a form of good manners. If you blurted out something it was seen as a failure in self-restraint, rather than 'being honest'.)

Snobbery was particularly potent among the British, because Britain had experienced the industrial revolution — that thing that changed the planet, possibly wrecking it — before any other country on earth. It did two things: it changed an established class system by pushing up people who suddenly had to learn manners and ways of dressing and eating and sitting they had never known before, and this made them very anxious; and it made Britain, which today may no longer even be a united kingdom, into a ferociously powerful dynamo of a nation, spilling out from itself vast floods of 'waste' population who spurted all around the globe.

This is how your New Zealand ancestors got to be in a place about as far from Britain as you could get. They were poor people who needed to leave an overpopulated tiny island and set out to find . . . anything, really, that might be better than the straitened lives they left behind. And when they set sail, they did leave the past behind. In the 1840s, very few people went back. Once you sailed off in a tiny boat, usually crowded below decks like cattle, nauseous and seasick, it was forever.

LEFT
Snobbery was rife in colonial society. My grandmother regularly consulted this etiquette book for guidance.

CENTRE
My grandmother's calling card.

BELOW
A saucer from the family tea set that miraculously survived the Napier earthquake.

But to go back to my grandmother, Jessie Isobel Purvis, as she was christened. (Christening meant you were introduced to the Christian church as a baby in a ceremony attended by family and friends. You became a Christian.) She is your great-great-grandmother, hence so distant to you as to seem a fantasy, a person of no possible importance in who you are. You are right. And wrong. Some tiny part of you will be informed by her, just because Geraldine, your own grandmother, carries part of her own grandmother's dynamic personality, her wry sense of humour and pleasure in the absurdities of life. Why is life absurd? Because we all live with contradictions and have to make sense of them. That is part of being human — matching up things that don't seem to match.

Jessie was born in Hastings, in Hawke's Bay in New Zealand. She was the daughter of a man born in Scotland, on the very border between England and Scotland. It was said he could stand with one foot in England and the other foot in Scotland. When my mother was small she thought this made her much-loved grandfather into a kind of giant, a figure of marvellous intrigue.

His name was William Purvis, and when Jessie was born he was a coachman. A coachman was in a way like a chauffeur, but different from a chauffeur in that he personally attended to the horses which were harnessed to pull a carriage along. A coachman needed knowledge of horses, how to groom them, how to look after them when they were sick. But a good coachman also had to look rather magnificent on a carriage. He was the personification of his employers. They could be miserable, misshapen people. But it mattered that their servants were fair-formed, handsome and capable. That was your great-great-great-grandfather William — a handsome, capable, even dandyish young man with a love of jewellery, tending to his magnificent auburn hair, which he wore in a wave high on his head.

He was born in 1850. He met his future wife Betsy in the fashionable town of Bath in England. Betsy was New Zealand-born. She was born in 1845, so was a very early New Zealander, or, to put it another way, a very early colonial child. She was born with the mud of Titahi Bay under her toenails. She could walk for miles and miles and miles. She knew no other land than New Zealand. And in fact my own mother told a story about her grandmother, Betsy, and her annual childhood outing. This was when the family walked the 25 kilometres into Wellington, which was 'town'.

There they attended a Sunday School picnic — probably with running races, juggling and some sort of sweet. It was the high point of a hard-working year. But at the end of a long day, Betsy had to turn into a beast of burden. She had to carry on her back a heavy sack of flour. Bowed down with the weight of flour, she would walk along the shore, climb hills, skid down banks until finally, exhausted and in the gloaming dark, the family would arrive back at their tiny wooden cottage, open the door and seek out their beds.

Betsy Bartlett was resourceful. There was very little work for poorer girls when she came of age — probably at ten or eleven — other than 'going into service'. Going into service meant becoming a servant for someone better off. You started off at the very lowest level, washing floors on your hands and knees, cleaning out fire grates, which was filthy work. You did this at dawn so that your rich employers could come into a room warmed by a fire that you had also set. You yourself got up in the cold. You did not have a fire. Only after a long apprenticeship did you graduate to other levels of labour. You also left home when you became a servant.

You lived life as a kind of indentured labourer, with only a few hours off on a Sunday — and then you might be expected to go to church. (In a way it is like the immigrants you probably see all around you — people used to working very hard for very little, but capable and taking it in their stride that this is the card that life has dealt them — but also these migrants have the expectation that they might, at a certain point, be able to deal their own hand. In other words, change their lives for the better.)

This early history of childhood labour formed Betsy into a hard-working young woman, capable. In fact, when she met William the coachman in Bath she had ascended the rungs of servantdom to the extent that she had become the personal maid of the wealthiest family in Hawke's Bay. You will hear of this place often in my story, so I will describe Hawke's Bay to you.

Hawke's Bay is both a physical place and a state of mind. As a physical space it is a rather grand wild area on the East Coast of the North Island (Te Ika-a-Māui). It is hidden behind mountain ranges and runs towards a ragged cut of coastline that then drops into the sea.

It is beautiful and wild. The land from a plane looks like a blanket dragged together in pleats. This is because earthquakes often occur in the area. (And in fact the great Hawke's Bay earthquake of 1931 changed the lives of your Northe ancestors forever. We will come to that.) It is a

LEFT

A fashionable West End photographer created these *cartes de viste* which William and Betsy exchanged while courting in Britain.

BELOW

Bess's grandparents, William Purvis and Betsy Bartlett.

dramatic and eloquent landscape, as vast as a Western and in some ways as mythic.

Very early on in colonisation it was judged to have very good land for sheep grazing and large sheep stations were established. Most of New Zealand's colonial settlements grew like topsy, unformed and anarchic. But society in Hawke's Bay was skewered early on by the creation of these large sheep farms. It allowed certain families to ape the aristocracy in England and see themselves as very grand. They often built big wooden houses in the country and then came into 'town', which was Napier, and there on the hill they built other large houses as kind of 'townhouses'. They were members of the Hawke's Bay Club. This class consciousness was unusual in New Zealand at the time.

Betsy was the maid for the Tanner family, who were by way of being nouveaux riche. When the Governor of New Zealand — who himself personified the Queen — came to stay with the Tanners they did up their already large house and, tellingly, the taps were lacquered with gold leaf. This says something about their lust for status. When the Tanners — such an unglamorous name — went to England they took Betsy along with them. She was a trusted servant, almost 'one of the family' although definitely of not 'of the family'.

Betsy Bartlett regarded this as the pinnacle of her career as a working woman. I have a photograph taken of her by a fashionable photographer in London — it is a *carte de visite,* which was the cheapest form of photography, like a small card you could put in an envelope. In this photograph she looks severe and proud and serene. She is someone who knows who she is. She does not wear a hat. Her clothing is fashionably tight-fitting, because it was probably important to the Tanners that their maid servant should look 'smart' — it reflected on them.

There is the small cross by her side, showing her pious Christianity, and her hands are large, the hands of a capable working woman. But there is something else. Betsy is verging on being a spinster. She is quite severe in this photograph, with her damped-down curled hair and simple faith of a face. There is a story here.

I don't know how she met her future husband, William, who was quite a few years younger than her, in Bath. But I would say they exchanged cheap little *carte de visite* photographs, as I now have this matching duet of images. In the one which I assume William gave to Betsy he appears without the beard that established his serious credentials — almost his manliness. In fact, with his high, slightly ridiculous curl on the top of his head, he looks effete, like a footman in one of Tenniel's drawings for Charles Dickens, as if he might lisp and be slightly dishonest. Which he wasn't. He was a god-fearing Scot who read the Bible on Sunday and refused adamantly to do any 'labour' on the day of God's rest. (God was resting on the seventh day from creating the world. People believed this.)

After this exchange of photographs, Betsy vanished back to New Zealand with her employers. The two probably thought they would never see one another again.

To get some idea of the constriction of Betsy's life we can look at her travelling trunk: the space she had to put all her clothes and worldly possessions in while she travelled from New Zealand to Britain and back again, a two-month journey by steamship. The trunk is no more than 75 centimetres long, 35 centimetres wide and 30 centimetres deep.

The fact I have it today is a comment on Betsy's pride in her attainment. Although born in a rural area outside Wellington, she had managed to make the return trip 'home' to England. (All the early colonists called England 'home' because that is where they or their parents had come from.) Travel for New Zealanders, as for any isolated people, has a weight, a gravitas — a heightened meaning, almost a magic. You who have travelled so much even as a baby cannot comprehend how fiercely isolated New Zealand was, nor how magical movement beyond its shores seemed.

Betsy kept the box, which is a simple enough kauri box with stout iron handles, because a box is always handy. It travelled out into her daughter's kitchen in a similarly ambiguous way — both as something practical but also a *memento mori*, a memory of both the constriction and attainment of her mother's past. It was fascinating, this box — as if you could have measured, quantified, weighed someone's social space. (For a servant, that box was their total private world, all they had.)

Typically, my snobbish grandmother — the daughter of a lady's maid — had the plain wooden box covered with a flowery slub linen. The linen was of a Jacobean flower design and expertly tailored with a roll. In other words, it was tasteful and the kind of thing my grandmother would have observed in the drawing rooms of the gentry. The box was kept in Grandma's kitchen and when she died, my mother — cautious, economical, indebted to the past — took the box up to Auckland. And when my mother's house was broken up I in turn took the box to look after it. I do not know what will happen to it in future. To the younger members of my extended family, its story is probably inert. It can no longer tell its rimes. Its song reaches the final note.

Betsy's story does not end here. She returned with the Tanner family to Hastings — a town Mr Tanner had effectively created. He had helped promote the town, sold off a large number of sections, and when the railway rode right through its heart, bisecting the long main street, he knew he had struck gold. Hastings grew to be a service town for the rural hinterland. Napier, 17 kilometres away and right by the coast, was the port and administrative centre of Hawke's Bay.

Hastings was Thomas Tanner's invention, one might almost say, his personal fiefdom. He and his family lived in an estate called Riverslea on its distant outskirts. It was antiseptically removed from the dirt and coal dust and sweat of working Hastings, and it mimicked a great estate in England, with elaborate gardens, tennis courts, carriages and, later, large motor cars. They aspired to be like the great county families of England, living in rural splendour. My ancestor was a very small cog in the machine of their pretention. I am sure, however, Betsy Bartlett did not see it like this. She probably saw the Tanners as good employers to whom she was emotionally bonded.

Here is what happened, according to my mother (who may have drawn her storytelling skills from Hollywood movies of the 1940s). 'Betsy was riding along in the carriage with the Tanners when she looked out the window and said' — intake of breath — '"There's *William!*"' Here, suddenly, was the young man she had fallen in love with — no longer in the streets of Bath surrounded by stone buildings, but in the dusty streets of Hastings, New Zealand.

There is something improbable about this story, however. Did a servant ride around inside a carriage with her employers? Betsy's position seemed to change according to my mother Bessie's versions. Sometimes she was that erstwhile figure of ambiguity — somewhere between the poor and the rich — 'a governess' like Jane Eyre. Other times she was 'a lady's maid'. Both imply she was a superior servant, which is an arcane distinction, but one of great moment to those cramped inside a rigid, competitive hierarchy.

But once again, in my mind's eye, I see this as a scene realised by one of the great Hollywood directors of the 1940s, when the Victorian era came back into vogue, and film directors looked back at their childhoods with loving regret. They celebrated — and mourned — its passing by making any number of films set in the Victorian period: *Gone with the Wind, Jezebel, The Magnificent Ambersons, Meet Me in St Louis, The Heiress.* These films were very artificial but powerful, often shot inside studio sets, with sumptuous costuming, expert lighting, make-up.

I can see the shot, inside the carriage, with one of the Tanner ladies' blonde ringlets swaying with the buck of the coach, while my ancestor sits closer to the door, lower in her seat than the ladies but more sharply observant of the outside world. And there, walking along, not even looking around him — lost in thought, as is someone who is suddenly plunged into an entirely new world — is William Purvis. He is dazed. In this memory-film Betsy calls out — her cry is like a stumbled inward drawing of breath — she is shocked — but the impact reaches him quickly, he feels it as a soft wind across his face. He isn't even listening or looking, but he looks up. It's as if he's heard a voice he recognises, or more than this, sensed a presence, the smell of someone, their physical essence. The carriage keeps moving, but for a split second their eyes meet, then the carriage draws the two lovers apart.

The next scene is the local church at Havelock North. Thomas Tanner, as befits a faux lordling, has donated money for the erection of the church, which is small, wooden and Gothic. It is the marriage day of William Purvis and Betsy Bartlett. And she is now on the arm of her employer, Thomas Tanner. He is giving her away. Her actual father, a one-time labourer in distant Lower Hutt, is too far away to be present. Perhaps anyway she doesn't want him there on her wedding day. This is much neater. It has a storybook neatness about it, like two small figures in a weather vane — male and female, eternal. Betsy Bartlett walks in on the arm of a grandee condescending to be her 'protector' and to give her away. She emerges on the arm of the man with whom she will live for the rest of her life.

Interestingly, inside the scrapbooks that William Purvis keeps — amid horse lotions and hair remedies and jam recipes (he is quite a flexible man) — is a small scrap of a newspaper announcing the wedding. But what is especially significant to me is that Betsy is described in the public announcement as 'Bessie'. Bessie is my mother's name, and it always seemed a mystery where it had come from. It was already old-fashioned by 1916 when my mother was born. But Bessie is a good servant's name, reliable — a brown name somehow, sheeny as the flanks of a good-natured horse. I never knew its origins, but once I saw this small strip of newsprint I became convinced she shared the name of her own grandmother.

'Bessie' Bartlett, as perhaps she was known familiarly by the Tanner family — a name to call out down a hallway, summon from another room, order to pick up clothes thrown on the floor, or find a hair tidy or locate a missing handkerchief, arrange for a carriage to be at the front door, quickly mend a rip on a silk dress, comfort, listen, manage the awkward silences — be present — be there — be a wall, a window to look out of, a door to walk through. Bessie, reliable, ever present — Bessie without bad temper, who kept her opinions to herself, who worked hard and finally, almost on the point of being an old maid, was released into the fecundity of marriage with a handsome man who was actually (secretly or not) five years younger than she was.

What a catch. What a lucky release.

But how *did* William happen to be walking down that dusty street in the same town as the maidservant he had fallen in love with? He had come to New Zealand as indentured labour. This meant his voyage out was paid for but he had to work for nothing until the sum was paid off. This is a tale of cautious lives, of lives lived with a fixed determination. We are not lordlings or great criminals or bastards. We're the people in the background of Dickens' tumultuous novels — *small people,* they were once called. Not physically, but called *small* for the space they took up on the social and political and economic stage. 'Of modest background' was a phrase often seen in nineteenth-century novels, and what it meant was a portion of respectability, of cleanliness, of hope. It also meant straitened. Straitened means made tense by the effort of making ends meet. To be always alert as to the value of money. To be watchful, even perhaps to be mean.

When Joan Didion tried to quantify 'self-respect' in relation to her own colonial ancestors (who lived in California), she said they were people who possessed 'a certain toughness, a kind of moral nerve; they display what was once called character'. 'Self-respect,' she continued, 'is something that our grandparents, whether or not they had it, knew all about. They had instilled into them, young, a certain discipline, the sense that one lives by doing things one does not particularly want to do, by putting fears and doubts to one side, by weighing immediate comforts against the possibility of larger, even intangible, comforts . . . it is a question of recognising that anything worth having has its price.'[1]

Your ancestors had this quality of toughness. They had to. There was no choice. In fact if there is one difference between our lives now and their lives then, it relates to the absence of choice. 'One lives by doing things one does not particularly want to do.' I doubt whether Betsy Bartlett as a very young girl dreamt of being a lady's maid, at the beck and call of women who may have been even younger than she was and who spoke to her in a certain tone of voice. But this is what she did — and she did it with a professional zeal, an excellence so she could take pride in the work itself. She may have been a servant but she was a good servant. She kept her self-respect.

Your colonial ancestors were always having to weigh up painful options. In Britain, hunger was a real possibility. Poverty was just around the corner. And with poverty came complete loss of power. My mother had a phrase — 'cold as charity'. I sometimes wonder if this concept travelled down through her family: the idea that charity was demeaning, chilling to the human heart, an affront to dignity. It was better to do almost anything than to end up in the 'poorhouse'. The poorhouse was a charitable institution in which families were broken up, children separated from parents, brothers from sisters, husbands from wives. They were given demeaning work to do in return for a subsistence diet. The idea was to make the experience so unpleasant people would do anything rather than go 'on welfare'.

Hence the desperate gamble of immigration. You are a descendant of people who shifted themselves from everything they had known, from a land their ancestors had lived in for so long nobody could remember any other world, from a place where relationships were so established that they seemed to come out of the Bible. They had to leave this all behind. They were projecting themselves forward into unknown places. This was a great gamble and, so far as any romance attaches itself to your colonial ancestors, it lies in this roll of the dice.

You will of course feel it is ridiculous to say that the tiny genetic inheritance from my family has anything to do with you. The wonderful thing about being young is the feeling of being a blank slate. You can be whoever you want to be. At least that is what people say on Facebook — that unreliable mirror. The strange thing about being alive for a long time is you continuously learn things about yourself. As you get tested more and more by life, you become defined — by your failures as much as your successes, oddly enough. Indeed, the way you meet a reversal can say a great deal about you. You have to reach deep down inside yourself. When 'in disgrace with fortune and men's eyes' you reach right into the very depth of yourself — maybe back further, even into your genetic memory. Somehow at the back of you, receding behind you, are those tough survivors who gritted their teeth, turned their faces into the wind and moved — bleakly at times — forwards.

Māori acknowledge this all the time: you are not who you are, you are a collection of all your combined ancestors who live within you — and you must pay your respects to all the people who led to your existence. This seems to me entirely sensible.

But let's talk more practically. It turns out the way you experience something as basic as food is a result of your genetic make-up. In other words, if your ancestors liked certain kinds of foods — fatty? salty? sweet? — you will have a disposition towards them. The very thing that seems to define you most intimately — the taste inside your mouth, your choice of food on a table (the way you 'instinctively' reach for something on a buffet) — turns out to be ghostwritten by ancestors you may not even know.

There are other things that are pre-written in your genes. Health is an obvious one, a predisposition to certain illnesses. But there's something even more ghostly here. A woman who has been pregnant is likely to be a 'microchimera' (a person who carries the cells of another person). Fetal cells have the imprint of her child's father and his ancestry.

What this is saying is we are all more composites than we thought. Interdependent even while being singular. Connected even when we are separate. Within each of us lies a ghostly trail of DNA which may point to the nature of our death, however far that is in the future.

Or this may all be bunk. We like to think of ourselves as free agents, unchained from the slavery of genes and social background.

BUT LET'S GO BACK NOW to that seemingly invisible force known as 'history'. The root of history is the word *story,* and history in essence is the story, or rather stories, we tell ourselves to make sense of what happened to us in the past. It is an entirely human fabrication, a form of dreaming, perhaps even a form of rationalising the anarchic forces that constantly assail us.

Let me tell you this: I was always a weird little boy, looking backwards as much as I looked forwards. This was because I was baffled by the present — let alone the future. I was a little cissy, Oliver. This means an effeminate boy. I was born into a confusing world, at the end of a world war that had emphasised manliness as a way of surviving.

My father seemed to dislike me — or the parts of me that were effeminate. I couldn't understand why; what I was appeared as natural to me as breathing or walking. It was how I was. But to my father it was perplexing and a source of shame. I had to learn how to cope with dislike. I grew up with a sense of not being as others were from a very early age. This either strengthens you or destroys you. Or it does both. I felt very insecure but I also noticed a lot. I was observant without being aware this was a characteristic to value. But I felt very unsure about the present. So I turned and looked to the past.

But what past? And what was the past?

The past often comes down to us through the stories our mothers tell us, murmur in our ears. Mothers tend to be the spinners of the threads of stories that bind us to the past. Hence the two matrilineal lines we are investigating here are my grandmother Northe (and her preference was for her own mother's stories — those of the Bartletts — and the way she managed to transcend her background and leave it far behind), and my mother, whose family were the all-powerful Northes, as I conceived of them. I grew up with a vivid sense of the realities of these people who were really phantoms — all of them were dead. Yet when my mother and grandmother talked about them they leapt alive again, or they became so familiar it was just as if they had walked around the corner and could no longer be seen. They were still there.

This is how the past is sung to us, murmured drowsily into our ears just when we are on the point of plunging into sleep. This borderline somewhere between consciousness and sleep is where these legends lie, like huge Neolithic monsters. They bathe in the sleety waters of memory and come alive under the tongues of our mothers. They form mysteriously, returning to human form and dancing before our eyes. They cry, weep with misery or a sense of sudden victory. They tell moral fables. They tell us how to be.

This is why I am writing this long letter, Oliver, so I can pass on to you some of these stories. None of them is particularly glorious. You cannot

TOP

Dad, loving but wounded and distant, with Russell in Point Chevalier, 1949.

CENTRE

Mum, protective and affectionate, with Russell and me on Point Chev beach in 1949.

LEFT

An absent father. Mum with me and Russell around 1949.

boast of ancestors who were either generals at the head of victorious armies or revolutionaries who inchoately understood where time was heading and stepped forward to lead a benighted people to a promised land. My stories are the stories of very ordinary people. But then, of course, nobody is ordinary. Every human has a mystery inside them.

JUNE 2015

Bess asked me this afternoon to look in the phone book to see how many Northes were living in Napier now. It was an astonishingly scanty list. Considering Robert Northe, my great-grandfather (himself one of five brothers and five sisters), had sired eight boys in the late nineteenth century, plus one daughter, the six names in the phone book were an almost melancholy diminution.[2] 'It was upon the population of variants that natural selection could act,' Oliver Sacks writes, 'preserving some lineages for posterity, condemning others to extinction.'[3]

My mother sighed and said, to the room, to me — to her past, certainly her future — something I thought I would never hear her say: 'The Northes have had their day.' (In her confusion in the downstairs lounge when I had come to interrupt her while slumbering through a film, she had introduced to me another old lady as 'This is my son, Peter Northe . . .' When I said, 'Let's go to your room and have a cup of tea,' she looked suddenly shrewd and said, '*If I still have a room.*') Now she was pontificating on the fact 'the Northes have had their day'.

'What about the Northeys?' she asked suddenly. As if grabbing at a straw. (The Northeys were another branch of the same family.)

I looked in the phone book again. 'There aren't any,' I said.

'None at all?'

'None,' I said.

I myself did not find this melancholy. I had long lived with the fact I would not have children, and in my heart of hearts saw this as a selfless act. I could never quite suppress a sigh of irritation at those people who rattled on about vanishing resources but saw their right to have as many grandchildren as possible unquestioned. I realised the supposedly selfless desire to save the world from future destruction was actually based on the concept that their descendants would have a future to enjoy. Entirely understandable, but in its most basic form it is a variant of self-interest, a form of appropriation of the future. But then is the world worth continuing with if humans are not here to enjoy it? (Of course I would argue yes.)

Then I decided to have a bit of fun.

'There's a Robert Northe down in Christchurch who has been found guilty of breaking into the houses of earthquake victims and selling weed.'

My mother took quite some time to synthesise this. (After all, the other day she asked her eighty-nine-year-old cousin, quite sincerely, 'And is your father still alive?' Only moments before she had been scandalised when I said her own mother had been dead more than half a century. 'But then you're ninety-nine, Mum.')

'Who . . . *what?*' she said of this recent piece of information.

'He must be a relative. Someone called *Robert Northe*.' (Robert Northe being the eponymous name of the family firm of coal and wood merchants of which my grandfather was the managing director.) 'It's online. He's a thief and a drug dealer.'

She made a comic face of horror, a million miles away from the stringent, even stony face she had turned to my brother and me when she reproached us for our homosexuality, not least because we risked offending the spotless Northe name.

'Yes,' I said, enjoying myself. 'Robert Northe to boot.'

She had nothing further to say, except to let out a small sigh.

Now, when asking whether a particular second cousin was married and had a family, and I replied he was gay, she just said thoughtfully, 'I don't understand it. So many Northes being gay.'

One could say life had defeated her. Or at her advanced age and state of deteriorating memory, she had come to accept what her conscious will and mind had always struggled to accept.

What more could be said? A shrug. A grimace intimating irony. 'Life is like that.' It delivers unacceptable news, or news you might never have expected. But this is why it is called 'news', after all. It is new.

THAT EVENING I SAW YOU, Oliver, on Facebook, that wonderfully shameless cupboard to which we retire to contemplate what fills the emptiness of the world: Pauline had put up a small video of you in your cot. The phone was held high above you and looked directly down at you. I gazed in wonderment — and also a degree of fascinated horror — as you pullulated in your cot, your arms squirming outwards, little bow legs continually moving, almost like fins trying to push through the air. You seemed neither happy nor unhappy. In fact what overwhelmed me was the sense of your beginning to wade through the oncoming textures of life. You were already sentient, a human with your own characteristics. Are you like Pauline's side of the family or like your birth mother, Nicole?

I gazed at you, amazed at this newcomer to the world.

FEBRUARY 2016

Time takes up a lot of time with Bess. Establishing the time. As in, 'It's your hundredth birthday this year, Mum.'

An appalled look on her face.

'Really?' She looks at me. 'What's the date of my birthday?'

'The twenty-first of April 1916—'

'Yes, that's right.'

'—and this is 2016, so on April the twenty-first you'll be one hundred.'

She smiles a little, almost in gratification.

'Really.'

'I'll have an afternoon tea for you, Mum,' I say, 'up at the house.'

'Don't go to any fuss' — the eternal mother's code for *please make a fuss*.

'There's aren't that many of us,' she observes.

'I've asked Philippa and Suzanne' — my sole remaining cousins, aside from Geraldine, your grandmother — 'and both of them have said they will come.'

Just before, she had asked not so much who they were as where did they fit in.

'Your sister — Aunty Jean's two daughters.'

'Where do they live?'

'They both have apartments on Oriental Parade,' I say. '*Our posh relatives.*'

She laughs a little, liking that.

'Good.'

'And Geraldine is coming out soon for a visit. From Canada.'

'Where does Geraldine live?'

Conversation is like this, a kind of waltz wherein the steps go back as much as forward.

'Ottawa. In Canada. She is out for the summer. And . . .' I draw in a breath, as this is the slightly difficult part, 'Geraldine's daughter Pauline is coming, too.'

Silence, almost a wary silence.

'Geraldine has two children, remember? Simon and Pauline.'

'What do they do?'

'Simon has a very good job at a university in New York. And Pauline . . . Pauline has the Foot genes, she's good at making money. Some kind of commerce,' I add.

Bess likes this. She likes people who are good at making money. Geraldine's father was an accountant with the surname of Foot, and he was clever at making money.

But I needed to familiarise my mother with some news. This was that Pauline was visiting New Zealand with her partner, Nicole, and they had brought with them the surprise package of . . . you, Oliver. And it was quite likely that Pauline, Nicole and you might come to Napier. There seemed an almost historic nicety in the member of the family who was oldest, at one hundred, meeting the member of the family who was youngest — only eight months old. Sort of one end of the family tree greeting the other.

When I first told Bess that Pauline had had a child, she had asked a single question: 'What does her husband do?'

This had pretty much put an end to the conversation — easy enough when Bess's concentration span is so reduced. But now I had to try to explain something that wasn't actually very complicated in a modern sense at all.

'Pauline is coming to Napier with Nicole, her partner.'

A lurch into silence.

'Two females?'

I noticed her disparaging term 'females' — not 'women' or even 'two friends'. It was the lightly veiled homophobia of a redoubtable heterosexual who, until she had had to come to terms with two sons who were homosexual, forthrightly paraded her small-town prejudices. She wore them as a badge of honour.

I let it lie for a second.

'Yes,' I took up as if nothing had been said, my tone consciously upbeat, 'and Pauline and Nicole have had a child — a son — and they're bringing him to Napier.'

She thought about this. A child is good news. A son.
'What is his name?'
'Oliver,' I said. 'He's eight months old.'
'Poor wee chap,' she said when I explained he had come all the way from San Francisco and promptly got a stomach bug which had then been communicated to all the relatives.
'I hope he doesn't have it when you meet him.'
'No,' I said, 'I'm sure he'll be all right by then . . .'
She sat in silence for a while, pondering it all.
'Oh well, we'll survive, I guess.'
There was in this the wisdom of a lifetime — the adjustments you had to make to come to terms with a world arranged differently from how you might have thought.
She pondered a bit further, shaking her head slightly, sighing ruefully.
'It's a funny old world.'

YOU ARE ALREADY SHAPED BY history without even being aware of it. So it is for every human born. We are born into history. Your history is to have two mothers who love one another. Once upon a time, and comparatively recently, it was impossible for two people of the same gender to produce a child. So you are the product of changes in society, not only of biological intervention but also of LGBT rights, a fight in which I took a small part.

Oliver, I hope this seems incredible to you, but in the past gay men and lesbians were regarded as evil creatures who should be punished for just existing. Men who were found to be lovers were imprisoned, even hanged. The most infamous case was the imprisonment of Oscar Wilde in 1895. This brilliant man had to work on a treadmill that moved perpetually so that he never got anywhere. He was destroyed as a result — he lost the human part of him, the tender core of being human.

This was a cage I grew up in, too. Its space felt very small, it pressed the breath out of your body. You could not move. At times it felt better to die — except that inside me, as inside every human, is this fiery instinct to seek a better life. *Life must be better than this.* It is hard to stifle this instinct, this swerve towards vitality. It is what has helped human beings create a better world.

In my twenties, along with other people like me, I began to fight for equal rights. At the time it did not seem possible. It only seemed right. It seemed unjust to live in a world in which you were always pushed back inside a box, could never talk about a thing like love, which dignifies all human beings. But if I am honest with you, Oliver, I am not absolutely sure I believed we would achieve equal rights in my lifetime. Nevertheless, it seemed necessary to fight for these rights, as the fight itself would educate people and say one thing: *We will never go away*.

None of this was obvious at the time. Looking back from the current high tide of marriage equality and legislated LGBT rights, it all seems destined to have occurred. But to live through change is to be regaled with all sorts of alternative routes, and even alternative beings. For example, for a long time I hoped desperately I would turn into the person my parents wanted: this meant I tried to model myself on a sports-loving Christian youth. I was politically conservative and a fervent monarchist.

Then in my twenties I went to the opposite extreme, reinvented myself and became a drug-taking party animal who effectively abandoned and rejected my parents and their values. In England I changed again and became a hard-line Marxist who favoured revolution. I became a republican. Gradually this persona ebbed away into a more reclusive, thoughtful person who was somewhere between the two poles, looking both backwards at the child I had been and towards the person I was becoming.

You are different things at different times, Oliver. This is a strange fact of being human — we are contradictory, at times complacent, at other times tormented, always presenting to the world a face behind which lie irresolution, secret passions, unsorted feelings we would rather not acknowledge, the rawness of love and the need for affirmation. Then there are physical appetites intimately linked to a search for what might prove to be an elusive happiness.

So when I say we are all shaped by history whether we know it or not, we also have our individual response to this shaping, whether we accept it or attempt to discard it — acknowledging at the same time there can never ever be a discarding of history. The past enters you at birth and you live out its rhythms — it is just a matter of the degree to which you become conscious of it. Rebel against the past and you are just reliving it in another form. You are still fighting its potency. The past is all around you and, as I have said, inside you. It's just you can't see it. Getting older could be said to be the process of gaining sharper perception of the shape of the past and its power over you, just as your optical sight deteriorates and loses precision. Possibly at your age history is a blur, like the shadow of a tree against a window pane. Let me sharpen its shape for you.

THE MOST IMPORTANT EVENT IN the life of your matrilineal family, the Northes, was the 1931 Hawke's Bay earthquake. This is the experience that was seared into the genes, and defined us most as a family. It implied both being tested and surviving. It also implied you had looked into the core of existence and taken from it some essential lesson. Whether this is true or not, I cannot say. I can only record my own memory of how the stories of the quake were passed on.

The 1931 earthquake was always shortened to the familiar, if ominous, name which was as much a musical note as a word — *the Quake*. *The Quake* and *the War* were the two musical notes of my childhood, with *the Slump* just behind them — all of them sonorous, grave, dark and miserable, as much reprimand as a forewarning. So when I say rather too grandly that 'we' experienced the quake, what I really mean is 'they'. But in a curious way it also means 'us'.

I am the son of an earthquake survivor. When I experience a quake, no matter how small, I feel a sense of utter dread. It is as if all the stories of disaster, catastrophe, violence flush through my system, causing me to sweat, breathe faster, in short shallow breaths. Children of earthquake survivors are more frightened of earthquakes than the children of people who have never known them.

This is partly because we were brought up (as you will be, too, Oliver) with stories that are so enormous in dimension as to be apocryphal, like something off a biblical tablet or the shard of an old shattered vase. Except for this: the actors in these tales of danger and survival are members of your family, some of whom are no longer alive. In these stories they are magically reborn, forever duplicating certain actions — lighting a fire on the front lawn, boiling the billy — and, as in myths and fables, there is something curiously foreshortened in these actions. There is definitely a *before* and an *after* — but there is also an interregnum of impossible actions, of heightened unreality wherein all that your eyes see and your mind takes for granted is withdrawn from you. You enter a magic realm which is, at the same time, so grindingly real you cannot escape, and the very existence in this world calls forth fundamental questions of survival like your ability to find food, water, shelter — even something as basic as being able to stand upright.

The story of my mother walking home from school aged fourteen is like a small movie I have seen over and over again, each time passing by the same sights: the houses with collapsed verandas and toppled chimneys; the Holts' maid sitting in the gutter with blood flowing over her face, just sitting there in shock. Getting nearer to the Napier Hospital, which was one street away from where Bessie lived, the film becomes quite frenetic — patients being wheeled in iron beds down into the Botanic Gardens. A scene of disarray. Inside a tent doctors conduct emergency operations. Smoke rises from the burning city.

Bessie walks up the slight hill towards the hospital, and here she passes by what was the Nurses' Home. Now the film gets very slow, becomes silent. The Nurses' Home had been a three-storey Spanish Mission-style building, new and stylish. Now it is a heap of collapsed concrete. It has pancaked. Here the film ticks by frame by frame with the slow galumph of a heartbeat. Now, suddenly, it breaks into sound. The sound is of a woman screaming, but it is muffled because it comes from under the concrete. Eight night nurses are trapped under the debris, along with three office staff. Now they lie crushed. There is no machinery to lift away the concrete. The victims can only cry out to indicate where they are. And then as the hours pass and it falls into night, they cry out in agony, frustration, terror.

This is the sound I hear thirty, forty years later. It's obviously a sound that penetrated my mother's childlike defences, lodged itself in her brain. It's a sound she can never forget. And unwittingly she passed it on to me.

There are other stories she passed on to me, too. The tea trolley, laden with the best china teacups, that sailed around the 'drawing room' in a dance with the piano — the only cups to survive the quake. The whole family ended up drinking out of cups that Bessie was normally never allowed to touch. How she walked up the lane two days later and came across two English immigrants who had arrived in Napier to work at the hospital on the day of the quake. They had not moved since, or eaten anything or talked to anyone; they just lay under a tree, not moving. Or the nursing sister who arrived at Bessie's home at 4 Lawrence Road, her dress stripped away to underwear; she had torn it up to provide tourniquets for

RIGHT

3 February 1931. In between shakes, people run down Napier's streets. The city is yet to catch fire. This will burn to death those trapped under the masonry.

BELOW

The hoses soon ran dry.

ABOVE

The death toll of the earthquake was 256.

LEFT

The Napier Nurses' Home, pancaked. Twelve people died there.

people whose limbs were broken, bleeding. She was covered in dirt and dust from the collapsed buildings. They had one bucket of water for six filthy people.

So many stories to do with the quake, the experience of it, its surreal juxtapositions, its trauma but also its distinction — a kind of tribal identification to do with undergoing something terrible but also, more importantly, surviving it and, to a degree, transcending it. *What might have happened if you had been standing there.* The miracle of chance. The fixed nature of fate.

This is in the genes, too, Oliver, a kind of survivalism. Pragmatic, basic: how to survive a kind of apocalypse. We live in dystopian times. An age of hurricanes, natural disasters and political upheavals. Call this a gift of the ancestors — an ability to survive.

FEBRUARY 2016

We sat in Suzanne's sitting room that looked out onto Oriental Bay. The splendour of the view was, in its own quiet way, an expression of power. Suzanne was there, as was Geraldine, with her second husband, a loquacious Scot called Jim, and there, on the floor, lay a soft, rounded bundle. I glanced into your face quickly and understood there was nothing of my brother there. Your face was round as a clock and everything within it seemed oracular — you were all wonder at the world. Sitting far away from me, like a chorus of mothers, sat Pauline, whom I knew, and her wife (I guess) Nicole. Nicole had a sharp triangle of a face, almost dramatically white, with a slew of black-black hair. (Later she revealed her ancestors were Irish.)

Introductions over, we settled down like combatants around the ring, all of us looking inwards to the miracle of you.

We immediately established the degree of our propinquity (how near or far we were related). Pauline and I were 'first cousins at one remove' — not second cousins at all. This recalled an ancient chime — I seem to recall that when I was a child in long-ago Wellington we cousins spent a lot of time tracing the arcane filaments of family. Or rather, the girl cousins did. This was by way of preparation for launching out on their own endeavours to enlarge the family. It was a way of peering into the future.

Now our future lay before us: you were levering your way by jackknifing rubbery limbs along a silk Persian rug, gazing at the pattern as you went. Your eyes were large. Jim explained how everything was a matter of wonder to you: the whirl of wood on floorboards, the colour of patterns in the rug. I suddenly remembered that sense of wonder that overcame me when I was tripping, and understood you were in a more peaceful version of this hallucinatory state. The world was wonderful to you, a 3D rippling waterfall of sensations, and you needed to put things in your mouth to taste whatever you were seeing — to taste was another way of seeing.

We were all looking towards you, following your antics in a wondering, good-humoured way and also, on Geraldine's part, a proprietary way: 'Put your hand over that glass edge.' She was more on the case than the two mothers, who were perhaps exhausted.

I felt baffled by the insistent glaze of adoration. I wanted adult talk — I resented you.

Later you were sitting in Pauline's lap. We were at a dining table that echoed back to our mothers' insistence on tablecloths and a silver place setting, and back further to our redoubtable grandmother. (Suzanne surprised me by saying she was now almost as old as her mother, Aunty Jean, when she died of lymphatic cancer. I remember as a thirty-four-year-old thinking Aunty Jean was very old. 'Well,' Suzanne said with elan, 'I am very old!') I noted she seemed relaxed with you in the house. Ebullient. She who had, for whatever reason, not had children, when she was a classic case of a woman who would have been a brilliant mother. The fact we never talked of this implied a hidden hurt.

Pauline seemed to me to be rounded out by motherhood, albeit by proxy. I remembered her as a resentful teenager being dragged through the intense boredom of family connections. She was always called Paul, and probably, looking back, she was coping with her intense sense of difference. Now she was older and much more confidently herself. Consequently, she looked better. When we fit into our skins it's strange how all the things that seem and look out of alignment suddenly slide together and, for the first time in our life, we look complete.

She was at ease, though tired, with you balanced plump on her lap. You were gnawing on a bread roll while we ate a chicken (stuffed, another echo of our grandmother from a time when food was parsed out to last longer and go further). The vegetables — corn, potatoes, beans, peas, beetroot —

all came from Suzanne and her husband Peter's vegetable garden, another echo of the past, when every family had a large vegetable plot.

Your slobbery bread roll suddenly fell from your grasp. Holding you, Pauline felt for it with her feet and picked it up. This happened again. It rolled under my chair. I picked it up, feeling its soft saliva snail-wet repulsion.

At this point your soft gaze turned to me. I understood I was just part of the never-ending waterfall of impressions, but it was the first time your gaze had actually come to focus on me. I smiled at you, or sent you an improbable beam of love. And in return your face melted into a smile, too, and for one second we were held there in paradise.

SO HOW DOES A FAMILY WORK? Willa Cather, in praising Katherine Mansfield's stories, noted the strangely ambiguous territory of love and resentment that is part and parcel of being in a family. Even in a happy family 'every individual in that household (even the children) is clinging passionately to his individual soul, is in terror of losing it in the general family flavor. As in most families, the mere struggle to have anything of one's own, to be one's self at all, creates an element of strain which keeps everybody almost at the breaking-point.'

Cather goes on: 'One realizes that even in harmonious families there is this double life: the group life, which is the one we can observe in our neighbor's household, and, underneath, another — secret and passionate and intense — which is the real life that stamps the faces and gives character to the voices of our friends. Always in his mind each member of these social units is escaping, running away, trying to break the net which circumstances and his own affections have woven about him. One realizes that human relationships are the tragic necessity of human life; that they can never be wholly satisfactory, that every ego is half the time greedily seeking them, and half the time pulling away from them.'[4]

This seems to me a very acute analysis of both the pleasure of being in a family (companionate, warm) and the terror of being in a family — that you will be submerged, obliterated, swamped, the secret part of yourself threatened and struggling for survival.

It is accepted that the earliest emotional patterns within families, between mothers and children and fathers and children, imprint themselves with a rebarbative ferocity that echoes forward in a person's life. I had read in Alan Downs' *The Velvet Rage: Overcoming the Pain of Growing Up Gay in a Straight Man's World* that 'the most important issue in a gay man's life was not "coming out", but coming to terms with the invalidating past'.[5] According to Downs, a father of a gay son can sense a son's erotic interest in him very early on. This leads to rejection, a seemingly inexplicable wall of ice behind which the human recedes.

The child, often no more than three or four, feels only a confused fracturing of the wholeness of his soul. He becomes aware of himself as something so loathsome he must face rejection from someone who, until that moment, he had blindly loved. The mother, sensing the rejection, tries to placate this icy fume of rage and dislike. She spreads her body out protectively, covering the boy in the mantle of her love. The child, however, has been wounded for life. So a father in his disdain almost murders the son he has bred — and may indeed still love, albeit in a confused amalgam of repulsion and fear and something still dormant and powerful: pride and wonder.

'They fuck you up your mum and dad'. There is a cruel truth to Philip Larkin's bleak line.

I seem like a bad fairy at a christening, I know. Why do I want to parade my own sores before you? What does it matter to you that I had a father who rejected me — and who in turn I angrily rejected? You have no father — not one who is present on a daily basis in that intrusive zone of interrogation and surveillance known as family. You are lucky in a way to have two mothers. The evidence suggests that children blessed with two mothers who love you grow into well-rounded humans. In the end there is only love. That is, love is the nourishing element for a child, as well as guidance and limits.

But why am I talking about such large issues here when your presence is precise, individual — to a degree, unique? I suppose because parenting holds the key to the future, or one of the keys.

Martha Nussbaum, the philosopher, talks of mother and child as two 'imperfect beings'. She talks of the subtle interplay of the 'ambivalence of love'.[6] This just about sums it up. I reflect on my own understanding of my mother and how this has changed throughout my life. As a child, and for a long time, I thought she was the most brilliant guiding star in my firmament. Everything she said I believed. I was credulous, empathetic and, understanding nothing of the world, took everything she said at face value. Bit by bit, through subtle emphases, significant silences, tearful moments of pathos, I understood she resented my father. Without any question I took her side and saw him through her judgmental, disillusioned gaze.

Was my father so bad? I do not know. It was not a question I asked myself until my father was facing death and we silently took steps towards one another. Be honest. It was I who took the steps. Chastened by my long alienation, I retraced my path back to him. Helping him in the very last moments of his life was made bitter-sweet by his disbelief that I was there to help him. But I was there.

My father, Gordon, died in 1987. Soon after, my brother Russell was dying of HIV-AIDS. Bess had a severe nervous breakdown. There can have been few more brutal ways for her to be outed as the mother of a homosexual son. Her breakdown was a human response to a conflict she could not endure. Now she was fractured, adrift, as if she had wandered so far away from her past, let alone her present, that she had lost the ability to find a path back. She returned to the child she had been after the earthquake — fractured, dislocated, friable and hysterical. Hysteria was a part of her personality I had never diagnosed as a child. Her stories to me were truth; I did not understand them as laments, wish fulfilment, self-justifications so extreme they amounted to lies.

Now I saw a truth that had escaped me all my life. I pitied her as a human in excruciating pain. But our relationship changed forever. It was as if, from now on, there would be two 'me's in relation to her. One was an artful ambassador always referring back to my deferential position as a child. This child was a believer, an affirmer, a listener. But behind this child was an adult who listened in a different way, understanding he might at a certain point have to deliver help, assist — actually take over her life and reshape it so she could continue to function.

MARCH 2016

Pauline and Nicole were now in Napier, and I had arranged with them to bring you over to my house so you could meet Bess. 'One end of the family meets the other.' I knew I needed to get a photograph. This was foremost in my mind as I drove down to PA (Princess Alexandra Retirement Village) to arrange for Bess to be picked up at 12.30 p.m. (This meant arranging for her to finish her midday meal early and be prepared. Any change in routine requires the awkward logistics of a tugboat turning around a liner.) You were arriving at 1 p.m.

Bess was sitting in her room and I noted she was well dressed for once, and was actually wearing both hearing aids. I gave her lipstick and asked her to put some on. With an expert hand she painted on the shape of her upper lip, then pressed it against her lower. (When I'd asked her to put on lipstick the day before, she had protested: 'Why? There's nobody to see it.' I realised she meant *There are no men here to look at me*. My mother, the heterosexual. 'Well,' I countered, 'there are still people looking at you.' And after she put the lipstick on she accepted, grudgingly, 'It does make you feel better.')

As we walked out to the car, I reminded her once more about what was happening. My heart was beating fast. I was aware, again, of how slowly she moved, more a shuffle than a walk — almost a propelling roll forward that her legs struggled to stabilise. Her eyesight was poor, so her movement through space suggested a cognitive greyness, as if she were enclosed in a wall of sensations and vague shapes.

At my house I took her into the sunroom, where the table was laid. We were having lunch (Bess was having only a cup of tea). I had set the table — wine glasses, soup plates, a crusty sourdough loaf. We sat and waited. Bess asked me again why she was there. Eventually your party arrived, Nicole and Pauline dressed practically, in trousers and puffer jackets. You were being held by Nicole, and both mothers had supplies in a backpack. Introductions were made, Nicole to Bessie. Pauline knew Bess from old — she had last seen her when she was a teenager resentful of the burden of family connections.

But Pauline had a personal connection to Bess: as a young girl she had gone for a walk on her own and found a stray cat and brought it back and given it to Bess. The much-loved cat had lived with Mum for many years, till it died. Now Pauline was an assured young woman and Bessie had shrunk into almost a mute figure. I had assumed that the sight of a baby would awaken something profound in my mother. I'd seen her in the past expertly crook her arms to cradle a baby, and I had experienced a wire of profound grief that the position of her cradling arms indicated how ready she'd been all her life to receive the grandchildren who never arrived.

I did a lot of thinking in the night before you arrived, Oliver. You made me think back all over my life. I counted back to the age my mother had been when I was born. I was surprised, adding up the dates, that she was thirty-four. I hadn't realised she was so mature. I was a lucky boy, Oliver. Like you, I experienced the endless richness that is unconditional love. It is something that will help you all your life; its echo will never die. So it surprised me that when Nicole carried you into the room Bess simply gazed at you unmoved, her face still and almost grim. It was awkward.

'How old is he?' became her stock question of the afternoon, to be asked again and again.

It was this which alerted Nicole and Pauline to the state of her mind. Younger people who are not used to being around the very old (and this means nearly all young people these days) don't understand how to approach and treat and listen to them. It requires tact and patience, even a sense of humour. I was more than a little stressed when I realised I needed to mediate between you, who were of course oblivious to the *mise en scène*, and my mother, who was being obdurate, separate, not dissolving back into the remembered role of motherhood as I had assumed she would. (Perhaps the truth was that she was deafer than I thought and her eyesight was worse, so she sat isolated, incapable of catching the quick idiom of our sentences, half completed and full of telegraphese. Perhaps she wasn't feeling well. But she seemed so disconnected from expressing her own feelings that she appeared inert.)

You were more yourself than I had seen you before. After all, you had serious business to conduct, which was being yourself, attentive to mood, hunger, distraction, attention. Your mothers, on the other side of the table, took turns nursing you — you were passed like a weighty parcel from Nicole, slightly yielding, to Pauline, who seemed entirely in love with you and who could not keep a broad smile from her face. You look like her, which is sweet, considering she is not your birth mother. We talked — that is, Nicole, Pauline and I talked — about gay marriage. They explained they couldn't get married immediately. Pauline said she would adopt you — and I was surprised, since she is so obviously your adoring second mother. When you got hungry and started grizzling, she picked you up, swung you athletically onto her shoulders, then danced up and down like a bear, so you had the distraction and pleasure of a circus ride. Your tears instantly vanished, you smiled, then the thought of tears returned like a tide and you were clearly trying to decide what mood you were in.

I asked Nicole how she was coping with meeting so many members of Pauline's extended family (the Feet, being Catholic, have many more relatives than the sparse, Protestant and picky Northes). She smiled quickly and said how pleasant everyone had been. But even the extended family seemed small to her, since she came from an Irish Catholic family with many siblings and branches and sub-branches.

Bessie sat silent through all this, uncomprehending, and with a rank, almost obstinate look of bad temper on her face.

'He'll have bandy legs,' she announced at one point when you stood up and pulled yourself along the seat of the couch — a feat Pauline, Nicole and I saw as so clever it was little less than a miracle.

It was not going well. The eternal question of your age was asked again.

I realised I needed to return Bessie to PA. She had had her cup of tea: 'A *nice* cup of tea, Pete' — her usual comment on tea brewed with tea leaves in a teapot, but here it was delivered like a challenge. Nicole and Pauline were silent a moment and agreed. 'This table is a mess,' Bess added. 'You'll never clean it up, Pete.'

You suddenly started crying — a small crisis solved by Nicole getting you a bottle filled with formula and water. You were transferred to the sofa to sit alongside Pauline. You glugged away with that intense concentration, as if in sucking you were pulling the whole world into your insides for your delectation. Somehow Bess came to sit beside you on the sofa.

Maybe she could see you better. Or maybe it was just your physical proximity spreading an aura. She suddenly became involved. You reached out, or perhaps your hand just projected out and your tiny fingers closed around her ancient hand. This engaged her further. 'Poor little fellow,' she murmured, I am not sure why. (Poor because defenceless? Or because so much lies ahead of you, almost certainly pain as well as satisfactions and times of happiness?) There was some further interaction with ancient and soft fingertips, and Pauline said to Nicole quietly, as one murmurs so as not to distract two wild animals grazing by a pool, to get out her iPhone. I did likewise.

I took enough photographs to ensure that at least one of them would be okay. After this, the occasion was exhausted. The goodbyes were rather hurried. Pauline was very likely never going to see her great-aunt again but in the brouhaha of marshalling a baby out to the car this went unacknowledged. But I felt I would be seeing you again, so there was not a weighted feeling to my farewells. Bess sat through it all with the abstraction of a tired woman waiting for a bus that would never arrive.

Later, reviewing the photographs, I selected one which caught Bessie's delight in her contact with the child. Her hand is out and you have one of your fingers interlaced around hers. She is laughing with delight, as is Pauline. I put it on Facebook, explaining the situation and relationships. ('One end of the family...'). Various friends commented kindly. I wondered to myself later the degree to which I was leading people astray. The Facebook photo was calculated to warm and charm. What did they know of my mother's cognitive problems? But somehow the juxtaposition of you, the youngest member of the family, meeting her, the oldest member of the family reaching the great age of one hundred, had a neatness to it that surpassed any equivocations. It was an image that said something about continuity, survival, change. You, like all babies, were a signpost to the future just as Bess was an implacable signpost to the distant past. Her being one hundred was a statement with its own gravity. As for your being eight months, this was such a fleeting attainment, it had its own poetry.

IT WAS THE DAY AFTER Oliver — Ollie — met Bess. The phone had just rung. It was PA. Bess had vomited in the night, had diarrhoea, and was not able to keep down her breakfast. She was not dressing. She was staying in her room, lying on the top of her bed. The nurse described her condition as 'very fragile'.

When I went down to see her, Bess awoke, then drifted off to sleep, and I suddenly saw a vision of my father in extremis, when the face becomes stripped of all outerness, seems to look inward at the vast distance over which the soul has yet to travel.

It's strange really, Oliver, but I can't help but feel Bess's character was formed by her grandmother Betsy Bartlett as much as it was by her survival and endurance of the quake and other horrors. Grandmothers can be a formative influence on a child, a kind of distant beacon emitting a powerful guiding light. Betsy must have been tough as a young woman, as well as hard working. (Think of the young girl who bore a sack of flour on her back and walked for miles.) There's some of this residual strength in my mother — a tensile quality — so that now that she is sick and lying in bed, her face devoid of make-up and somehow returned to a puritanical mask, every feature registering pain and yet endurance, it is to this woman, Betsy, that I return.

WHEN THE YOUNG NURSE TALKS to me about the severity of Bess's condition — she is frail anyway, a tiny bird of a woman, and now she is constantly vomiting as well as suffering diarrhoea — I suddenly think, in a clutch of panic, she may not last. But the nurse, who is kind and can see my concern, shrugs and says, 'We don't know what the future holds . . . but what we do know is *she's a trooper.*' That just about says it, this inheritance of a plain peasant strength. Bess is of the earth. She doesn't have enough strength left to acknowledge me or play the slightly flirtatious game of being overjoyed to see me. She is almost mute. And when I leave her she is turning over in her narrow bed with the slowness of a sick animal, and she says to me something that I feel is almost symbolic: 'I hope I can get comfortable. I just want to go off to sleep.'

Is she lying there . . . dying? I am loath to use this verb, as she has such powers of recovery and I have rehearsed this moment so often when she seemed to reach the point of just-before-departure, then miraculously pulled back. This keeps me as a perpetual ageing child, a comic figure, an absurd creature, I know.

But yesterday, I looked at her in her overheated room — it was thirty-two degrees outside, windless, part of a long summer drought which at times seemed as if it was part of the earth itself dying — and she was drifting in and out of sleep, her mouth open, her hair scuffed up behind her small skull. She looked to me like someone dying. When I walked into the room I received a shock. Her nightie was pulled up almost to crotch level and I saw her withered limbs. She barely opened her lids to glance at me, angling her head with difficulty. We exchanged little more than a slight greeting. I offered to plump up her pillows so she could sit more comfortably. She leaned forward so I could do so.

'If this is dying, I wish it was over,' she said.

I thought back to my childhood, when I was in bed sick. It was the side bedroom at Point Chevalier, so I must have been very young, possibly five or six. It was when I still shared a bedroom with Russell. That room was always dark in the middle of the day, shaded by the house next door. The doctor was coming to visit. But what I recall is my mother coming into the room. I was lying in the muddle of a bed I had been in ever since I'd got sick, straying endlessly through sleep, in the timeless murk of not feeling well. She asked me to get up and perch on the side of the bed opposite — Russell's. I did so while she remade my bed. The soft winnow of air as she fluffed out the sheets. Time slid down a slope. And when I got back in the bed there was the most delicious coolness. I lay back and felt a spasm of deep love for this person who looked after me, whose sole focus was me, who had given birth to me and whose love I depended on.

Now it was me smoothing the pillow of my ancient mother.

She had recently murmured to me, taking hold of my hand with a surprising strength, her fingers so soft and shiny, 'I'm just so grateful for all you do for me, Pete.' I tried to pull my hand away, feeling a rinse of guilt that I had not done more (perhaps I had organised to wash some clothing she had spilled some food down, or I had combed her hair or found her missing hearing aids). I saw that in a situation of drifting aloneness maybe any attention meant a great deal. Perhaps for a moment she surfaced back into her own life, where she was a person again, even a person who meant something, had some value.

'You're my pride and joy, Pete, you know that.'

These words were quite genuinely said. But I felt only guilt, or, to be honest, a sense of pleasure lined with guilt, because some impatient part of me wanted her to be dead so I could get on with the rest of my life — in essence, be freed from this state of superannuated adolescence. Here we were, locked together still, both of us getting older and older and older, each one getting nearer the precipice, yet both of us, it seemed, holding onto one another, unwilling to let go.

This is one version of the bond between a child and his mother, Oliver. Just one. Some people would say it is an example of the unhealthy closeness of a homosexual son to his mother — a staple of homophobic prejudice. Why cannot it just be called what it is — love?

Lucky you, Oliver, who I saw bathed in the gaze of not only your two mothers but also grandparents, aunts, uncles, even distant cousins like myself, so far away from you genetically as to be an echo of an echo. Of course to be loved too much can be its own curse. If my soul was twisted and perverted and hurt by a father's lack of love, this also put iron in my soul. It hardened me and gave me strength.

Where is this taking me? To this moment now when I consider the death of my mother — the cessation of all the murmuring stories, half-truths, distortions, fairy stories of the past. But the fact is the reality of her death terrifies me.

I could not understand where my mother's digestive problems had come from. They began the day after she came to my house and met you, Oliver. It was not unusual for her to have what was euphemistically called 'an upset stomach' after eating at my place. This was, I worked out, because the food I cooked was so unlike the retirement village's bland diet. There was probably too much fibre, too much 'real' food content. But this time she had eaten only a tiny portion of paleo almond cake. Would that have upset her so badly?

Then I remembered 'the stomach upset' you had brought to New Zealand, one that was so volatile that everyone you came into contact with came down with it. It was two weeks at least since you had arrived. But could a very susceptible and fragile almost-one-hundred-year-old pick up a nascent bug from touch, or even the atmosphere? There was the photo of an intrigued and smiling Bess, her fingers interlaced with your fingers.

In engineering what was essentially a photo op, had I in fact killed my mother?

MARCH 2016

She has been in bed for more than a week now. When I say to her, 'You must get up. You'll become bed-bound,' she just looks at me. She has trouble hearing me, so I have to yell. 'You'll lose the use of your legs. They won't work if you don't use them.' Then I make my threat: 'You won't be able to stay in your room, Mum. You'll be shifted to the hospital.' She reacts to this: her eyes focus on me and she says, 'I've got to get up.' But she makes no move and lies there, breathing shallowly. She forgets what I've just said, and when I say, 'Mum, *you have to get up and get dressed,* even if it's just to sit in the chair,' she replies, 'Why? Why do I have to get up? There's nothing to do,' and she settles back into her bed. I can't argue with that.

Her hair is standing up at the back of her head. Her lids close and she drifts off into a light sleep. I look at her. I can see she's tired of living but doesn't have the will to die either. I have to tell her I am going away for a week. I have work to do in Auckland. This will end my attempts at supervision, of trying to persuade the nurses they must dress her, get her out of bed. A tray of entirely unsuitable lunch sits there — it is a meat stew, a large amount of mashed potato, not an invalid meal at all. She has eaten whatever the sweet is.

I try to do what I can. When I come in I put some mānuka honey on a spoon to give her some energy. As I approach the bed she opens her mouth like a child and I place the spoon there and she sucks the honey off the spoon. Then I make tea. Talk is difficult and I have to fight hard not to look at my iPhone, a battle I often don't win. I take some photos of her. I'm frightened — no, not frightened, but apprehensive she might slip into some other world while I'm away.

'It'll feel like a month,' she says when I explain I'm away a week. I lie and say I will be back the following Sunday rather than Tuesday, knowing she won't remember the precise day. I keep looking at her face intensely as if to memorise it — and the strangest thing happens. She suddenly changes back into the young mother I knew, the woman in her forties who was always rushing into rooms, or out in the car, hurrying along, full of energy. I can see her clearly. I say to her fondly, 'You were always so full of get-up-and-go, Mum,' consciously using her own mother's highest term of approval. But here she is now, shipwrecked in old age.

She often asks me, 'Do you know people down here?' I don't say who I see or how I see them, on what terms. I think of her own mysterious sexual past, when she explored life to the depths. But when I sit close by her on her bed and say to her fondly, 'You were always so full of get-up-and-go. Do you remember? Rushing here. Rushing there. Playing tennis. Cooking. Going out,' she nods in a vague way, as if that were some other person, separated from her by a vast chasm of time.

'Put the cup up there,' she says to me in her old voice, not exactly of command, but do-what-I-say I-know-best.

'Old bossy britches,' I say to her fondly.

'What's that?'

'Old bossy britches,' I repeat. 'You.'

Her face for a moment shines: she becomes beautiful to my eyes, and she smiles. She does what she has always done. She raises her fist up, clenches it and shakes it at me in a playful fashion. 'I shake the fist,' she says, the age-old words of a game that goes right back to childhood. (Was it cod-Māori or did it come from Nino Culotta's *They're a Weird Mob*?)

We smile at one another.

'It's only a week, Mum, I'll be back.'

'I'll miss you,' she says in a small pettish voice, but she looks up at me with absolute love. 'You have been good to me, Pete, coming in here to see me, it must be very boring.'

'It's no trouble for me,' I say. 'Besides, I like doing it.'

I do not say that I have begun to wonder if she will ever die, whether I will ever be free.

I reach down and take her hand.

I'm not amazed that these thoughts can co-exist — I felt a strange kind of transporting love for her, consciously remembering her even as I looked at her. We touched hands as I leaned forward to kiss her; she jumped slightly, as if I was going to kiss her on the lips (which of course I never did), and instead presented a rather boney cheek. I kissed her soft skin, the texture of which I remembered from my grandmother. We looked at one another like lovers parting — or people who love one another. I can say this without shame.

'See you soon. Only a week. Bye.'

She lifts a hand to wave.

I do not look back.

N.Z. AIR MAIL
LETTER CARD

If anything is enclosed this card will be sent by ordinary mail

4/9930
Gunner Gordon L. Wells
R.N.Z.A.
6 Fletcher Regt.
2nd N.Z.E.F.
Middle East Force

When folded the letter card must conform in size and shape with the blue border

How to Read a Letter

OPPOSITE

A wartime aerogramme from Bess Wells to her husband Gordon: 'We edit our persona as much as we put up a front.'

It seems obvious how to read a letter. You open it up, start at the beginning and read through to the end. But a letter is not just a collection of sentences, a bundle of facts. A letter, if seen in the right light, is a kind of biography.

EVEN WHEN A LETTER APPEARS to be banal, language is such a slippery medium that the human spirit slithers in between the letters of a word and, elfin-like, introduces its presence. Besides, life is made up of endless small decisions. We edit our persona as much as we put up a front. Letters have the virtue of being imprints of an identity that occurs just on the particular day the letter is written. They can be candid, duplicitous, straightforward, or a mask through which a conflicted self speaks.

'For all their apparent simplicity, [letters] are complex documents,' the biographer Janet Malcolm has written.[1] The significant thing with a letter is that it comes without the corollary of things we use in face-to-face conversations to verify, test, back up or question (eye movements, instinctive jerks, a feeling of unease). But even an everyday letter may be chucked in a bag or purse and re-read at a later, more leisurely moment when we can — so to speak — unpick it and look for the hidden meanings that survive as a kind of subtext. That is the true richness of a letter. It is not only what it is; it is also, if we know 'how to read it', a midden, a treasure chest, a mystery revealing the human heart sliced open in the rawness and indecision of a moment in time.

I'm prompted to these thoughts by the single letter that survives from my parents' wartime correspondence. It's an aerogramme sent by my mother, Bess, to my father, Gordon, in the chaotic days following the end of the Second World War. They had married in December 1939, just after war was declared, their marriage hastened by the sense of impending global change. None of the other letters from my mother survived apart from this one, because my father's truck, carrying his belongings, was destroyed by a bomb in northern Italy. Bess, living in civilian Auckland, did not save a single wartime letter from Gordon. Make of that what you will.

By early 1942 the war was going badly for the Allies. Singapore had fallen to the Japanese, and on 19 February the Japanese bombed Darwin, killing 235 people. Suddenly Australia and New Zealand were vulnerable to invasion. My father, a thirty-four-year-old bank clerk, was called up. He went overseas in late 1942. By the time this letter was sent, the newly married couple had been apart for three long years. My mother was twenty-nine, my father was thirty-seven.

The aerogramme shows my mother making tentative approaches to the man with whom she was going to have to live for the rest of her life. But she had been separated from him for longer than she had lived with him. How could she tell him what had happened to her in his absence?

This aerogramme certainly looks its age. It feels grubby — after all, it has gone off to a Europe reduced to rubble and ash, been flown back to New Zealand in a military aircraft (probably stuffed in a canvas sack), then laid relatively untouched in a handkerchief drawer. It has been re-addressed crudely by someone in a hurry. The crayon scrawl seems to breathe impatience. Part of the letter is typed, using a ribbon almost devoid of ink. (Wartime shortages.) The rest is handwritten in ink that has faded with time. But for all this, the letter is curiously resilient. Paper worms are only now starting to eat it. So in one way this piece of writing is both archeology (bringing something dead back to life) and, more profoundly, an act of emotional rescue. Something my mother wrote in a state of agonised indecision has lasted more than seventy years, delivering itself into my hands as something to parse, ponder and reflect on.

In 1945 an aerogramme was a relatively recent invention. A lightweight self-sealing single sheet of paper, usually coloured blue to signify air transport, it was a breakthrough in communication. (Previously the quality of a letter was denoted by the heaviness of the paper stock. Heavy equalled good.) The essence of an aerogramme was lightness and speed; it was also cheap to send. The needs of war had accelerated acceptance of the aerogramme, and by 1941 it was widely used in the British Army in the Middle East. But there were further reasons for its quick acceptance. It created a private form of correspondence, and the very fact it did not allow much space in which to exchange information meant it was ideal for a certain kind of letter writing. Aerogrammes were not for love letters or an endless flow of thought. They demanded containment, economy of expression, almost a mundane form of discourse.

This letter from Bess to her husband displays these attributes. It is prosaic in its use of language and tone; there is no sense of Bess gushing out pent-up feelings. Yet looking beneath the surface reveals another whole world. At a glance I can see their future lies exposed. They were a man and a woman at a particularly vulnerable moment. In fact, the very first sentence is a harbinger of the rest of their lives together: of missed connections, misreadings, secret feelings and things unsaid.

'*My Dear Gordy, Well I have missed writing to you for a couple of weeks now for that letter of yours of the 28th June mislead me* [sic]. *I thought from* [the letter sent on 28 June] *that you must have been on your way but on*

Sat I received one dated 30 June and you just seemed to be still at Trieste. Suppose you too were mislead by wild rumours.'

Wild rumours, as it turned out, were a worrying possibility for Bess. Both she and Gordon were trying to communicate in a zone where information was still strictly monitored and rumour was as much a part of reality as fact. Behind their communication problems lay the movement of troops returning home just at a time when Europe was full of stateless beings, people without shelter. This aerogramme survived simply because it did not arrive while he was at the European theatre, as it was then called. It was forwarded back to Tekapō, a military camp in the South Island, then sent back to my mother who, for reasons unknown, saved it.

The aerogramme was addressed with the specificity necessary for identifying an individual during a conflict in which approximately 690 million humans fought. It began with my father's ID number (472930), then ran on to his personal identity: *Gunner Gordon L Wells RHQ 61 Field Regt 2nd NZEF Middle East Force*. For three long years — in Egypt, Palestine, Libya, Tunisia, and then Italy and Austria — this had been who he was, all he was. His military role had subsumed his identity entirely.

The aerogramme is dated 30 July 1945. Everyone knows what 1945 signifies. At one minute past midnight on 8 May 1945, war in Europe was declared over. Dad was in Venice that night, and I have a worthless Italian bank note with his ebullient words written on it: 'The Night of peace'. It is signed all over by New Zealand comrades. (There is also a phrase he has gone to a lot of trouble to rub off. What did it say?) With the war over, Gordon could look homewards. But first he was to go with his regiment to Trieste to hold insurgent communists at bay — it was the start of a new war, the Cold War — and also to enjoy three months' rest and recreation.

The official artillery history notes the soldiers' 'enjoyment of their Adriatic paradise'. It talks of Trieste in terms of 'an enchantment'. It was the height of a European summer, and the weary men who had spent eighteen months in Italy 'serving their guns in anger and anxiety', fighting through snow and blizzards, could now relax, swim, flirt and dance.[2] There is some evidence Gordon had an affair in Trieste. (The sexual double standard almost expects this and evaluates this entirely differently, as we shall see.) The soldiers dressed up in the 'smart clothes worn to Groppi's cabaret or garden restaurant in Cairo or similar places', and had the time of their lives, celebrating their survival. 'There were anguished looks and

LEFT
Dad as a carefree bachelor.

CENTRE
Dad wrote 'The Night of Peace, 7 May 1945' on a worthless Italian banknote.

BELOW
Dad (centre) — as suave as Cary Grant and as insecure — embarks for war.

TOP

Her husband overseas at war, Bess sunbathed and relaxed at Point Chev.

CENTRE

Bess kept this photograph of her and an unknown man on a road trip somewhere in the North Island.

BELOW

In the first few years of marriage Bess had already left Gordon once, returning to Napier.

tearstained [female] faces at the roadsides as the gunners said goodbye to Trieste and the Triestini,' the historian notes.³

It seems typical of the way Bess's letter was all about missed connections that Gordon had already left Trieste the day before she even started writing it. He was part of a convoy making its slow way down the leg of the Italian peninsula. (He was actually in Bologna on the day she dated it.) The ability of a couple to correspond, to keep in touch, to keep up to date, was as severely tested during this time as it was during the war. But it needs to be noted that, even then, Dad had sent Mum two letters in quick succession, while she had 'missed' sending him a letter for a relatively long fortnight. She then delayed a further week before adding a postscript. It is possible she was agonising over what she could say — and not say.

When I first read this letter without any knowledge of the background, I was disappointed that it appeared so prosaic. It struck me as hardly the letter of a woman who had been married comparatively briefly, then been separated for three years from a husband she loved. It was business-like, distracted, even if couched in conventional phrases of affection. It was only later I grasped that the entire letter was a masquerade. Like many letters, what *was not being said* was more important than the few sentences that seemed to provide meaning.

What was not being said was that she had fallen in love with someone else.

The letter talks about ordinary concerns, darting here and there, following her thoughts. But at times it also, and unavoidably, displays her unspoken anxieties about what is going to happen when her husband returns. As with all things repressed, these anxieties have a way of emerging in a different form.

This is most clearly expressed at the beginning of the letter when Bess raises a subject of great importance to them both. '*I think you only get 28 days free travel and it can be taken any time within a year.*' She is referring to a train trip they have planned to take around the scenic South Island. They will spend time together, reacquainting themselves one with the other. Unofficially, this has the status of a second honeymoon. (In fact, the government thanked returned servicemen by offering a free rail double pass, second class, to them and their wives. It had to be taken within a period of thirty-six days.) But if Bess is nervously anticipating it in words, she demurs in thought: '*However, the longer it is before you actually get* under way the more chance we have of getting our holiday in the summer — that is if you are not too long of course.' So she plays off her secret wish that he may be delayed coming home — the reckoning — with the lustre of a promise that they will spend time together on a summer holiday. She then immediately goes into negative territory: if they were going then it would be *'pretty cold and miserable in the South Island just now — they have had a terrific lot of snow — 8 inches in Christchurch — all transport held up etc etc.'* That is, conditions of the human heart are freezing and hostile to the prospect of intimate time together.

Then she goes into another apology — she wasn't keeping up with his world, she was thinking of other things, subconsciously trying to block out the inevitable: her husband would return. *'Sorry I didn't post those things to Beth and Muriel [Gordon's favourite niece and only sister] before but when they arrived it was the time of the Italian and German capitulation.'* These were gifts and trinkets Gordon sent to the women in his family, including his wife, as tokens of affection and love. I recall elaborate and very pretty mosaic brooches and rings and bracelets sent from Italy. *'Gloves to your Mother, and the bracelet and badges to Muriel and Beth.'*

The tone is light, at times slightly flirtatious, but there is also a sense that she is thinking aloud in an attempt to quiet some inner uncertainty. Never once does she talk of her feelings, or of how she has missed him, or even how much she is looking forward to seeing him again. She does not say she loves him, except in a formulaic way as a sign-off at the very end of the letter where to leave it off would itself raise awkward questions. The plans for their railway trip instead represent anticipation, and she crowds out any exploration of her feelings with plans, gossip — her friend Nora and her mother *'are still disagreeing — it's a pity she doesn't get her own house back. Mother even quibbles about the supper Nora's visitors eat'* — at the same time managing to say nothing directly about her own life.

Yet in one key passage she seems to reveal an inner self. She is talking here of a pair of Italian leather gloves Gordon has sent her. The gloves represent a *billet doux*; they signify *I am thinking of you, I am imagining your warm hands inserted inside the living texture of animal skin.* On the most basic level they signify her presence in his thoughts. But her response shows that he is not in *her* thoughts at all. Or rather, that she has put off placing him centrally in her mind. She hadn't got around to sending the gloves and trinkets on to his relatives. *'I thought I'd keep them for you to* deliver yourself, but when I received your letters enquiring about them I sent them along,' she writes dutifully.

But this is followed by what amounts to an unconscious disavowal. '*I haven't worn any of mine yet for I use hand knitted woolen [sic] gloves all the winter and never wear a hat in the summer so hardly ever use them, but they'll be very handy when I leave work and play ladies again.*' Wartime conditions had freed her from the clothing constraints of a middle-class woman: wearing gloves and a hat in public, stockings rather than bare legs. But it goes beyond this: she chooses not to put her hands into his gloves, preferring her own self-constructed gloves — by inference, being her own woman, making her own choices.

And the explanation swiftly follows. She has had the best period of her life, without a male — father or husband — directing her on how to live and, to a degree, what to think. She has become a working woman. But like so many women who were, to a greater or lesser extent, liberated by the Second World War, she now faces a looming crisis. She will have to return to domesticity — '*playing ladies*', as she says dismissively, a childhood game of tea parties and idle chatter.

She is very clear about what she feels. '*I hate that thought for I'd be so bored just mooching around the Point. I've got used to a busy life now and I'd miss all the company.*' She does not specify what company, implying in a vague way it is her working environment that she will miss. The gender of her co-workers is carefully left undisclosed, just as she is not explicit about the fact she enjoys being her own agent, meeting whoever she likes, whenever she likes and on whatever terms.

Then she abruptly changes tack and goes on the offensive: '*What is the point of double spacing your typed letters? Maybe I spoil you, for I try to get as much as possible on the one sheet. It must be my very Scotch instinct don't you think? (You see I haven't changed). Groans from you I guess.*'

This is the closest she comes to badinage. She can twist him around her little finger is the inference.

BUT NOW THERE IS A break in the letter, which up to this point has been typed. Had she been writing at lunchtime in the office?

She had a secretarial position at a grocery and dry goods importer, Hutchinsons Wholesale, near Auckland's railway station. During a time of wartime shortages, when New Zealand was cut off from British imports, this was an advantageous place to work. It was a desk job, meaning she could not be manpowered into a factory or a farm, expected to dig up turnips or milk cows at dawn. It also gave her access to food that was strictly rationed.

She was a woman used to getting what she wanted. Before her marriage, she had been a receptionist at the Masonic Hotel, Napier's one luxury hotel. There too she had an advantageous position, not working in the winter months and taking time off to play tennis and golf. She was the daughter of well-to-do parents in a small town and she had high expectations about how her life would roll out.

Bess, according to her two elder sisters, was 'spoilt'. She was the youngest in the family, and the 'pet' — hence her nickname 'Chick' or 'Chicken'. She had been sent to a private school, Solway College, after the earthquake, unlike her sisters who attended state schools. Unusually for the time, she also had five years of secondary education. She had a sense of entitlement about who she was and what she expected of life. 'I could do no wrong,' she told me recently, a hundred-year-old looking back almost gloatingly at a younger self. She was good-looking, with a lively sense of humour, and used to the attentions of men. As a young girl and teenager she had been the favourite of a childless couple, the Burtenshaws, who lived next door to her parents in Lawrence Road. Bess became their goddaughter. At fourteen she had learnt to drive the Chrysler car that 'Mr Bertie' (Mr Burtenshaw) owned as a commercial traveller for Campbell & Ehrenfried. She received gifts from the Burtenshaws and at times travelled with Mr Burtenshaw to luxury hotels like the Chateau. Today we would look askance at the relationship of a man in his forties with a girl on the verge of being a young woman. In the 1930s, people were less suspicious or perhaps more contained by an expectation of codes of behaviour. But I do not know if this was not part of my mother 'being spoiled', with all this implies about an uncertain moral compass.

These thoughts are my own creation of a possible past for Bess, but they could well be wrong. Marguerite Duras, the French novelist, has commented: 'In existence, I think one's mother is, generally speaking, the strangest, most unpredictable and elusive person one meets.'[4] What strikes me now is that Bess made her own decision about shaping her life during the war. She had not gone home to Napier when her husband went overseas, as her parents expected. (There is a letter from Jean, her eldest sister, written after the Japanese bombing of Darwin, which says Bess should abandon Auckland, bury anything valuable in the garden and go to family friends who had a farm in Taranaki. '*It's no good getting panicky,*' Jean wrote, '*as I feel if the Japs ever get to New Zealand we will have lost the war.*')

But Bess stayed in Auckland and got a flatmate who happened to be a glamorous blonde woman separated from her husband, a golf professional. This flatmate had some of the recherché lustre of a Wallis Simpson: she was a mistress of Tibor Donner, a modernist Czech architect working in Auckland as a wartime exile. He was a married man. Times of war are notoriously complex morally. The fixed nature of society tends to come unstuck under the duress of separation and the anxiety of impending death. People grab at life with both hands. This was the morally neutral world Bess came to live in while her husband was away overseas. In escaping her small-town background she had also escaped the opprobrium of small-town eyes. Possibly for the very first time in her life she felt free.

Her flat was at the end of the tramline in the seaside suburb of Point Chevalier. She lived in a mini-estate created in the 1920s by a rumoured black marketeer who had made a fast fortune as a plasterer in the rebuild of Napier after 1931. In Point Chevalier he created a Shangri-La of sorts, building a plaster Art Deco mansion with its own private cinema, tennis courts and boat shed by the water's edge. It had a certain film noir character to it, morally hazy, at once smart, slightly cheap and rather loose.

It was in this environment that Bess met an American who became her lover. She was pretty, seemingly abandoned by a husband who, she later told me, regarded the marriage as a dead end by the time he went off to war. (I never heard my father's version of this story.) He had apparently told Bess that 'if he returned', it would not be to her. But what people say when they go off to war may not be the same when they come back. Perhaps the long wound of war had made my father rethink. Perhaps he thought of his wife more fondly now he no longer saw her. Perhaps he remembered only what he loved. Perhaps he was just looking forward to coming home.

TIME HAS JUMPED FORWARD WHEN Bess takes up the letter again. (Remember it is already a fortnight in which she has received two letters from Gordon. It is now a week later — three weeks since she has written. Is she thinking what to write? How to fill in the empty space when she cannot say what obsesses her? Is she like Emma Bovary who, as she walked home to her husband, mused, 'What am I going to say? How am I going to begin?') She mistakes the date, putting in July for 6 August 1945, by which time Gordon is at Lake Trasimene: '. . . [S]ince starting this,' she writes, '*I heard from BBC that the 2nd Div was on the eve of departing from the European theatre so I didn't bother to continue writing but apparently all that meant was a 4 day journey to another part of Italy.*'

This is her explanation for the delay, perfectly justifiable in itself. She is also trying to work out exactly where to send the damned letter. But she still has about three-quarters of the aerogramme left, so now she reaches out for the kind of gossip that is essentially filler. At the same time she is unconsciously evoking a morally grey world to which Gordon will be returning. Servicemen have already started coming home: '*Doug Flett arrived home yesterday — big party at the Commercial last night & a lot of sore heads today. Tom gave me a lift into town this morning — he reckoned they had all tried to get him under the table but he was the last on deck. All so darned silly for I guess Doug Flett is not a bit interested in . . . that crowd.*'[5]

This is a world I recognise as a child in the immediate post-war period — alcohol being used to tranquillise unquiet spirits, deaden anxieties, steady the nerves. There is no acknowledgement of post-traumatic stress disorder (PTSD), not even of the concept. Instead heavy drinking is presented as 'hilarious', a continuation of the 'high spirits' of wartime. But already this is starting to come into collision with the expectations of the post-war world ('*all so darned silly*'): '*Doug reckons Jock is on the water now — Nora is going to get a rude awakening I think for she imagines Jock will just stay at home & look after the children while she holidays — parties etc — Jock doesn't seem to come into her plans at all.*'[6]

Bess then reverts for a moment to a metaphor for anxiety. '*Old Ruapehu & the other Mts are all erupting quite fiercely — the grey dust has ruined all the snow for skiing I believe. Personally I'd be a bit dicky if I lived within coo-ee for each week seems to see them grow fiercer.*' The grey ash from Mt Ruapehu was soiling the beautiful white snow — snow as white as a wedding dress. To live nearby would be dangerous. '*Hope we can visit the Franz Joseph.*'

Unknown to Bess, Gordon was himself having to get used to rapid change. The 2nd Division was on the point of embarkation. The embrace of army life, with its frustrating rules and regulations, its discipline and orchestrated moments of insanity in which a human was suddenly meant to regard killing as a normal part of everyday life, was at its end. It was unsettling. The 'next few weeks and months were full of pathos', the regimental history notes. 'A great fighting force and the powerful loyalties surrounding it slowly disintegrated, and even the thought of going home could not make this process agreeable.'[7] Whatever great body had held these men in its death-like clasp was about to release them back onto civvy street. A great many of them were damaged. Gunner Gordon L. Wells — 472930 — boarded HMT *Strathmore* on 5 September 1945 bound for home.

THERE IS LITTLE SENSE THAT Bess was aware of Gordon's state of mind in her superficial, almost prattling letter. (But then she was essentially talking to herself, nervously making it up as she went along.) And Gordon, typically for his time, would have considered it both unmanly and unbecoming to write to his wife about his fears and uncertainties. Possibly he lacked the language.

The rest of the letter is written in Bess's competent workaday handwriting. It is easy to read and there is no ambiguity about the meaning of a word. Gordon's handwriting (very little of which remains) was by contrast gorgeous and elegant. In one way his handwriting was like an inner semaphore of a ghost-being. As a young man he had been stylish, with Brilliantined hair, smart clothes and the body of an athlete. He projected his bachelor status in the peacock shades of his rayon dressing gowns. This was the man Bess had married and who had gone away to war. The man who returned would be different. His medical notes describe him at one point as 'a walking case'. He returned as one of the many walking wounded.

This is who Bess addresses in this aerogramme. She is feeling out towards someone she no longer knows. Just as she, in her turn, is a changed woman with experiences she has not shared with her husband. (Is that why she kept this missive? It was a moment in time — between what has happened and what would perhaps never come to light? Was it precious in some way, or was it something she instinctively just tucked away in a drawer and, through some species of inertia, forgot about? Did it remind her of an earlier self? A more innocent self? Or a more deceptive self?)

The last flap of an aerogramme is always the most important. By this time you know you are running out of room and you have to cram in whatever is left, as you do a suitcase that is already full. Here Bess raises the question of Gordon's future employment, an issue that will dog their married life. She asks whether 'Head Office' at the English bank for which Gordon worked had asked where he would like to 'serve' once he is demobbed: '— *are you going to pick? Guess you will hate the Bank — I wish we could branch out into something fresh but it's hard to know just what.*'

This was not a small matter, despite the casual way she introduces the subject so late in the letter. Bess came from an upwardly mobile family. Not to upwardly mobilise in your turn was, in a way, to defame a shared religion. It was to ignore a central tenet of your being. It was one of the disappointments of Bess's life that she married a man who did not produce the upward mobility she needed for her sense of self-worth.

But the issue was deeper than that. Dad's wartime experiences scoured out of him some earlier being. He had gone off to war a handsome man with some of the lissome qualities of a Cary Grant. The photos of him taken during the war show a prematurely aged man, exhausted, drained, just hanging on as a grunt. He had turned down any chance at promotion, even though it was offered to him. Some sea change had happened to him during the war years. He became a bitter and sarcastic man.

For the meantime, believing him still to be the person she knew before his army experience, Bess wants Gordon to consider another career — but she leaves the reality vacant, as she cannot think what it would be. So this was a juncture, theoretically, at which they could have changed their lives. Bess, in this scenario, is looking to the future positively, if tentatively, accepting they will be together henceforth.

But now she has only a tiny amount of space left. There is still room to abruptly change the tone of the letter and say something personal to him. Like she loves him and misses him. Like she longs to see him and touch him. But she writes, in rather large letters to fill up any remaining space, '*Cheerio — good sailing — hope you get a chance to at least ring your brothers [in Australia] — Miss Flynn is at Hotel Styne — Manly — Sydney — See you soon, Love Chicken.*'

See you soon.

I FIRST FOUND THIS LETTER as a child, foraging in the hall cupboard. My reading of it then differs almost entirely from my understanding of it now.

The hall was decorated for that extremely rare moment when someone knocked at the front door. (If a tradesman like the Rawleigh's man came, he was always told to go to the back door, where negotiations could take place in private.) The front hall was, to a degree, formal, with an expensive embossed wallpaper, and had presentation objects in it, like the dark carved box that had come from 'the Far East', and an imposing clock that ticked out the minutes and chimed away the hours.

Around the corner, away from the evaluating eyes of the visitor, was a tall, thin cupboard with stacked shelves and a closed door. Inside the cupboard (I am tempted to call it a closet) was a compendium of my mother's past, a small museum of items ranging from never-opened presentation boxes of handkerchiefs, the lids decorated with 1930s maidens dancing along with Art Deco nimbleness, to boxes of photographs and rarely used table linen. Every square inch of the cupboard was wedged with memorabilia. Just like a library it had different levels of rarity and usefulness. The bottom level was given over to items of practical use — like the Electrolux. But as you rose up, you seemed to be climbing a ladder into a mysterious past.

Russell and I came across the aerogramme on the second to top level. We were always sorting out what was hidden in the house, restless as animals roaming a veldt. It was a way of trying to uncover our parents' past, of trying to get to know these mysterious beings whom biology and history had placed right in front of us, blocking the light. (I think I became an historian and writer on these forays into the backs of drawers and inside musty boxes, lifting up creased bridesmaids' frocks and carefully packed, elaborately knitted old pullovers. There always seemed a secret ahead of me.)

We had no way of knowing that this aerogramme held such a potent secret. Yet we had, unknowingly, already found other clues — or rather, separate parts of the same puzzle which, if the parts were put side by side, would make up a picture of our mother so diametrically opposed to what our childhood eyes saw that it would have seemed startling, even shocking. To the point of disbelief.

Let me describe one of these clues. It was a studio photograph of a man neither Russell nor I had ever seen. By now we were familiar with the core cast of most of the family photographs. 'Who's that?' and 'Where is that?'

were staple questions to ask our mother, and it was always a pleasure to perceive the infinite depth of her knowledge of family members, recognition of whom often led to a story or an incident. Just by looking at her face you knew these incidents had a reality that our mundane house, and even we her children, lacked. But this man never had a name.

Russell had managed to feel something behind the tablecloths. Tightly wedged into the shelf was the hard edge of a framed photograph. He triumphantly brought it out, and we looked at it in uncomprehending silence. It came from the 1940s (we did not know that, but intuited it came from the past, as the past was always black and white). The frame was slim, wooden, and had come apart along the left-hand side. The subject, a man, was wearing glasses, and looked to the right. He was not particularly handsome. He did not look like any known relative.

Our mother was on her way from the kitchen to the bedroom when she saw what we were holding.

'What are you doing with *that*?'

Before we had time to answer she veered towards us, her hand out.

'*Give it to me.*'

She was angry, we could see that. But not only angry. There was some other feeling in her face, trapped there like a slide caught in an automatic projector. She snatched the photo out of Russell's hands. At the same time, she raised the hem of her apron, and with one tender move wiped it across the glass of the frame, removing the dust. She seemed to sink down a shaft of memory for a moment.

'Who is it?'

Russell was always bolder than me. I knew it was better to wait, to ask her in a weaker moment, when her guard was down. She held the photo away from us, above our heads, so we could no longer see the man's face.

'Never you mind,' she said sharply. 'It's none of you kids' blasted business.'

The use of the word 'blasted' indicated her dander was up.

'Yes, but who is it?' said Russell

'Someone I used to know once. That's all,' she said.

We watched her put the picture on a higher shelf in the cupboard. We would need a stool to have another closer look at it.

She had her back turned to us as she hid it under further layers of cloth. 'Just don't ever show it to your father,' she said.

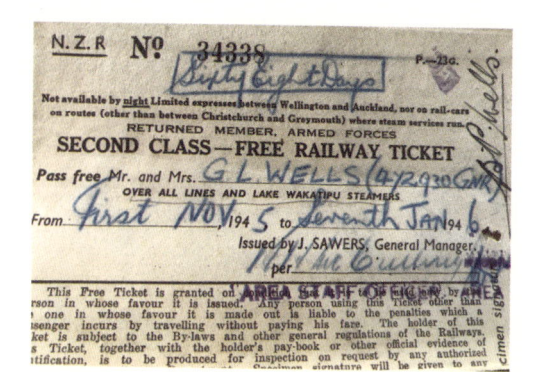

ABOVE

Bess and Gordon's rail pass for their trip around New Zealand, just after the war.

CENTRE

A second honeymoon after the wounds of war.

BELOW

Doc Barker's dog tag, secretly kept by Bess for decades.

She turned and shot Russell a look of exasperation.

'Why don't you kids go out and play in the fresh air.'

She shooed us further out of the hall, towards the kitchen.

'I don't understand you kids,' she said. 'You have a beach down the road to play on, a park, swings. Why do you always want to hang around indoors, fishing inside cupboards? *Get outside.*' Then, in a steely voice which meant we had definitely done something wrong, she said, 'I don't want to see either of you for a good hour or two.'

That was the last time we ever saw the photograph.

But in time I would discover that our house was littered with objects that had a particular resonance to my mother because they related to past love affairs. If the lover had vanished, at least he had left a small token behind. And just by glancing at this object — a perfume bottle, an aluminium plate from the US canteen — you received the charge of a long-buried secret.

THE TRUTH ABOUT BESS'S AMERICAN lover came to light in a way Tennessee Williams would have approved. It was at my brother's twenty-first birthday party. The woman who 'told us the facts' was a family friend. Her name was Aunty Margaret, no real relation. It was her sister-in-law who had shared Bess's flat, giving Aunty Margaret a ringside seat to my mother's life during the war. By the 1960s, Aunty Margaret was an alcoholic. Nobody, of course, said this at the time — many people drank heavily at social occasions. It was simply said she 'drank too much'.

Aunty Margaret could be funny and generous, but when the booze went sour on her she became querulous and serpent-tongued. I do not know why she made the occasion of my brother's coming of age into a truth-telling moment. But it could not have been worse timing. I still remember the shock. The whiteness of a wound before blood starts seeping.

I don't remember my father's reaction, or indeed my mother's. (Aunty Margaret was ushered out stage left by her husband.) Nor do I remember Dad ever overtly referring to the incident again. But it is hard not to think it was a source of his roiling unhappiness, the bitterness which marked his character. It might have been better if he had not loved my mother: but this was a stark fact.

What did I think about my mother's American lover, her sexual experimentation during the war? The new information demanded a difficult revision of her persona. I had assumed she went into marriage as a virgin and had stayed monogamous since — a confinement I would now regard as punishing and monotonous. But at nineteen I was a prude, a repressed homosexual. I was having trouble coming to terms with the explosive force of sexuality in myself, let alone in the family, with a volatile older brother who was also homosexual. To have a mother as a fraught, uncontrolled sexual force was too much to take on. I felt betrayed. I felt disillusioned. I felt I had been sold a pup.

As I got older and understood more about the complexity of a sexual persona, I was much more empathetic. I understood more about the power of social mores and how, at times, an individual has to explore his or her sexuality, even if it is directly against the norms and laws of the time. I now saw those wartime years as the one period in Bess's life when she was free to act as she wished. She herself told me later that she thanked God (a strange being to thank in the circumstances) she had this period to look back on. I understood it to be a time of romance and sexual fulfilment. If she never ever used the word 'love' in connection with my father, it was because she had experienced the bewilderment and enchantment of love with another man.

She did lie. That is how you live when you're cornered in a relationship. She did tell 'different kinds of truth'. But I have lied in similar situations, as have probably most people on earth. I would be a hypocrite to make any censorious comment.

IT WAS ONLY AFTER MY father died that Bess returned to being her own woman. She could talk freely now. But Gordon's death was followed swiftly — too swiftly — by Russell's dying. This led to a complete collapse. Yet once Bess recovered, she could talk frankly about the moral dilemma that had underlain her married life.

According to Bess's version of events, when Gordon had his final leave before going overseas, he deliberately left her on her own. He went off, played golf, partied and turned his back to her. And he said: 'If I return, it will not be to you. You are free.'

Some instinct made her stay in Auckland. It was the one time in her life when she lacked a male authority figure — she was not a daughter living with a father or a wife living with a husband. She was working and she could make her own decisions. She had resisted going home to live with her parents in Napier.

At some point she volunteered to serve food at the American canteen set up in the old ballroom at Government House. It was only a matter of time, I imagine, before she, an attractive young woman, caught the attention of a lonely — randy? — American. His name was Dr Taylor Wallace Barker. He was from Ohio. She referred to him as 'Doc Barker' — a name I became familiar with after both my father and brother died, and Bess and I would settle down for several hallucinatory-strength gin and tonics and talk about life. He was, she said, 'the love of my life' and 'thank God I had had that to think of', presumably during the long and difficult marriage with Gordon.

Forty-five thousand American servicemen came to New Zealand between 1942 and 1944, when the country served as the base for the American war effort in the wider Pacific. Auckland was a major supply base. But it was also a rest and recreation centre (and hospital) for the ever-increasing number of young men being fed into a brutal killing machine. The Pacific War was infamous for its ferocity: the Japanese fought till death and gave no quarter. Wounded flesh was also vulnerable to tropical diseases. Boys off the farm went insane under pressure. It was not all Glen Miller and moonlight.

Barker was a medical doctor and it was his job to attend to the wounded, the sick and, possibly, those driven mad by the horrors of the Pacific War. If he found comfort in a warm and passionate young woman who possessed a wry sense of humour and a thirst for life, it is understandable. That both of them were married may have just been part of the problematic landscape of war. Certainly the fact he was an officer would have soothed my mother's social anxieties. The officers had more select clubs and access to better goods, and were keenly sought after by young New Zealand women. Yet this intense love affair — at least on my mother's part — was relatively brief. The Americans were in New Zealand for only about two years. But when can intensity of feeling be measured by a clock? She was, on the other hand, married to Gordon for forty-eight years. It is a long time to hold a secret.

Later when I did some online investigation into Dr Barker, I found out he already had two children by the time he was in New Zealand. Whether Bess was the love of his life, I do not know. He sent her nylon stockings for a long time after the war. (I imagine Bess had to watch the post very carefully on a Saturday, when Gordon was home.) He lived in Cincinnati, Ohio, and was a Roman Catholic, and when his own son died in February 2014 Taylor Wallace Barker Jr. was described as 'a devout christian [sic] man, following the Catholic faith, and was a Pro-Life advocate'. This does not point to an especially liberal background.

My mother never forgot him. Even in her eighties, still a vibrant and lively woman, she tried to find out what had happened to Dr Barker. One day at the bridge club (at which she reigned supreme) she played a game with some Americans from Cincinnati who were on a Pacific cruise. She gave these sympathetic Americans her address, the name she used with Doc Barker (Betsy) and asked them to look him up in the phone book. They wrote in turn — it was still a time of letters as precious disseminators of personal information — that he had died.

But if Doc Barker had been the love of my mother's life, Aunty Margaret intimated with her serpent's tongue on that long-ago night that there had been others. Many others. Perhaps once Barker left, Bess did not refrain from taking other American lovers. Aunty Margaret talked of Paddy's Puzzle, a notorious house in Parnell (and not far away from where Bess worked), where rooms could be rented by the hour.

It was possibly at this very worldly period of her life that Bess plucked off all her eyebrows so she could paint on the high cynical raised eyebrows of a Marlene Dietrich or any of the other 'love goddesses' from cinema. Maybe she was mourning the loss of a man she had fallen deeply in love with. It's not uncommon to try to bury loss in the arms of another man or men. Who am I to point a finger? But ever since that signal moment when she eviscerated that natural growth of hair, so she stayed for all time — a woman without eyebrows. Even at age one hundred there was no sign of them. Their absence gave her face a curiously puritanical look, naked, slightly gaunt.

What Gordon thought when he saw her without her eyebrows I do not know. This is the thing. I have no knowledge of what happened when they met. After Dad died, she told me that she had had trouble going down to the railway station to face him, but that her women friends had said she had no choice. Even the newspapers of the time, briefing wives on the incoming difficulties of men damaged by years of war and killing, advised: 'You are in their debt. You must pay that debt in a form they can accept

. . . time, patience and tact are needed . . . If with understanding in your mind and sympathy in your heart — and not forgetting due gratitude on your part for what he has done for us all — you may make an appeal to his sense of fair play, he will seldom let you down. His behaviour may have temporarily changed, but his heart is sound.'[8]

So perhaps she packed away her thoughts and cares and erotic daydreams — the burden of her past — and turned to face the future, ironically in the form of the past, a man she had married six years before, during three of which she had had neither sight nor sound of him.

Yet the photos we have of them on their second honeymoon — and this is the conundrum — show a radiant couple. Clearly the honeymoon was a success. It was what came after that was more gruelling.

MANY YEARS LATER, WHEN I was packing up Bess's house — she had the beginnings of dementia and could no longer give me any answers to the questions I still wanted to ask (had my formidable grandmother ever known about Doc Barker? How much did Dad know of Barker or the other men my mother had known?) — I happened to look inside her sewing box. By this time I knew enough about my mother's obsessive hiding of things to search for them forensically. My fingers slithered inside a small pocket on the right-hand side of the interior of the sewing box. My finger pads felt the coolness of metal. I took out a small rectangular object. For a moment I was nonplussed. Then I looked at it more closely. The name *Taylor Wallace Barker* was stamped into it, followed by a long series of numbers, then a letter (his blood type). It was Doc Barker's dog tag. It had been hidden in a place my father would never have thought to look, and she had kept it all her life.

ANT
is not valid

raph of holder
by issuing

elow
and signed

is valuable.
fely and
when
as proof of
membership.
ferable.

PETER N. WALKER

(Term) INTERNATIONAL HOUSE
& UNIVERSITY OF WARWIC

(Home) 35 ST LEONARDS RD

The Coming Out Letter

OPPOSITE

My Warwick University student ID card: 'Hindsight is an erratic, even duplicitous gaze.'

Just before Christmas 1977 I decided I had to send a letter to my parents to bring them up to date with a significant development in my life. I was gay.

IT WAS ONE OF THE most difficult letters I have written in my life. And yet it is, in its raw basis, a letter that hundreds of thousands of young women and men — perhaps by now millions of young and not so young people — have written to their parents.

'London
  '5/12/77
  'Dear Mum and Dad,
  'I don't know why I've found this letter difficult to get down to write when all it contains is good news. But there it is. I have found it difficult to write.
  'Partly this is due to the fact that I have found it difficult to keep you up to date with other developments in my life, and this fact is due primarily to my being gay, and we three, between ourselves, never acknowledging it. This means that things which are important to me — like finding someone I am happy living with — I cannot share with you. Or haven't been able to, up to the present. This seems silly to let the world and the world's way of thinking about things stand in the way.
  'I do hope you can see in this letter my respect for you, my wish for you to keep up with my life, and not drift apart. I want to include you in my life, so you know what I am doing, and so we can feel friendly with each other and not as strangers.
  'Probably all this comes as a shock to you, but I will continue on.
  'Part of the happiness of finding someone to live with has been that it has made me more aware of what I want to do. I can imagine you will say that it is perfectly obvious what I want to do. Complete my thesis and start lecturing or teaching. Well, it's not true. And it's a long story...'

This does require a bit of backstory. In 1974 I had won a postgraduate scholarship to attend the University of Warwick's celebrated School of Social History. (Celebrated because this is where E. P. Thompson wrote *The Making of the English Working Class*, a work of history as passionate and imaginative as a novel, reinventing a libertarian working class for a socialist Britain.) But I was actually more attracted to Warwick by the fact that Germaine Greer, the charismatic author of *The Female Eunuch*, had lectured there. Greer had toured New Zealand in 1972, stirring up a nascent feminist movement. Gay Liberation ('The Gay Liberation Front') had swiftly followed. I joined, and I came out to my friends, my brother —

but not to my parents. We lived, as many did then, in mutually exclusive or parallel realities.

By the end of 1975, I'd been at Warwick University long enough to get over my first sharp culture shock; I had been to Paris with an Auckland friend, Tim Blanks, then Morocco with a new English friend, Bruce; and in the summer Bess and Gordon had come to visit, and this was a qualified success. Then two important events happened at Warwick: signposts pointing in diametrically opposite directions.

One of them was a paper I gave at the School of Social History. This looked at the press reactions to a sexual scandal which occurred in 1870, when two female prostitutes were arrested at a theatre and were found to be upper-middle-class men in drag. Their names were Boulton and Park. One of them lived as the wife of an aristocrat closely associated with the royal family. The revelation led to a moral panic about British masculinity, with effeminacy seen as a symptom of imperial decadence. Like all moral panics, it says more about the society in which it occurs than the incident that sparked it. But the panic was sufficiently explosive for a new word — *drag* — to enter the global vocabulary.

Writing to my brother Russell, I said, '*I suppose it might look like some anecdotal piece of joke-pulling; but it's not. I regard it as a really fundamental piece of history, Victorian history, shedding great wads of light onto sexual roles, expectations from what is male, female; things very important in an incipiently imperialist Britain.*'

It was, I said, '*rather like a proclamation of existence of an historian doing work in a serious area of historical investigation (no small thing, it seems to me, in the field of homosexuality which is usually consigned to dull books by unreadable authors: or irrelevant books by dull authors — take your pick).*'[1]

Explaining to my brother by way of explaining it to myself: '*Perhaps I should explain how good I've found it being at Warwick academically — that's to say at the Centre for the Study of Social History: which is like a mini-School in the French sense of the word, extremely professional in its method; in fact above all, strict in its historical method, religious.*'

I was responding to the intellectual stimulus of a new 'scientific' way of looking at history, as well as the intensity with which social history was regarded. In its own way I was also feeling towards something that became, twenty years later, queer studies. '*I feel I've grasped so much more clearly what history is all about, in its doing, and because laboriously, with utterings of agony and groans of pain, frustration, I've at long last started my own doing, I value this very highly.*

'*As you can see I feel on the very brink of things — perhaps an illusion — but I don't want to traipse back to NZ midsentence —*'

This was the crux of the situation, even in 1975. My scholarship was negotiated year by year, and ahead of me loomed the possibility of having to go home. '*I can only see going back to NZ as 1) cutting me off from sources I will need to refer to . . . 2) returning to a peaceful pond atmosphere, where the stimulus is very minor and the perils of intellectual isolation (not to sound too snobbish — but it's true for all sorts of reasons — mainly NZ's undeveloped colonial rawness) very great . . .*'

The fact was I was loving Britain with '*its free atmosphere, its largeness . . . England fairly vibrates, or shakes at the moment; it's like an ancient machine whose inner workings are working up into a tumult, out of sight.*'[2] In fact, it was not the anticipated socialist revolution that lay ahead but Thatcher's neoliberal Britain and, as ominously, AIDs. At the time, however, there seemed to be momentum towards social change. '*There seems a real surfacing of films about gay people,*' I wrote in October '75. (I was thinking of Fassbinder's *Fox and His Friends*, *The Naked Civil Servant*, *A Bigger Splash*, Derek Jarman's *Sebastiane*.) And I was starting to register as part of the new English intellectual establishment. '*Jeffrey Weekes, a lecturer at the London School of Economics* [and a mentor], *has just published an article on the historiographical problems of studying sexuality, especially homosexuality. He mentions my work, which is nice of him. I think I'm the only person in England doing work in this specific area.*'[3]

So this was one signpost — pointing in the direction of an academic career as a lecturer or historian, working in a pioneering area of what would later be conceptualised as queer studies.

But there was another signpost pointing completely the other way. In March 1975 I had entered a short fiction competition held by the University of Warwick; it later became the prestigious Warwick Prize for Writing. It was, I told Russell, who was both confidant and sounding board, '*a story I had based round the experiences at Brown's Bay, which I had written in the midst of winter when all I could do was remember back to long sunny dusty days full of radios in cars, swinging coloured lightbulbs in Norfolks along the parade, and the wail of hymns inside suffocating tents . . . a mixture*

LEFT

My brother Russell,
full of charm,
kindness and brio.

CENTRE

A proud Bess and
Peter, graduation day,
Auckland, 1974.

BELOW

Warwick University,
England, where
Germaine Greer taught.

OPPOSITE

A letter to my
brother Russell from
a father I forgot.

THE NATIONAL BANK OF NEW ZEALAND LIMITED

Jean Batten Place,
Off Shortland & Fort Streets
AUCKLAND, C.1.

Dear Russell,
 I suppose by now you won't want to come back to Auckland, 'tis a wonderful life on the farm, have you been for a ride on a horse yet? I'll bet both you and Peter have been good boys for Mummy. I saw little Brian last night and he wished he could be with you boys on the farm.
 See you on Saturday
 x x   xx Daddy

of pathos and grotesquery: and an odd wavering kind of beauty.' To my delight, the short story won first prize.

Something was happening to me almost uncontrollably. Separated from New Zealand, I had begun to think about it obsessively, reconceptualising it. This is what happens to all expatriates — you suddenly come to comprehend the country that formed you. For me this took a primarily fictional form; or rather, I attempted to come to terms with my past through the writing of fiction — fiction, however, based very closely on my childhood experiences in New Zealand.[4] (I was feeling my way towards being what would later be called 'a gay writer'.) This flooding back of memories, after a period when the past seemed frozen behind a wall of ice, became unstoppable — it was a time of unthawing.

Perhaps not coincidentally, I had also fallen in love. At Warwick University I met a young man, a Londoner of emphatically working-class background. He had a shock of coal-black hair, very white skin, red lips made for kissing. He spoke with an exaggerated Cockney accent, was full of braggadocio and, for me more winningly, transparent insecurities. He was younger than me, intense and passionate, and he came — illegally — to live in my tiny room at International House. Like all first love affairs, it was rhapsodic, idealistic and overwhelming. He had only just come out. This highly sexual affair, with its hurricane-force intimacy, reoriented my life. If my memory was unthawing, the almost constant sex had a way of knitting my personality together so I became whole. So when I wrote to my parents about 'things that are important to me — like finding someone I am happy living with', I was introducing them to a man I thought of as my long-term partner. And even though it was the mid-1970s and pre-AIDS, when promiscuity was virtually prescriptive, I subscribed to monogamy without giving this too much close inspection.

My letter to my parents continued: *'There's an old cliché, you're only alive or young once. Well it's true. I feel I have to get my courage together sufficiently to make a great change in my life, and start doing something I want to do. This is something which I've wanted to do ever since I was a kid sitting in my bedroom scribbling away like a maniac into my diary. It has never really changed. I just lost sight of it in the immense period of upheaval when I first began to come to terms with the fact I was what other people call homosexual. Anyway, what I have always wanted to do, and am doing now, is write.*'

I had made a decision that I would abandon my doctoral studies, which had begun to lose momentum anyway. Following the Boulton and Park paper, I had drifted along, uncertain of where I was going and what I was doing. I lacked the analytic tools.[5]

'I have started writing in the past year. I very much wanted to get some stories published, win some prizes so I could assure you that my going into such a new field, inexperienced, would be worth it. Well I haven't got much to show for a whole year's concentration and effort — except perhaps my determination to keep writing, my joy in it, the pleasure it gives me . . .

'I can imagine that this decision of mine, which is to finish at university without a doctorate, will come as a shock to you. Most of all to your expectations. I can imagine that you will immediately start worrying about me. But don't. I'm not worried about myself, so why should you? I am aware of the great step I am taking, the great gamble, but I want to take it.'

I wanted Mum and Dad to know the most important thing that any parent can give a child:

'I've found something which makes me happy. I think this is a great and beneficial gift — one of the greatest gifts anybody can give anyone. I am deeply grateful to you both having provided the circumstances which make it possible — and I want you to accept that what has happened is good.

'This letter comes out all of a lump but it is something which has been constantly on my mind day and night for the last year. I have wanted to confide in you, share with you some of the enthusiasm I feel for what I'm doing. Above all I want to put you in the picture, so we don't just grow apart. I do value you as parents, as friends, and I don't want that to happen.'

These words had been typed out on my portable Remington, on the thin folio paper that I used to write stories. Then I handwrote in pencil:

'In all fondness and deep love,
Pete'

TWO DAYS LATER I SENT a letter to Russell. '*My dear Russell*'. By now we were writing to each other reasonably regularly, though by no means with the metronomic monotony that dictated my letters to our parents. (The coming out letter above ended, somewhat anticlimactically, '*PS Received yours this morning. Many many thanks.*') In the abstract space that is distance, Russell and I had achieved the seemingly impossible: we had removed the sibling rivalry that had been so destructive when we were younger. Instead we treated each other with relative courtesy and interest, and the powerful bond we shared had room to flourish.

'*After a great deal of indecision and loss of nerve,*' I wrote to Russell, '*I wrote to Mum and Dad last week, saying I thought it was time they acknowledged the fact I was gay . . . I'm not sure if this is incredibly foolhardy, even cruel . . . I am worried that they will both punish each other, apportioning blame out, breastbeating in the silence etc. Both of them have a really strong line in emotional terror . . . I only hope not. I tried to make the letter as good and kind and hopeful as ever, pointing out I am not sad or anything, that it is just a part of my life, like a limb on which I walk . . . I don't know what sort of Christmas you will have in Auckland. I can imagine my letter will cause a major adjustment in the lives of us all — perhaps . . . I've told them these facts in my life, not from a wish to be brutal or anything, but just so that . . . we don't grow totally apart. Surely a family should be based on understanding each other rather than just pure familial links.*'

Russell kept every one of the letters I sent him while overseas, right from my first letter sent from Hong Kong. I didn't keep a single letter from him. This is a neat encapsulation of the terms of our relationship. I was the spoilt younger brother. (I was also moving around a great deal, the usual reason for jettisoning 'excess baggage'.) In many ways he was an ideal older brother. There was nothing he would not do to help me, and I relied on his constant faith in me without ever quite acknowledging it. That he loved me obsessively was something I could overlook when we were twelve thousand miles apart. And the fact that he kept my letters (which came back into my possession after his death) meant, when it was time to reconstruct this part of my life, I had a contextual bed of fact to check against the inexactitude of my own recollection.

Hindsight is an erratic, even duplicitous gaze. What makes us uncomfortable we remove from the gaze of others and then slowly from ourselves. We end up preferring the narcissism of an unreal image behind which we hide our insecurities, secret unhappiness and doubts about whether we have done the right things in life. I was — am — no different. And when, forty years later, I re-read the letters I'd sent my brother, I cringed at my apparent self-confidence, my self-assurance in believing my opinions were interesting.

There is also the syntactical awkwardness of the coming out letter itself. I have no memory now of how many copies I wrote before ending up with the one relatively clean version I sent my parents. But the first two sentences are an obstacle course in awkward locution. At the same time I have to acknowledge something that remains with me only vestigially now: a young person's grace — or naivety — that the world can be improved, and that as humans we will evolve into a better space. What strikes me now with this letter is my affection for my parents. I was trying to make things easier for them, so our relationship could keep growing. I was very naive.

THERE IS IN FACT ANOTHER backstory behind this relatively simple, even earnest coming out letter, one that this letter effectively screens from the reader.

When I murmured the word 'perhaps' in relation to the thought that my letter would dramatically alter the relationships within the family, I was acknowledging a sense of reality about how our family worked. If my parents' marriage was built on a secret, they had unknowingly created a house of secrets within which we had all accustomed ourselves to feel at home. Speaking out in this context was treasonous. So when I murmured 'perhaps', what I was really saying was I doubted anything would change.

Twenty-three days later, the other side of Christmas, I wrote to Russell again. He had rung me — which gives some sense of the crisis: *'I was so pleased to hear your voice . . . You seemed so distant and I had trouble hearing . . . I wonder how your Christmas went at home.'*

The fact was that every Christmas we spent together as a family was tense. There was always a sense of dwelling in a minefield, that at any moment a tripwire would accidentally set off an explosion. (Christmas still makes me apprehensive; it carries a sense of impending misery from which I have to actively shake myself awake.)

'I hope Mum was not too upset . . . She wrote to me three letters day after day, after she received my letter. Each one progressively more mellow, in a way. More supplicating. I hope she realizes that her non-recognition of my gayness — in effect — for barring Dad from any knowledge is this — is her own choice, and she does it from her own sense of weakness — the flaws in her own relationship with Dad. It's a horrible irony that these have to re-

occur so late on. I hated the thought of causing her any pain; in some ways she has so few defences; she is pure Tennessee Williams; but some amount of truth is necessary to my own life.'

My memory of Bess's response is visceral. She sent me a letter saying she 'thanked God' she had got to the letterbox before Dad and she had read the letter first. She implored me never to raise the issue again. Dad above all must not be told. This to me was a shocking, a dismal, response. In my mind's eye, I saw her ripping the letter up into a thousand small pieces and flushing them down the toilet. I have no memory at all of the three letters she sent day after day as she thought the situation through. This in itself is an interesting statement on the unreliability of memory. Or was it that the first outright rejection blocked any memory of further communication? I have no memory, either, of her letters becoming more mellow, ending up as 'supplications'. (Or were the supplications *Please do not speak to your father*?)

Bess was then aged sixty-one, and suffered from a duodenal ulcer — all that keeping silent, all that stress. Gordon was a prematurely aged sixty-nine-year-old ex-serviceman, self-medicating with alcohol and the heavy tranquillisers (Valium, Mogodon, Seconal, Tuinal) that were part and parcel of the period. Yet in an unexpected and long-term way, the letter was a success. Such was Bess's unconditional love, she supported my decision to embark on the risky business of becoming a writer. She had no interest in the arts and knew that being a writer was practically a form of financial suicide. But she had experienced Dad's frustration at spending his life doing a job he did not like: they had never branched out, as she suggested they might in that long-ago wartime letter, written at a crossroads of their lives. Dad had spent his life in drudgery at a bank. She was determined that I should be supported doing something that I was passionate about. That she could not accept my sexuality related to her understanding of morality — or, as I would see it, her misunderstanding of morality.

Or was it a case that she could support me in one area of my life as a way of saying she could not support me in the other? Whatever, supporting me in my choice to become a writer was one way I felt the depth of her love.

Bess and Gordon were older than many post-war parents, although I had no sense of that growing up. In their style and values they remained emphatically pre-war — on the surface, a sporty, fun-loving couple from the 1930s and '40s who enjoyed a party, a swim, a good drink. It may have

ABOVE AND RIGHT

Russell struck down by HIV, 1988.

BELOW

Bess vulnerable and struggling with the blows landing on her.

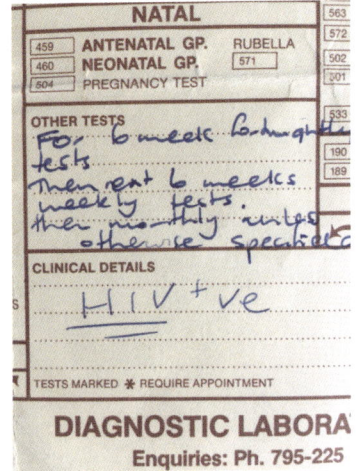

been that the ambiguities buried so deeply in their marriage made them delay having children. Bess's version was that Dad never wanted children anyway. According to Bess, the classic unreliable witness, Dad's first response to her saying she was pregnant with Russell was a very basic one: *Get rid of it.*

I am not sure about this. Dad was a kind man and it sounds like a rash statement in the middle of an argument. Or was a child the bandage that Bess produced, unasked, to hold their shaky marriage together? It is a classic ploy. When I wrote to Russell, '*I am worried that they will both punish each other, apportioning blame out, breastbeating in the silence etc. Both of them have a really strong line in emotional terror*', I was not exaggerating. My parents went on terrorising one another for the rest of their marriage. In this sense, the coming out letter was a failure.

IT WAS A GREAT COMFORT to me that I could be candid with Russell in a way I could never be with my parents. He in his turn talked to me about the anxieties in his own life. We are talking the 1970s here, when homosexual relations were still illegal. He was a solicitor and lived a double life, as we all did, with the consequent strains and tensions. A promising Labour politician had had his career ruined by National's Robert Muldoon on the basis of gay innuendo, introduced inside the safe-house of Parliament. The sense of surveillance in Muldoon's New Zealand was never far away after the so-called Moyle Affair.

In an undated letter to Russell concerning the arrest of his current lover, we talked about the realities of the situation. The reason for the arrest was not made clear, but my supposition is that 'John' was caught 'cottaging' by a policeman — a common tactic in the repression of homosexuality at this time. Attractive, well-hung policemen would often be chosen as bait to lure men who had few opportunities for meeting other men for sex into public toilets: the result — arrest and publication of details of full name, job and address — was deliberately destructive.

'*I can never quite work out with Mum and Dad whether our relationship to them, vis a vis, our homosexuality, is based on the thin veil of illusion that our sexual bias does not exist. Is invisible to them. Of course an occasion like this speaks it loud and clear, and to a very wide, interested, beery-breathed, sharp eyed, scissor tongued, and notch-in-the-belt public.*

I imagine people where you work must have put one and one together and worked out a gossipy sum totally one thousand and one days of Sodom. These are all public-personal issues of course, and I have no doubt your personal credibility, and the esteem in which many people personally hold you, will carry you over, so long as you yourself hold tight.

'I can't see you, or how you are, so I am talking in the dark. How are you surviving in it? . . . You are in a very vulnerable position. You are a public servant, and reasonably prominent, hence, exposed. Please write and tell me what is happening with the case; also what your approach will be to Mum and Dad, if any . . . As far as I know, they know nothing. They've made no allusion to being worried or anything in their letters; in Dad's last one, sent on 30 January, he just said you were very busy, they didn't see much of you. We are really in the position of parents with children, seeking to protect them. One has to be careful of putting too much strain on Mum above all, she is a real whirlpool of worry. Also she values the mirage of social life so much that she would never question, in her rational self, its laws . . . the whole thing brings it home to me the minute pressures of NZ life.

'Well, I must be off,' I added at the end of the letter, *'I envy you swimming, and don't get caught in any rips.'*

I FEEL MANY THINGS WHEN I now look at my 1977 coming out letter. It seems to encapsulate a past self that I look back to almost with longing. What do I mean by this? At twenty-seven you think you know the world. At that time I thought you came out and that was it. Today I see life is a constant state of becoming, of essentially coming to terms with unexpected changes that go on throughout life. Ageing itself is an intense philosophical process as much as a bodily experience.

But I also feel a deep and residual sadness reading this letter, as I know how it was received. Bess was terrified of what Dad would say. Herein lies, at the very least, a deep ambiguity. I was being asked to return to silence to protect her relationship, itself ambiguous at best, with her husband, my father. Why was she so frightened of him? It's hard not to think that the secrets of her wartime life made her extremely vulnerable to a kind of emotional blackmail. She was always, so to speak, on the back foot. Contemporary popular psychology did not help. Its 'explanation for the origins of homosexuality' was singularly punishing for the mother of a homosexual son. The son was classically meant to be feminised or castrated by an overpowerful, anxious mother. In other words, she was to blame.

Imagine then, if you had by some freak of nature mothered two homosexual sons — and these were your only children? And you yourself had issues to do with guilt and secrecy? She wished to keep my homosexuality secret, or at least unnamed, so that she did not have to face further obloquy from her husband who had every right, according to contemporary theory, to blame her for 'turning' me and my brother into homosexuals.

But I have another theory, and one my mother did not know about. (And surely in a house of secrets, there are always further locked and barred rooms, rooms without exits, rooms sealed up, rooms that only the imprisoned individual knows and feels at home within.) Long after Dad died, I asked to see his war records.[6] I wanted to try to understand more about this man who was always deeply mysterious to me, a man who I could claim never to have really known, not intimately, not closely. What I did know about him was that his war experience was central to his identity, to his core of masculinity. *It was who he was.* But when I finally got his medical records, I came to a different understanding of him.

At first I found it hard to comprehend what they were saying. ('Sick leave without pay'. 'Reverts to ranks at own request'. 'Battle casualty and accidentally wounded' struck out and 'Sick' left in. 'Nil abnormal seen'.) But gradually I began to understand the pattern behind Dad's behaviour. One thing was that he was offered promotion at least three times when away overseas, but each time he either took the promotion momentarily and then asked for it to be rescinded (one time the night before a battle), or he refused the promotion completely.

Why was this? As a bank officer and an intelligent man, he was probably considered potential officer material. But instead he stayed back in the ranks, as a grunt. He became a gunner, part of a small team of men whose job it was to load the weapons, fire them: he was a human attached to an infernal machine. (This led to a premature deafness that added to our communication problems. He could never *hear*.)

But there was something else, something much more troubling. I began to work out that Dad, rather than being a macho male who responded to army life, had the record of a malingerer. He was sometimes ill immediately before a battle (as at Cassino), and during battles he suffered forms of

TOP AND CENTRE

Dad, exhausted and worn thin, photographed on service in the war.

LEFT

Some part of my father never came home.

diarrhoea — the shits, not to put too fine a point on it. Was he frightened? It is only human to be terrified at sites of mass slaughter. He was often sent away from the front with unspecified medical problems which may have been as much psychological as physical. ('This man looked rather pale & drawn'; he is 'a walking case'.) He was constantly being screened for 'Sandfly fever', a common 'vector-borne febrile arboviral infection' for men fighting in the desert. (This also led to diarrhoea, but often no evidence of sandfly fever was found.) It is also notable that Dad asked to revert to the ranks two days before his first experience of battle (at Medenine, in Tunisia). Medical problems which plagued his later life — a bad back, pleurisy — manifested themselves during the war.

Dad had a hair-trigger sensibility. He was a champion sprinter whose attention was pinpointed to the explosion of a gun: instantly, he accelerated, and in a short brilliant spurt passed through the ribbon. A winner. But here, in battle after battle, year after year, he was surrounded by gunshots, bombs, explosions, strafings. The analogy is of a racehorse in a war zone. I believe the experience really disturbed his entire psychological mechanism. His war service was not glorious, was not macho — indeed, could almost be characterised as cowardly. (I find it very hard to write that word down. I feel my father's presence freezing in dismay that I would so betray him.) But this is the thing: I don't think any of my father's comrades saw it like that. If he had tried to portray himself as a hero, or falsely claimed some similar status, yes, he would have been heavily stigmatised. But it was perhaps the humanity of shared loss, of a communal experience of horror and death and constant killing, that broadened an understanding of the varieties of human response.

Dad, I think, was gathered into the bosom of the army, was accepted for what he'd contributed. Hence the army, long after the war had ended, remained the one irrefutable refuge for this man who had been changed forever by his experience in the war.

So what did this mean for my mother and my father's deeply troubled relationship? What worse fate could a man who wondered if he was a malingerer, even a coward, have than to be presented by his wife with two 'unmanly' sons — sons who are not even men according to his understanding? To his generation, a homosexual man could not be brave, manly or true. He'd have preferred anything rather than accept he had fathered, or was the father of, two sons who were homosexual. It was like a ghastly revenance from his wartime experiences.

You can see how difficult it was for my mother and father to read the letter I was sending them. It was impossible.

This is one of the reasons I feel a deep sadness when I read this letter now. There is my own bright shiny naivety, my lack of knowledge of what troubled them both. I did not understand. I did not know the wounds each of them carried. On the other hand, I was young enough to believe in the malleability of human nature. I thought we could break through the caul of secrecy and untruth, and get to know one another as we humanly were. '*Surely a family should be based on understanding each other rather than just pure familial links,*' as I wrote to Russell.

THIS WASN'T TO HAPPEN TILL the implosion and collapse of the family. This was all clustered, significantly enough, around Dad's death in November 1987. Fortunately, he and I had a rapprochement before then. In a notebook a week before he died, I wrote: '*Then I realised there was no time left. I either had to begin talking or it would end with both of us silent till the end. And as soon as I launched out I realised it didn't matter what I talked about . . . the stock market crash, the cat, the weather — what mattered was that we were looking at each other and our bodies were near. And I thought of all the years, the decades really, when we simply hadn't been able to talk. The fact that I was gay lay between us like a huge wall, almost as if one or the other of us was in prison and the other person was the visitor: we were forced to communicate thru' a small gap in the wall. And the strange thing is — once I began talking — he began answering in a way he wouldn't have before. (Which one of us was in prison, I wonder?)*'

A year later, in October 1988, I wrote: '*I thought the saddest day in my life was telling Bess Russell was antibody positive. The second saddest day is acknowledging, no, saying yes to Bess having ECT.*' Bess had tried to commit suicide, then she had a breakdown. '*It all takes the pathetically Freudian form,*' I wrote to a confidante, Jude Henderson, in an undated letter, '*of an obsession with the drains in her house, which she is convinced are blocked up . . . she foresees landslides, eruptions, demolition and complete poverty. It is truly awful and very pathetic. What makes it worse is she is aware of how pathetic she is being. Naturally it all relates to Russell (and her complete conviction I'm also dying of AIDS) . . . I am totally overwrought.*' I added:

'*Part of her problem has been not being able to tell her bridge-playing friends what is obviously obsessing her and upsetting her enormously.*'

It is difficult these days, when HIV has become a treatable condition, to comprehend what it was like when AIDS first appeared in the 1980s. As the Broadway producer of a revival of *Angels in America* said recently, 'It's hard to remember now just how frightening and how all-engulfing AIDS was,' especially for gay men.[7] 'A society's attitude to disease reveals more than its state of medical knowledge,' A. N. Wilson has rightly said, and the aggressive homophobia AIDS whipped up — just when gay men were at their most vulnerable — was horrifying.[8] In the longer term, gay men and their allies learnt to advocate for advances in medical treatment, laying the groundwork for other people to confront political conservatism disguised as medical inertia. But at the time it was a dark, confusing period in which friend after friend, acquaintance after acquaintance, first got sick, then died. In my diary at the time I acknowledged the dramatic changes we were living through: 'The whole gay world has collapsed — inwards . . . It is no longer possible to be "gay" in this world. We have to retreat into being homosexuals again.'

Russell died in September 1989. The loss of a child is one of the greatest wounds life can deliver to a parent. But once Bess came to terms with it — that is, if one can ever come to terms with such a terrible blow — it deepened her compassion and understanding of life, including her own. She became an integrated person. She acknowledged publicly she was the mother of two gay sons and at HIV events spoke, sometimes with tears running down her face, as the mother of a son who had died of AIDS. I still cry when I think of this period in my life — not only for the pathos of it, but also for the way we were all forced by events towards that rapprochement I had wanted so much as a twenty-seven-year-old.

In the aftermath, when Dad had gone and Russell had gone and Bess had recovered, I really got to know Bess as a human. I would go to her place for dinner, which was always preceded by dynamite G & Ts. (Bess: 'Pete, you do know how to pour a good gin.') It was at this time in her life she told me about her American lover. She levelled, as we once would have said. One evening after a few gins she said she'd 'run upstairs' to show me something. (In her eighties she still cleaned a three-bedroom, three-bathroom house and did the garden, without any 'help'.)

She brought down a piece of paper and handed it over to me. It was what she now called 'your wonderful letter'. All those years — for thirty years I had believed she had destroyed that letter. But no, she had kept it safe, hidden away in the house of secrets. 'The deliciousness of a letter had to do, in part, with its ability to hold a spiritual or physical portion of the self,' Deborah Lutz has written in *The Brontë Cabinet*.[9] Bess had kept that part of my soul safe all those years and cherished what was true in its sentiments — its wish that we would know each other as we were.

I didn't re-read the letter when she showed it to me. I felt a kind of shame for what I assumed would be its false tone, its meretriciousness. It was only when I was once again sorting through Bess's possessions, to shift her from her townhouse to the retirement village, that I came across it. As I sat down to read it I felt many things, but one of them was a particular feeling — you might call it a sense of farewell '. . . as in the rearview mirror, you glimpse a familiar figure who is your younger self passing into history'.[10]

Solway College.

The Principal and Staff request the pleasure of
the company of

Mr & Mrs Northe & friends

at the following Functions:

SPORTS—Saturday, Nov. 26th, at 2 p.m.

DRAMA—"The Countess Cathleen" (W. B. Yeats)
Saturday, Dec. 3rd, at 7.45 p.m.

CONCERT AND PLAY—
Saturday, Dec. 10th, at 7.45 p.m.   1931

ELOCUTION, DRILL & DANCING—
Tuesday, Dec. 13th, at 7.30 p.m.

BREAK-UP—Friday, Dec. 16th, at 7.30 p.m.

To Whom It May Concern

OPPOSITE

My mother's letter of reference from the Solway College headmistress and an invitation to Solway's end of year activities: 'The ordinary virtues still define us as humans.'

The reference letter was a staple of the letter-writing genre and arose from a time when information on an individual was difficult to access. (A digital trail, courtesy of Google and Facebook, with its potential for whiplash, did not exist.)

SUPPLYING WRITTEN REFERENCES WAS A necessary preliminary to obtaining a job, and employers took them seriously as a basis on which to make a judgment call. At the same time, everyone knew they were artificial puffs which routinely excluded any negative comment.

But a reference had to have some correspondence with truth, otherwise the referee, the person who wrote the reference, brought themselves into disrepute as an unreliable source. A reference could also be deepened by its writer's insight, giving the document a more rounded, even novelistic quality.

When I was sorting out material for this book, I came across Bess's references from the 1930s, kept as part of her overall inclination to 'save everything'. The first of them, stiff and thin in its cadence, did not offer much insight. It commended '*Miss Northe*' as having '*the highest character and . . . the advantage of an excellent Education and Home Training*'. But then there was the give-away: '*I have known her Parents for many years. They are highly esteemed Residents of Napier — her Father . . . being the Managing Director of R Northe & Sons Ltd of this Town.*' It was typed in the vivid purple of a carbon copy, signed by A. E. Renouf, JP.[1] The date was 16 October 1936.

The Renoufs were family friends. I knew Mr Renouf from the decorated handwritten verses from the 1930s that my grandmother had saved. (She seems to have had the hoarding gene Bess inherited, but then she lived in the same house all her life so it was easy to just tuck something away.) Mr Renouf wrote doggerel to mark birthdays, gifts of a cake (one delivered on the same day the reference was written, as quid pro quo), and even the breaking of a vase. One, addressed to 'Mr & Mrs W E. Northe, Lawrence Road, Napier', marked the occasion of my grandparents' silver wedding anniversary, 27 April 1935. (Jess and Ern's wedding date coincided with King George V becoming king, hence the royalist sentiments):

> *The King preserves our Empire fair,*
> *Across the far flung waters;*
> *But Ern and Jess have done their share,*
> *To wit — three bonny daughters.*
>
> *From then, King George has ruled the State,*
> *While Ernie ruled his Wife,*
> *Each possessed a loving mate,*
> *And spent a happy life.*

If anything, this pointed to the way the British Empire, with a royal family at its apex, formed a pyramid made up of 'similar' families of all sorts of different classes and races throughout its many lands. In the 1930s, people like the Northes and Renoufs did not see the Empire as a racist construct: they were still insulated inside the belief systems they had inherited. The weakness of the British Empire lay ahead, when the Japanese inflicted the biggest defeat on the British Army in history, in Singapore in 1942. As Lee Kuan Yew, later prime minister of Singapore, said, this was the day the British Empire ended. The defeat of 'the white man' by a 'coloured people' had profound ramifications for the future.

Mr Renouf's doggerel depicts a smaller, more intimate provincial world, more humble in a way, more connected. It was of course entirely Pākehā. The women, who are called 'Balquhidder Belles' in one of his poems, dressed in long evening gowns and met every Saturday night to play bridge. Their husbands ('Ruddenclau Roughs') dressed in suits and ties to play snooker. But since it was the Depression, the men all paid one shilling a head for electricity and my grandfather brought along the milk. Later there might be a supper of various home-made delights baked by the women. My mother commented in a handwritten note I found among her effects: 'They were a lovely group of friends and we young ones would often call in for supper after the Sat. night pictures'.

The venue was 'Balquhidder', a large house belonging to the Ruddenclaus, who had at one time owned a number of sheep farms.[2] By the time of the Great Depression these farms were all mortgaged to the hilt and the Ruddenclaus had withdrawn to their large house in Napier, which was, in fact, one of those grand houses built by the gentry in the nineteenth century so their wives could 'come to town', enjoy a little urban life — and escape the monotony and isolation of their 40,000-acre spreads.

This is the tightly interwoven provincial context, then, of a reference supplied by a family friend during the Depression.[3]

ANOTHER REFERENCE WHICH DREW MY attention, partly because of the elegance of its script and the impressive embossed letterhead, came from a hallowed source: Solway College. Solway often cropped up in my mother's reminiscences. Her tone made it clear that the school was virtually sacred. Everything to do with it was good, fine, fun and also, on another level, inspirational. It is not too much to say that Solway College was an enduring inspiration to Bess throughout her life.

And because Bess's influence on Russell and me was so strong, Solway had an effect on us, too — on how we saw her, and hence how we saw ourselves. The school gave her, in the context of the egalitarian blue-collar suburb of Point Chevalier in which we grew up, a distinction, an air of exclusivity we craved. It also gave her a kind of confidence, a breeze of assurance, something almost quietly distinguished — as good, in its way, as marrying into a family with an ancient ancestry. Because that is what a private school offers: an illustrious genealogy which you adopt just by paying a fee. That's the theory anyway. But I think what made Bess's experience of Solway College exceptional was its first headmistress, Marion Thompson.

Marion Thompson was 'one of a distinguished group of University of Otago women graduates of the 1890s, most of them former pupils of Otago Girls High School and many with strong Presbyterian connections, who combined high academic achievement with a sense of Christian vocation'.[4] 'Mrs T', as Bess always referred to her, was actually a proto-feminist. Obtaining an MA with First Class Honours as early as 1898 (and, in the process, supporting herself by private coaching and teaching), she could not help but be anything else. Later, she had also to slip into the role of the main wage-earner when her husband, a Presbyterian minister, had a serious heart attack and had to give up the ministry.

The offer to become headmistress of a new Presbyterian boarding school in the Wairarapa in 1916 was 'not wholeheartedly welcomed by the Thompsons who held that fee-charging schools were incompatible with the democratic principles of the Presbyterian Church'.[5] This is the crux: earnest Presbyterianism mixed its love of education and core democratic values with a sense that one existed in the world to make it better. This gave Bess's private school experience a particular set of values, broader than the purely aspirational aspect that is the normal part of a snobbish 'private school education'.

Bess went to Solway under exceptional circumstances. After the quake, the school took in educationally displaced girls from the private schools of Hawke's Bay, and offered them the first term free. In one way this displayed Mrs T's characteristic shrewdness: the roll was dropping so dramatically thanks to the Depression that Solway came close to closing. The influx of

— To Mrs W. E. Northe —

— Napier —

How sweet of you, for Friendship's sake
To make for me this Birthday Cake.
I'm sure it is the nicest way
For you to mark my Natal Day
Be sure your work will not be wasted
Tis the finest Cake I ever tasted.

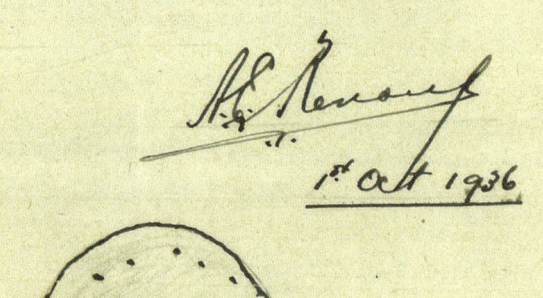

1st Oct 1936

ABOVE

Bess, fourth from left, as a prefect at Solway College, 1933.

RIGHT

Solway College in the Wairarapa.

BELOW

The Masonic Hotel, sleek and modern, in the new Napier.

OPPOSITE

A handwritten thank you in the form of a poem.

Hawke's Bay girls (sufficient for them to have their own railway carriage when they returned at the end of term) saved the school.

But there is an interesting nano-detail relating to Bess going to Solway. Mr Burtenshaw, her godfather, had read about the free term offered in the newspaper. His role in her life as fairy godfather advanced when he took it upon himself to register her interest. Bess had been floundering at Wellington Girls' College, still in such a state of shock from earthquake trauma that she could remember nothing of her favourite subject, algebra. Solway accepted Burtenshaw's application and Bess was sent off to Hawke's Bay.

Jess and Ern were left with the impression that the tuition was free. Mr Burtenshaw himself paid for a further term, then Mrs T persuaded him that, on ethical grounds, it was wrong to leave 'Mr & Mrs Northe' in a state of ignorance. I am unsure what happened next. Did Ern at first refuse to pay? He was, after all, in the throes of trying to re-establish the family firm of R. Northe & Sons after the disaster of the quake. The outcome was that Bess attended the school on the lower rate of a 'daughter of a clergyman'. It was essentially on a charitable basis, a fact of which Bess herself remained ignorant until she was in her eighties.

Writing as a mature woman in a book that celebrated Solway's Golden Jubilee, Bess noted, 'We were indeed fortunate on our arrival at Solway to find awaiting us a Principal as sympathetic and understanding as Mrs Thompson, who was guide, philosopher, friend, and certainly always a mother to us all. Where else, but at Solway would you find the majority of the girls queuing up outside the study door at the end of the day for the Principal's good-night kiss.'[6] It was a small, even intimate school of one hundred girls with, unusually, a family at its core. As the prospectus described it, Solway provided 'the happiness and comfort of a refined home'. Note that adjective: 'refined'.

Bessie's time at Solway framed the rest of her life. Mrs T's high ideals gave her something to aspire to: she kept the letters Mrs T sent to her, as you keep anything which amounts to a sacred text. I have them now. Their capable, strong handwriting, never varying, highly legible, driven by the broad nib of a fountain pen, is full of good advice: *'I remember getting a letter from one of my professors at the end of my University days in which he wrote: "Keep learning, ever moving, don't stand still!" and I have been glad to pass on that advice. Life is full of interest and always there is something to learn.*' This was sent to Bess just after she had left Solway. Again, when sending Bess's fulsome testimonial: '*Life is so much more interesting when you feel that you are making some contribution to the World's work and its happiness.*' Bess was right to see in Mrs T a philosopher and guide.

Of course Bess often failed to live up to such high ideals, most notably during her marriage. But Mrs T's testimonial for Bess showed some insight into the positive aspects of her pupil's character: '*As a prefect here she was most helpful. Her invariable courtesy made her a delightful pupil. A girl of high ideals of life and conduct, of pleasing personality and dignified presence, Miss Northe will uphold the tone of any institution or firm with which she is connected.*'

Was this a coded way of saying that, because of her private education, she would lend 'class' to wherever she worked? Certainly when she applied to become a receptionist at the Masonic, Napier's new luxury Art Deco hotel, Mr Chesney, the manager, thought so. She was even given privileges beyond those normally given to working women: time off when she wanted it. Part of the ambience of staying at the Masonic was that guests were greeted by a young woman educated at a private school, who spoke well and was, to boot, good-looking and courteous. This would have meant nothing if she was not efficient, but Bess brought her formidable memory to the task, always remembering customers even if they had not returned for quite some time.

She made a conspicuous success of her new role, and was even offered a position at the ultimate glamour hotel in New Zealand at the time, the Grand Hotel in Auckland, where visiting celebrities like Noël Coward and opera singers stayed. (She did not take up the offer.) She was voted 'the second best receptionist in New Zealand' at this time. (I am unsure how this was administered and I am reliant on Bess's own version of events here. She often paraded her glories before us children when she felt a little let down by the shrunken perimeter of her life as a 'home maker' in Point Chev in the 1950s.)

When Mrs T sent her testimonial on 30 October 1934 she added a personal note: 'Thank you for all the gracious courtesy you showed when you were our pupil. I love every thought of you and I know I am going to be proud of you and of the work you will do.' It was a more than formulaic response.

Did Bessie do work of which Mrs T, she of the high ideals, would be proud? Not really. She was a receptionist in a hotel and then in a dental surgery, and Mrs T had something higher in mind (in a moral sense) for her favourite pupil.[7] But Bess only became a working woman after she revolted against the role she was consigned to when she came home from Solway. Three years after the quake, and possibly in a delayed response to it, Jess, Bess's mother, developed a serious diabetic condition. '*I'm sorry your Mother is not well, and I think your first duty is with her,*' Mrs T advised. '*It is a good idea to go on with your Commercial work if you can find the time but I know that housework is exacting, and you will want to spare your Mother as much as possible. Give her my love.*'

Bess had earlier been handicapped by two elder sisters, Jean and Patti, who were scholastically high-achievers. They were successive duxes of Napier Girls' High School, and Bessie trailed in their shadow, shrinking from having to over-achieve just to keep up. (The 'Commercial' stream was a low-ranking option in the hierarchy of a school.) Solway gave Bess the chance to recreate a self: she became a prefect and a popular student, a role model perhaps remarkable for a girl who had arrived traumatised by the quake. The complication was that she now expected the rest of her life to unroll with the same degree of success.

Her marriage, of course, led to compromises and ever-deepening moral complexity. Did going to Solway help her there, or limit her understanding of the issues by exacerbating her snobbishness? But snobbishness flowed in both Bess's and her mother's veins, irrespective of the influence of Solway. Or rather, Bess and her mother thought so much alike it was as if they shared the same brain — just as I seemed to share the same consciousness with my mother, finding it difficult to establish my psychological independence. (Indeed the conjoined way we thought, spoke, saw the world was what made her approaching death so alarming and painful for me. It was as if part of my own brain was dying or going into darkness.)

There is a final interesting reference in one of Mrs T's rather moving letters: '*I like to think Solway girls go home enriched by their experience,*' she wrote in December 1933, just after Bess had left the school. '*I will not tell you how much I have appreciated your courtesy and helpfulness, and as you carry these into all relationships of life all must be well with you.*'

In the end, Bess became patron of the Solway Old Girls' Association, meeting Mrs T's high expectations of the 'dignified' and 'gracious' girl who left the school in 1933. Often, when coming into the lounge at the retirement village, I saw Bess struggle out of her seat to get a cup of tea for someone who might be decades younger but incapacitated. She kept that courtesy and helpfulness all her life, and it guarded her and gave her qualities that protected her, made her special in the eyes of the people around her, who in their turn looked out for her. Courtesy, after all, is one of the human virtues, or at least it was.

Written references no longer have the validity they once had. Employers have a more Mephistophelean way of scrutinising possible employees. The web has wrapped itself around us as efficiently as a spider seeking to imprison then embalm the insect captured in its clasp. Yet the ordinary virtues still define us as human beings — how we speak to one another, how we offer sympathy, extend empathy. Even something as simple as a handwritten sympathy note has a power far beyond the gesture it makes. '*What a sad world we have happened on!*' Mrs T wrote to Bessie in April 1942, in the depth of the Second World War. She ended the letter on a fond note: '*Yours lovingly, Marion Thompson.*'

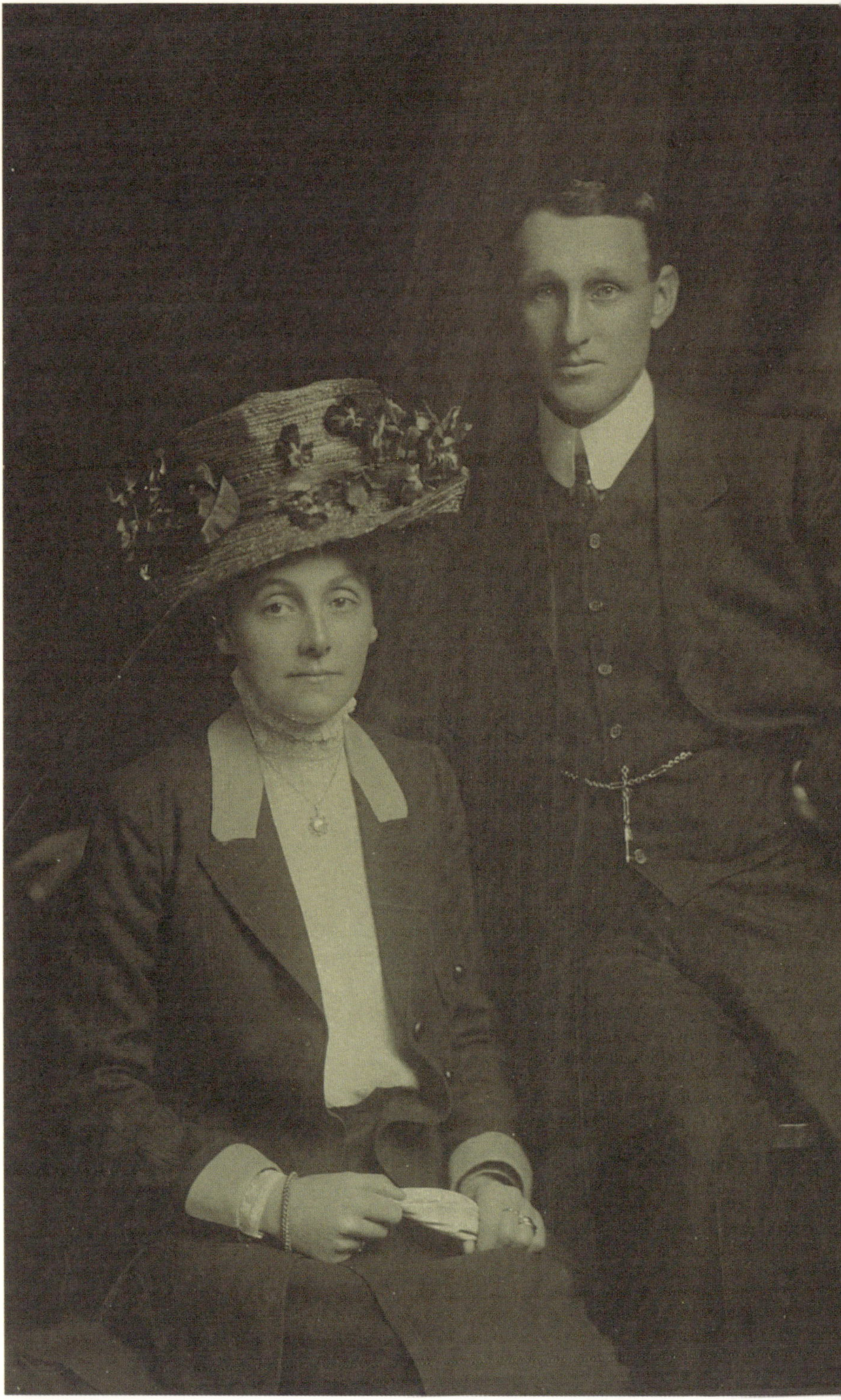

How to Write a Letter

OPPOSITE

My grandparents' wedding photo, 1910: 'Upward mobility is the fuel that powered the colonial quest.'

Jessie Northe was my grandmother, the daughter of Betsy Bartlett. Her photograph sits on the mantelpiece in a guest bedroom. It's a kind of informal altar to the piety of family.

THE PHOTOGRAPH WAS TAKEN ON my grandparents' wedding day, 26 April 1910. What really takes my eye is her hat, a large Edwardian hat — the size of her social aspirations, I think. It's like a galleon under full sail.

My grandmother already has her uppity look. She's definitely superior. She knows she's good-looking. She has made a success of working in Thorp's shoe shop in Napier. It might not be much, bending over, wedging new shoes onto smelly, puffed-up feet. But she is a good saleswoman, one of the best. She is a self-confident young woman, not exactly a New Woman, but she knows her own worth.

But there are other things this portrait does not tell us so overtly. It is relatively small and so it required only a modest financial outlay. Moreover, there is a very important detail: Jessie did not marry in white, with bridesmaids. The wedding was very small, 'private', done after work. White weddings were not 'for the likes of us'. For all the stylishness and handsomeness of my grandparents, this is a portrait of a lower-middle-class couple starting out in life.

There it is — *lower-middle-class* — that terrible aspersion, an unlovable category, universally tainted and abused by those immediately below, and by those above. The coarse working class don't aspire to or need such laughable fanciness, which of course is a comic parody to the secure middle class. To the middle- and upper-middle-class woman, a lower-middle-class lady is someone to be snide about, because she simply doesn't get what these folk effortlessly get as part of their birth, breeding, understanding of the world.

So while this photo is touching — here's a young couple about to embark on a new life — also it displays the couple's vulnerability to insult. Still, my grandmother shows her chutzpah — she will wear a magnificent, slightly mad tea-party hat, hoisting the flag of her aspirations even while she sits there quite modestly, in a tasteful civilian suit that will do for best. Let's face it, a white wedding dress is an extravagance, an unnecessary coda for 'people like us'. And 'people like us' is what we are, what we cannot quite escape, no matter how hard we try.

Yet Jessie was also a master of disguise. In her own way she would escape. By the time she was an old woman, which is when I knew her, she was universally recognised — *outside Hawke's Bay* — as a particular type, a Hawke's Bay lady. But within Hawke's Bay she was recognised in a different way: her parents were known, as was her husband's occupation, where she went to school. If she ever did anything wrong, this was keenly remembered.

For example, many years after her death I heard about her very first 'at home'. This was part of an arcane ritual by which genteel women visited each other's homes and left a visiting card. On your visiting card you wrote the particular afternoon you would be at home. Then you prepared an afternoon tea for an unknown number of women, and you sat and waited. A woman who knew of my grandmother reported to me, with a still-keen relish, how Jessie had prepared a magnificent afternoon tea for her first such occasion, but nobody came. How did she know then? There must have been someone who attended and couldn't wait to get home to spread this tasty morsel of gossip.

So while my grandmother was 'a Hawke's Bay lady' in Auckland or Wellington, in Hawke's Bay she would always be the woman whose very first 'at home' was a failure. In time she had her revenge: she was smart, had a good sense of humour, was nobody's fool. A depression, an earthquake and a world war also dealt to the security of many of the women who regarded her as beyond the social pale. Coal and wood and property have a hardiness other more genteel occupations might lack during times of extremity. She was an ace bridge player, too, which gave her social reach. And after her husband died she had what was then called 'a private income' — the *sine qua non* of gentility in those days.

She also wrote letters. She wrote letters in the way other people breathed. She was a beneficiary of the 1870 Education Act under which reading and writing were taught universally throughout New Zealand. And although she left school at fourteen, she had the basis of a supple literacy she never lost. She had been introduced to the pleasures of letter writing as a nine-year-old. One could almost say she was seduced.

I know this because of the charmingly eccentric letters sent to Jessie by one Richard Mercer, a family friend. He worked as a clerk, and he lived right in the heart of Napier in Mrs Bird's boarding house, wedged between the American Steam Coach Factory and Wilson's Boot Factory.

On a Sunday evening Mercer usually sat down with a steel-nibbed dip-in pen and a variety of coloured inks, and he created fantastical worlds in letter form which he posted to Jessie, then a child living with her parents some 17 kilometres away on the Frimley estate in Hastings, a semi-feudal domain of one of the Williams family. J. N. Williams was the third son of the missionary William Williams, the creator of the first Māori dictionary and a translator of the Treaty of Waitangi. For many missionaries, their intimacy with Māori and early arrival in New Zealand meant they could pick and choose the very best land when they decided to mix teaching of the gospel with a bit of upward mobilising. By the 1890s, the slightly ambiguous class background of the Williams family was replaced by a perception of them as landed grandees. ('Top drawer', as my mother would have said.)

An astute nineteenth-century observer of Hawke's Bay noted that families of straitened circumstances back in Britain often tried to reproduce the status of being 'county families'— that is, leading families of great antiquity and status — in their new environment. The Williams family was an example of this. Jessie grew up in their shadow, imbued with notions of deference quite different from the egalitarian ideals we normally associate with New Zealand. But the fact was Jessie's father worked for the Williamses, first as a coach driver, then as a manager of the orchards, until he accumulated enough capital to buy his own land and retire and live off the income, thus reproducing in miniature the gentrifying trajectory of the Williamses themselves.

This is the framing of this series of artful letters, all beautifully written in copperplate handwriting. The letters were carefully archived and placed in a writing box, and were among Grandma's possessions when she died. The letters are in effect playful seductions, all aimed at attracting a child's curiosity about written language. A form of education was silently taking place. Jessie was learning the art of letter writing. This was not a small thing, as letter writing was the basis of virtually all non-verbal communication between humans at this time. Letter writing also involved a kind of arcane etiquette. To those who learnt the etiquette in childhood it seems obvious and clear. Today, the internet has to inform people 'how to write a letter'.[1]

Jessie learnt this etiquette by receiving letters and — an integral part of the exchange — by writing letters in return. The first Mercer letter to survive is dated 26 June 1892, and is written in vivid green ink, using deliberate misspelling as a ruse. It is headed in telescoping order, *'New Zealand, Hawke's Bay, Napier'*. Mercer drops immediately into the business at hand: *'My Dear little Jessie, Your welcome note came to hand this day, and therefore Konsider it nothing but right to acknowledge it at once. I know you are all the tip toe of expectation wondering when you are to get an answer, and am afraid, you will be a little disappointed at getting it so soon. However try and bear up.'*

This teasing epistle was by way of educating her about the nature of letter writing. A letter sent is a letter requiring payment in kind. And payment in kind sets off long-term consequences. At the age of nine, Jessie was being broken into the habit — the sometimes delicious habit — of forming words that convey feelings and establish a personal view of events and people, part of an ongoing written conversation spanning space and time.

'You also tell me you have red the Books through and also like them, you don't tell me, what you thought of Alice, or any of the queer people mentioned in the house of Glass, or wonderful Alice. Have you learnt any of the funny poetry.'

This introduces an important, inescapable motif. When Lewis Carroll, a thirty-year-old man, wrote his books for Alice Liddell, aged twelve, he was creating some of the most enchanting tales in literature. In 1892 *Alice Through the Looking Glass* was twenty-one years old. It was a psychologically astute 'nonsense' tale of great richness.

There is a further shadowing here: of a clearly adult male sending the book to a nine-year-old. Today we are so accustomed to the brutality of paedophilia and to looking around us for signs of 'grooming' that it is impossible not to be discomfited by some of the emotions nascent in these adult letters to a child. '*Bless your ringlets,*' Mercer writes at one point. Many of the letters end on a cascade of kisses: '*Just 3 and a half times as many, sweet ones, as you have sent which will be 121 which you can half with dear Emily giving her 60 & a half & keeping 60 & a half for your dear self,*' one letter ends, before opening to a more formal and proper farewell: '*With kind love to you all, I am, My Dear Jessie, yours affectionately, R Mercer.*' I cannot verify what compelled a bachelor (there is no mention of a wife or children) to send these fervent notes to a clearly enchanting little girl.

But maybe in this case we shouldn't look beneath the surface, but rather look carefully at the surface. The letters are all written in coloured inks, which Mercer sometimes playfully interwove. In one particularly splendid letter, the lettering is a pyrotechnic display of different colours, forming a kind of intricate mosaic. It is an artwork in itself. Layout is often unstable, at times almost Sterne-like in its breaking of linearity. The intention was simple — to make reading and letter writing fun (and, with the 121 kisses, to encourage subdivision and the skills of arithmetic).

The content of the letters was usually fantastical and consciously entertaining. On 17 August 1893 Mercer tells Jessie he has ordered her some new books but they have not arrived. Once they do, '*I will send them along either by Balloon, Under Ground Railway, Steam or Sailing Ship*'. An 1892 letter, the first to survive (an interior page appears to be missing), opens a second page with a small upside-down note saying, '*You can turn over*': that is, you turn the page over and the writing is now upside down. It begins a broken-off sentence with '*smelling salts, and anything else she might have to hold. And the coach along with your Auntie Florry to hold her Fan . . . with no outriders or footman. There was a young footwoman and there was exactly 4 wheels under the Coach . . . I don't know how many horses there were.*'

It is hard to make sense of only part of a sentence, but it appears to create a fabulous universe in prosaic Hawke's Bay of coaches, footmen, smelling salts and a '*young footwoman*' — perhaps nine-year-old Jessie herself. '*I must now tell you I am very much pleased with your writing,*' he ends his letter, '*it is very good. and I think you and me are about eKal in spelin. never mind we will grow better in time.*' This gentle humour is meant to be instructive. Jessie did not yet spell correctly. '*Hoo ra it's bed time*', this lonely bachelor writes late on a Sunday evening in a small town in which there was probably very little to do apart from listening to church sermons and the mournful tolling of a church bell, '*and I'se getting so sleepy. So good night and pleasant dreams (as usual) to you.*'

The central whimsy in these letters is in the form of a circus, itself based on a book. *Our Noah's Ark* was printed in Bavaria, under an imprint of Frederick Warne & Co., a company which specialised in quality children's books by authors like Kate Greenaway and Beatrix Potter. The book opens up to reveal a diorama of stand-up animals, and in Jessie's copy the flyleaf is inscribed with the characteristically whimsical Mercer brio: '*Madamoiselle J. Purvissimo's Unrivalled Collection of Wild Animals. etc etc. N.B. The only collection of its magnitude ever exhibited in the Colonies. Admission 1/-. Pay here.*' Jessie, her sister Emily and Mercer were going into business together, showing the circus animals, charging one shilling and hence making their fortunes.

By October 1893 Mercer displays a slight vibration of annoyance, playfully based on the lack of profits from their enterprise, but as much for the lack of attention from his correspondents.

'October 31 1893

'My Dear little Partner,

'Your very, very, very short note duly to hand this afternoon, and I lose no time in replying to it. to let you know that if you are as half as sorry as I am about the menagerie, you are "sorry"! Here I am, been waiting patiently for part of a year, for an account of the Show. And the monies taken at the doors. But no thank you No for Joseph, not a Bronze as come my way and then told the Hanimals have all been laid up. Whats been the matter with em, I suppose the Elephant is gone dead lame with corns on his toes, never been looked after the Giraffes have had the Croup, the monkeys the measles & hooping cough . . . It wont do you know. I am getting tired of waiting for my monies . . . perhaps your dear sister may write saying how, why, and wot for she did not write sooner. With Kindest love to you all, I remain, Yours very sincerely, R Mercer.'

It was a harmless correspondence, an entertainment on both sides. As to whether Jessie herself ever felt uncomfortable with it, it's significant that she attached this particular explosion of a letter to an album of signatures she kept as a young woman. She clearly prized the letters as part of a vanished childhood.

But this does not mean there is not something painful in the letters, foreshadowing the abrupt way a child can change his or her affections as they grow older. For the lonely adult, the warmth of a child's regard has great meaning. For the child, an adult's attention can be precious and educative — if only too easy to forget.

'23 June 1895

'My dear Jessie

'I cant tell you how sorry I am that yourself in connection with Your dear Sister should have wasted so much good time at the School where they don't teach young Ladies to write how soon we forget all we have been taught. As in the case of you two girls having entirely lost all idea & use of pens, ink, paper & postage Stamps & the Post Office. Tis human nature to forget.'

But R. Mercer could have taken pleasure from the fact he had educated Jessie in the delights of letter writing. I would assert that this is where her facility with it began. By 1958, when she was seventy-five, she had no trouble turning out an eight-page letter — only one among three that she wrote weekly to Jean and Patti, her two daughters in Wellington, and Bess in Auckland. She wrote with a complete lack of self-consciousness. From childhood onwards, she was at home with letter writing as a way of communicating across space and time — forming a self out of words.

She was born, after all, at the high water mark of literacy, when the written or printed word was at its maximum extension of power. Cinema had emerged but was not yet influential. Words were what mattered. And words needed to be correctly spelt and clearly legible within a letter for the writer to be 'correctly dressed' in the costume of language. Poor grammar and spelling pointed to a poor background. (Although not exclusively: upper-class people could spell and write appallingly. But then they were often badly educated, too.)

If I can conceptualise my grandmother, it is through her strict adherence to matters of etiquette. She was tightly corseted in person. A lady did not go out without her stays. She had what was regarded as a good carriage, which meant you had a rigid backbone and your shoulders sat back (this related to horse riding originally). She was also almost obsessive about observing the niceties of table manners, dressing a table with a table cloth, setting a table, using a butter knife, not putting pots or jars on tables. You could say this was a typical lower-middle-class trait, expressing anxiety about where to fit in. Or you could say it was a branch of aesthetics, about how you liked things to look.

I think of a book that sat in her bookshelves. It was called *Manners and Rules of Good Society — Or Solecisms to be Avoided*. Written by 'A Member of the Aristocracy' (1922), it was a guide to such niceties as 'calling', precedence at dinner parties, and so on.[2] (Jessie may have learnt from this the rituals of card leaving: 'Leaving Cards upon New-comers. — In the country the residents should be the first to leave cards on the new-comers, after ascertaining the position which the new-comers occupy in society.')[3] This esoterica wasn't native to her; she had to learn it. And she learned it sufficiently for it to become almost second nature. Likewise, she knew exactly how to set out and end a letter.

But as for the rest of the letter's contents, they remained a wide, open prairie over which she could range at her leisure, constructing a world as she saw fit, holding forth with her own opinions fearlessly. The fact is, a letter, for so long as you are writing it, is one of the most personal statements about the world you can make. Because it is enclosed and personal, one to one, this often raises the stakes even higher. Letters can and probably should be indiscreet, opinionated, soaked in the very essence of a personality; the letter is, in fact, a kind of flag floating in the breeze, utterly individual to the writer, at that moment of time.

THIS IS ALL BY WAY of introducing a letter written by Jessie on 24 July 1959 and sent to my mother. It is closely written — eight pages in all, both sides filled with words. It was written on unlined, thick, good-quality notepaper that denoted 'class', one of Jessie's abiding obsessions. Thick paper implied you were not worried about the weight of the letter and thus the price of postage. Unlined paper showed you had perfect balance and control of the medium (a bit like sitting in a saddle, you could ride at an easy canter). Lined paper, on the other hand, inferred you were slightly uneducated and could not control your handwriting, and hence needed ruled paper to maintain an ordered script.

The letter was folded in half, then that half was folded into quarters, to fit snugly within the envelope, which was of the same quality paper as the pages within. It was like a well-tailored suit overall. It was part of the *bella figura* of letter writing.

Jessie used a fountain pen. She would have regarded a ballpoint as new-fangled and inherently inferior ('common'). A good-quality fountain pen displayed its high status by the sheen and elegance of its gold-plated nib. A pen from a company like Sheaffer was a gift often given to a young person as a sign of reaching maturity.[4] It was a status symbol, not unlike a high-end cellphone today. It was also utterly personal. You wore your nib in as you wrote: the nib gradually accommodated itself to your writing style and became smooth and fluent. It was personal as a pair of shoes. It might be kept for a lifetime. It is clear that Jessie filled her pen with blue-black ink several times while writing this letter, so the pen was possibly quite old.

By 1959 Jessie had been writing letters for decades, so she followed the etiquette of letter writing effortlessly, putting her address — 4 Lawrence Road — at the top right of the page so the reader could both locate the origin of the letter and know where to reply to. Below it was the exact date, down to the year. (The year was gradually dropped as a younger generation recognised there was no longer any possibility that a letter would take more than a month or so to reach its destination. But Jessie's mindset was essentially from the nineteenth century, so she kept the year.)

Jessie begins the letter with an intimate salute: *'Dear Chick'.*[5] Immediately below this, and indented, she wrote, *'I received your welcome letter on Wednesday.'* This was convention — a letter was always welcome — but it had a practical purpose. Bess could now work out how long the post took to reach Hawke's Bay and space out her next letter accordingly. In a letter-writing relationship, you unconsciously obeyed the rhythm of letter sending, parsing out the communication equally. An unexpected letter presaged a crisis.

Jessie then drops into the great standby of all letter writing: the weather. *'I have never felt colder mornings & that is the opinion of everyone I have asked.'* A seemingly early spring had been followed by bitterly cold winds and snow down so low the route out of Hawke's Bay to Auckland was closed off.

Before we look at what follows, it is worth remembering the letter's overall context. It is one link in a long chain of letters passed between mother and daughter that first started when Bessie left the family home and went to Solway College. Once Bessie left Napier as a bride in 1939, the letter writing effortlessly recommenced. In one sense, this letter is just part of an ongoing conversation between two talkative women whose intimate, easy tone reveals little sign of hesitation or deliberation about how the contents will be received. (The assumption was mother and daughter thought exactly alike on nearly everything.)

In this way the letter operates on something like a choral level, one voice ceasing when the other takes up, leading to a solo moment of near *coloratura* intensity. Both mother and daughter were great talkers. (My female cousins share this propensity, so family meetings are raised almost to the level of talking duels.) And because mother and daughter wrote to each other weekly, this letter has a speedy, almost sketchy quality to it, grabbing out at passersby, firing a scattershot of opinion, then moving swiftly on.

'I meant to say to you,' Jessie fires up the moment she has dispensed with the weather, *'I hope Kath McDowell strikes people like herself, never make up their minds what they want & go from shop to shop.'* (Kath McDowell was an Auckland friend of Bessie's who was a saleswoman in the 'dress salon' at the department store Milne & Choyce. She was also an indecisive and endlessly quibbling shopper.) *'Then she will know what it is like.'*

A subtext is Jessie's sense of self-possession, of knowing best as well as sharing information on shared acquaintances, all conveyed with a smack or a pat on the back. Jessie had 'run into' Kathleen Willis in the street.

'I said I was sorry about Mrs Stack passing away. She said they were so sorry, she had been ill for so long & she was just like her old self & taking an interest in things, & looking so bright. Her leg was still bad, she had had ulcers, but Dr Fleischel thought she should have blood tests, she was only at Hospital one day. He said she had better stay & have treatment for her leg. She had Physiotherapy one day, she was dead the next morning. She must have had a clot & the treatment shifted it. Now Kathleen wishes they had never taken her to Hospital. She seemed so sorry. I was too because she has had a hard life.'

This is like a small Chekhovian tale: '*She had Physiotherapy one day, she was dead the next morning.*' Jessie is clearly enjoying delivering the dramatic arpeggio of her tale, and the coda of the sad Kathleen, who delivered Mrs Stack to her death, gains further extrapolation through Jessie's explanation that it was all part of the woman having had a hard life. Mrs Stack was one of life's losers, whereas Jessie, as annunciate or chorus of the tale, is absolved from guilt by feeling '*so sorry too*', while secretly feeling vindicated by the fact she is sitting there, alive and functioning, gold-nibbed fountain pen in hand, driving blue-black ink over quality paper and enjoying a life of financial ease.

Another subtext here is Jess's own potential ill health. She had a serious diabetic condition. She lived on her own and always faced the possibility of falling into a coma.[6] She knew the dreadful lure and power of 'Hospital', as she called it. Napier Hospital had played an important symbolic role in her life. The collapse of the Nurses' Home during the quake was one of the traumas of her life. Her husband, Ern, had carried their daughter Jean up there on his back when she had caught diphtheria as a six-year-old. She herself had run up the road to the hospital in her apron when she was told Ern lay dying.[7]

The hospital was only 20 metres away, and towered over Lawrence Road with the omniscience of a Kafkaesque castle, just as its nearby laundry and smokestack, where dressings were incinerated, reduced the status of 4 Lawrence Road. But Jessie should not be backed into a corner as a remorseless snob. Her anxieties tended to focus on the ambiguity of her social standing. For example, she had R. Northe & Sons, the family firm, construct a porch at the back of the house at Lawrence Road so callers did not experience the unforgiveable social lapse of arriving at the kitchen door.[8] Jessie wanted to preserve the ideal that these visitors — who? — would arrive in a sitting room before being escorted down the hall to the drawing room, which was at the very front of the house: the ideal space for conversation and tea parties. This was the framework of her psyche or playground of her anxieties. At the same time, she was an intelligent, lively woman with a vivid life impulse.

'*I met Bill Popplewell & his wife in town on Thursday,*' her pen drives on. '*Sirett is in Hospital again. I cannot think of Bill's wife's name. She said they thought Sirett was going to die one night. George always gets her off to Hospital, he gets panicky. You remember how Rochie* [a neighbour] *was at times, & they get over it. She is always in Hospital, [getting] proper food & attention.*' A few lines later she philosophises: '*I would go mad with a life like Siretts, but then I have never been lazy I would rather try & work & not just give in.*'

This is like a hymn to Jessie's energy and ambition. She looked after herself, and rather despised people who gave in to ill health — 'enjoyed ill health', as she used to say.

Before moving on she looks closely at her contemporaries the Popplewells, who were an established family in Hawke's Bay: '*Bill looks old & rather uncared for. I thought Mrs Pop. looked rather shabby & a bit dirty. She is always nice. Good catholics have had five children & then learn no more.*' (Note the small 'c' for Catholics.)[9]

She continues: '*Monday I took Mrs Cato's place at Bridge with Mrs La Roche. We got quite a good score, I enjoyed playing with her.*' Bridge allowed Jessie to deploy her quick intelligence and redoubtable memory to great effect. She was a founding member of the Napier Bridge Club, and also played contract bridge at her women's club, which met in the sleek Art Deco elegance of rooms in the T & G Building on the Parade. In another letter she commented caustically on an acquaintance who was '*always crawling after the so called upper class*', but Jessie's skill at bridge meant she was a sought-after player around the card tables of the affluent and leisured of Hawke's Bay. It gave her social reach far beyond the status of a coal merchant's wife.

This needs some explanation. Nancy Isenberg opens her book *White Trash: The 400-Year Untold History of Class in America* by saying, 'We

ABOVE

Little Jess (left), an enchanting child.

RIGHT

Richard Mercer's calligraphy art.

BELOW

Animals from Noah's ark.

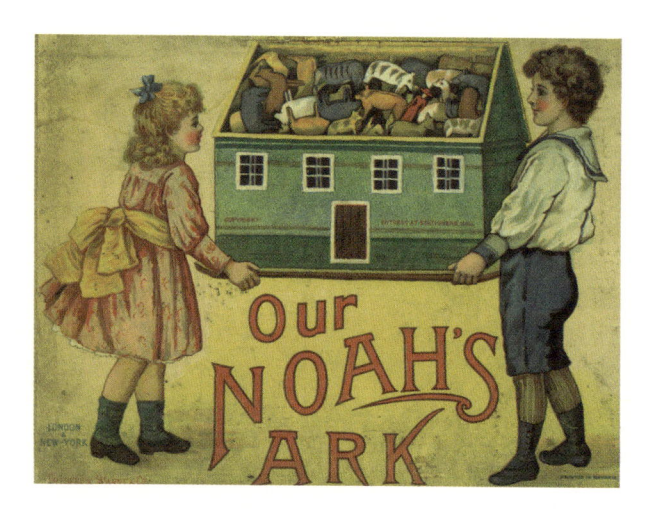

TOP

Jess the well-to-do widow.

CENTRE

A white wedding at last; Bess in 1939.

LEFT

In step and *simpatico*: Bess and Jess out shopping in Napier.

know what class is. Or think we do: economic stratification created by wealth and privilege. The problem is that popular American history is most commonly told — dramatized — without much reference to the existence of social classes.'[10] It is the same in New Zealand. Theoretically, social class does not exist as a lens through which we view our apparently stoutly egalitarian country. Race, yes, most definitely. But not class.

Possibly Hawke's Bay, like Canterbury, was unusual historically in having long-established sheep-farming families who intermarried and adopted the self-assured tone of an English upper class. It was not unusual for these families to send their sons to Oxford or Cambridge to be educated. The women shopped in Sydney and London, and featured in the social pages of newspapers and magazines; their children attended the same exclusive private schools; their sons married the daughters of sheep-farming families in Canterbury or Australia, perpetuating a sense of superiority over anyone involved in 'trade' (let alone a business as dirty as coal). By 1959 New Zealand had been enjoying a sustained period of affluence, helped along by the demand of wool for uniforms for the Korean War. This period was really the high-water mark of these families' wealth and influence. In the foreseeable future the protection they enjoyed would be removed and the vision of a rural aristocracy living in splendour on great estates would fade away.

Generally speaking, however, under the long and stultifying reign of the conservative National Party (which came to power in 1949 and had three terms in government), New Zealand regarded itself as successful, peaceful and racially harmonious. In fact it was a stifling period of socially enforced conformity in which Pākehā enjoyed the highest income per capita in the world, while most rural Māori lived in poverty.

This general sense of ease felt by well-to-do Pākehā — it could also be called obliviousness — is present in the letters. Jessie attends a farewell party to '*Mrs Chisholm who is going to Australia till October*' by ship. She also talks of Audrey, a young woman who inherited a medical practice from her father. Audrey is in the process of selling it, and has decided to go to live and work in New York (as a modern touch, she is flying there). '*They may come back in ten years but she does not think so.*'

A strange detail attaches to Audrey, who by common consensus '*was one of the nicest girls*' anyone knew. '*Audrey does everything so naturally and so quiet. She did all for her father. Everyone admires her.*' She was marrying a man who had no arms, whether as a result of injuries suffered in the war or some other cause is not made clear. To make matters even more complicated, the marriage crossed the religious divide, so there was a compromise: communion in an Anglican church (St Matthew's, where Jessie was married in 1910), followed by a marriage ceremony at the St Peter Chanel Catholic church in Hastings. '*I did not know he was a catholic,*' Jess writes, ruthlessly demoting the religion again with a small 'c'.

Jessie touches here on the collusive, even vehement opinions typical of a small-town environment. Her venom centres on an unfortunate woman by the name of Mrs O'Meara, whose sin was surely to be of Irish and Catholic descent. '*Mrs Baillie thinks just like I do about Mrs O'Meara,*' writes Jessie, standing breathlessly at the parish pump. '*Everyone knows Mrs O'Meara has never been known to do a thing for anyone. It is Mrs O'Meara first, second & last.*'

Mrs O'Meara dealt with, Jessie's relentless social whirl moves on: '*I played with Mrs Hindmarsh & I did enjoy it. She did too & said she would like to play again with me. I meet her a lot at bridge. Her husband is a cousin to Jack Hindmarsh* [a noteable cricketer] . . . *They lived in Selwyn Road, but have moved to the Bluff. She is always very charming.*'

This is what Jessie would have liked: to be 'always very charming' and to move from the equivocal status of Lawrence Road on Hospital Hill to a much better address on what was virtually nob hill. Other women, meantime, get a sharp rap over the knuckles. '*I can quite see how people hate playing with Mrs Renouf. I could not put up with her chatter & jokes all the time & talking to both tables.*'[11]

Then Jessie casually flourishes a feather in her cap. On Thursday '*Clinton Holt called for me at a quarter to seven in a great big sumptuous Jaguar car, a real beauty.*' The Holts ran a much more successful company than R. Northe & Sons. (Robert Holt's business went on to become part of Carter Holt Harvey in the 1980s.) Clinton Holt was a descendant of Robert Holt, for whom Jessie's father-in-law Robert Northe had worked in the 1860s. Napier was a small, incestuous town in all sorts of ways, with interconnections streaming back into the past. People generally knew what your grandparents did for a living, and your standing in the community was based on this knowledge of set social and economic gradations. The geographical isolation enforced this rigidity. There was a saying — in fact there is still a saying — that you are not 'a local' till your family has lived in

Napier for three generations. The three daughters of Jessie and Ern Northe escaped this parochial world by going to live in bigger cities.

But Jessie, who had lived in Hawke's Bay all her life, was comfortable with the world she assumed she knew, and a world in which people knew her and respected her — even if this exacerbated her social anxieties and kept her perpetually on edge. It was a world with a very small circumference.

After going to the Services Club in Hastings to play bridge (in this era Hastings, a service town, was conspicuously more affluent than Napier thanks to high wool prices; it had much better china, crystal, clothing and hat shops, as well as better tearooms), Jessie runs down a list of socially notable women with whom she has played bridge — '*Mrs Von Dadelszen . . . Mrs Herrick is back & just as charming as ever*' — before describing a micro-crisis in her world. There was a big party occupying '*our supper room & we had to go to the tearooms through a small passage. I did not like it all, no one did. Now the worst news.*' We pause for a crisis. '*Mr Franzssen is giving up the tea rooms & going to manage the new Mayfair Hotel which is being built . . . he is going to cater for weddings their* [sic]*, but no nice tea rooms, & we will never have supper for the E.S.K. or afternoon tea for our committee meetings & nowhere nice to go for lunch. Everyone will be sorry I am sure. Hastings has always been so proud of its Tea Rooms.*'

By now the letter, written on a Friday, has been running on for six tightly handwritten pages of tittle-tattle, observation, reflection and wry humour. Jessie has even informed Bess about calling a plumber: '*I really thought I would have gone silly last Sunday with the drip, drip & really running tap. I rang the Plumber & told him if he did not fix my tap, he would hear of me going to Porirua* [a psychiatric hospital in Wellington]. *He said he would hate that, & came that morning. He fixed my taps . . . I said I would pay him, it was too small for an account. He would not charge me as he said, it is always such a pleasure to work here & for me. He thinks my garden is lovely. He told me my house is a credit to me . . .*'

This is Jessie ruffling her feathers with pleasure at being acknowledged by a younger man as an ace housekeeper, with a beautiful garden and everything 'just so'. *She* was not dirty; *she* was not a panic artist. She did not sit down and mope. Her immaculate house and beautiful garden were all part of her identity as the redoubtable 'Mrs Northe' — a local institution on the hill. She had lived at 4 Lawrence Road for fifty years.

She could enjoy a leisurely life now, with an assured income from the interest from her husband's estate (which, in customary practice, she had for life, so long as she did not remarry). She still did all the housework for the roomy three-bedroomed villa, and cooked for herself. Jess also employed a gardener, Mr De Leuw. Whenever he worked in the garden she baked him a morning tea — a madeira cake, or scones with home-made jam — which he ate sitting at the outside table on the porch. She was always 'Mrs Northe' and he was always 'Mr De Leuw'. It was part of the understanding of a more humanly connected, if hierarchical, world.

On the seventh page Jess wrote '*Sat*' to indicate a break in the stream of the letter. She also refuelled her fountain pen. The weather had worsened into '*rain hail snow & a bitterly cold wind. One of our bleakest days. I am so tired of the cold.*' It seemed to alter her mood. (It is equally possible she was feeling hypoglycemic, which expresses itself in feelings of irritation.) The following page is filled with trenchant criticisms. She is about to go and stay with her elder daughter, Jean, in Karori, Wellington —'*I hate Karori I'll die if it is weather like this. I wished I was not going now*' — and she criticises her second daughter Patti's decision to sell her house before finding another, without due regard for the fact Patti is a widow of slender means who will need to sell a house in order to buy another. There are quibbles about sinus trouble following flu: '*You will have to take care.*' She does not have time to write to 'Pete' (I had picked up the letter-writing habit but she dispatches me without too much regret): '*I really have no time to write this week & next week I will be in Wellington & so it goes on. Never a spare moment in this home for some reason.*'

The final page is devoted to very specific instructions to Bess to purchase some silk stockings for her. By 1959 silk stockings were an anachronism. Nevertheless, Jessie writes: '*. . . through old Nash*' (a dismissive reference from a seventy-six-year-old to the seventy-eight-year-old Labour prime minister — Labour had come into government in 1957 and introduced steep taxes and severe import restrictions) '*we cannot get any more* [silk stockings] *& I simply can't wear nylon stockings. I would like 6 pairs the best you can get.*'

With this imperious injunction to a daughter who is struggling on a budget — '*I will send a cheque straight away, if procurable*' — Jessie backs out of the letter with a few asides: '*I hope Gordon is better. You are like me I always think men are the worst patients*'; a sudden thought that her washing is not yet dry; she is going away soon '*& it looks like it is going to* *rain for ever'*; then a very swift nod to her daughter's health: '*Hope you are feeling better.*' This is followed by a ritualistic farewell that also has a degree of truth to it: '*with fondest love, Your loving Mother*'. The surprise to me was the series of kisses — four — '*to the boys*'.

It is an epic letter, perhaps arising from her loneliness in a big empty house and the need to 'converse'. It is almost breathless in parts, but it also illustrates her vitality and energy levels. 'Get-up-and-go' was a term she used approvingly. She was an intelligent and insightful woman in her own way, achieving within the parameters of the small-town goals that mattered to her. She was highly opinionated and she managed her ill health and the risks of living alone with some panache. Like my mother, had she been able to invest all her energy in creating a career or running a business, there is every chance she would have been successful. But the times dictated that all her energy was put into managing a house and garden, into self-adornment and maintaining a lively social life. Her driving ambition passed to future generations. Suzanne, her granddaughter, became the Deputy High Commissioner in London, for example. We, in turn, realised goals she would have liked to pursue. Upward mobility, after all, is the fuel which powered the colonial quest.

YOU CAN PROBABLY TELL THERE is an ambiguity in my attitude to my grandmother: love, but also something that seeks to critique her. Maybe this is because she was a resident deity in my repressed youth, so came to seem part of a false religion. As a young man coming into his own, I felt a need to shrug off her baleful influence, with all its snobbery and small-mindedness. At the same time, I loved her with the unquestioning love of a child. It is not too much to say I adored her. (I think of how as a wee boy I would not leave the bathroom in Point Chevalier when she bathed till I saw the rose embroidered on her brassiere. What was that all about? It was as if I was seeking to understand the code to her enigma.)

While I was musing on how to express all this ambiguity, I suddenly recalled that I had written something about my grandmother in 1975. She had been dead for seven years; I had matured and was now a know-all twenty-five-year-old who was trying to feel my way towards some personal truth. I sat down and wrote out my thoughts. And what form would this piece of writing take — but a letter?

ABOVE

The perfect Hawke's Bay lady: Peter and Bess meet Jessie on the Auckland Airport tarmac.

LEFT

Jessie's drawing room, spick and span and with not a speck of dust.

BELOW

Jess's garden, kept tidy by a gardener.

'Dear Grandma,

'You have been dead 8 years now. You are almost forgotten. We are allowed to express our feelings for you, like disrespectful children. My cousin called you a vicious old woman; and even worse, for you — "a plumber's wife". Oh Grandma how my heart even then summoned up a sigh of protest in your defence: though I laughed too, glad to hear these defamations against your karma. You, a plumber's wife! You would have risen up and struck down even we your grandchildren at this. Yet why was it so unmentionable? Because it was true. Because you did not wish to know it. Because your starved imaginative nature demanded some other romance, the key to which I found in your dusty, shadowladen bookcase, filled with books of ex-empresses, eccentric American millionairesses of the East Coast variety; because you created your own universe within the perimeter of a small provincial town on an isolated island flung off like a piece of spit from the British Empire and made yourself its empress, its duchess . . .'

This was really the first piece of imaginative writing I'd done that addressed a central obsession: Who am I? Where do I come from? The letter was written in pencil, in the microscopic handwriting I used at the time. It runs on for three and a half fullscap pages, and is an explosion of thought and pent-up feelings.

How did this 'letter' come about? I was on my way to Britain to begin my doctoral studies at the University of Warwick. It was my first real time away from New Zealand. I was profoundly stimulated by a sense of distance and that curious, almost magical way omnipotent New Zealand shrank back to reveal its specifics. I was staying with my cousin Philippa, whose husband was second secretary at the New Zealand Embassy in Vienna. Philippa and I got drunk one night, and freefalled about the person who, like some holy figure, seemed to join us together: our grandmother. It felt freeing to spit on the icon. But among the galloping illiteracies of this letter was a clutch of very different and often conflicted feelings.

'I never knew you well enough . . . I was your slave . . . Perhaps naturally I identified your extraordinary advent into our domestic tensions and straitened circumstances [when Grandma came to stay in Auckland] *as something almost mythical . . . I wonder now if this perception owed so much to you as to my feverish need then to locate some type who was different to all who surrounded me, and who would, by your extraordinariness, explain my difference.*

'This is important to me. Because for me, as for all my cousins, came the disillusionment consequent on encountering the hard empirical fact of "builder's wife" "plumber's wife"; not the grande dame at all. The actual process was something . . . I used against you. I taunted you with it in my mind even as I grappled to accept it. Oh you have no idea how hard, Grandma, it was to accept that this imaginary, almost visionary woman who brought so much happiness to our house when you visited . . . occupied an unimportant place in the social environment in HB. It always surprised me that people coming from Hawke's Bay had not heard of you or your family name. I was positive our family name (by irony my middle name) was a great dynastic name like in a British novel.

'Meanwhile our family waited for your death to release the inheritance which would make my mother's life so much better.

'I waited for your death with almost unbearable impatience. If I was your slave when I brought your tea to you I was also your invisible poisoner. When I picked up your pink rug and placed it over your knees, in my mind I wrapped it round your feeble neck and quickly tightened it. My guilt only drove me to deeper piety. I did love you somehow but I seemed to see my entire youth dissipate before this old woman full of quibblings about manners, who had never brought up boys; who hated to see bare feet; also regarded coloured shirts as offensive because labourers wore them. You used the word "common" as others might use the word "wicked" and it extended to a range so infinitesimally minute that even the handling of a teaspoon was not beyond your surveillance. Ah the unconscious things we do! I know you will take a step back before all this, shaking your head with horror, saying no, no — I didn't know I was doing this; that it would lead to this; that it would affect you in that particular way. My love for you is so confused with hate, I resent so much my implication in this guilt.

'You never touched me. You never clasped me, or cradled me, or caressed me. With you I didn't expect it . . . Yet I loved you . . . Your self consciousness was limited by a kind of selfishness. A narcissistic selfishness . . . You were a shop girl . . . Yet you had a sense of humour. A delight in life. You had your own individuality, I recognise. I admire it. Yet . . . You were so unbendingly ambitious. You had a back of iron as regards "getting on". You worshipped what you yourself possessed in abundance — "get-up-and-go." This is what I mean by my carrying on unconsciously what you aspired to. I feel an enormous weight to achieve, pushing behind me. I push myself beyond my capabilities — hence I achieve so much less than I imagine I can that I detest my own capabilities. "I have achieved nothing": how often this has crossed my mind. "I have achieved nothing." No. My entire life has been taken up in an attempt to extricate myself from ... the ludicrous sack of ideas I inherited from you.

'Yet wait. Here I am in full cry against you — yet "you" ... I am thinking of my own mental image of you . . . You cannot answer for my over-identification with you: or my revolt from this over-dependence.

'Why did I seek to make you responsible? I wish I suppose for you to re-enter that stage, to sit before me so I can announce my homosexuality to you. I wish to kiss you on your cheek, kiss your tears away, hold your hands and say it is alright; it is alright; I am happy. I lift my head up and out through my eyes I see the world. If I taunted you and made you to blame it was as a child would, who wishes to return a deeply embedded hurt. I resent so much the inequalities of my situation as a gay man but not the fact I am gay. Ah, yet even as I talk to you I see its impracticality. You cannot understand. You cannot see, or know, or understand what this world is like. You are in the imprint of your world. Me in mine ... If you were unimportant there would only be silence.

'This is my hymn of burial to you . . . I want to place you parallel to the child which has become the man, I want to place your image, your reality beside the man I have become. I want you to see me as I am ...'

WHAT CAN I SAY NOW about this vituperative letter, written forty-two years ago? My grandmother was an intelligent woman who wrestled against the confines of her ambiguous social position: her parents Betsy Bartlett and William Purvis began life as upper servants and suffered from the bound-foot nature of that world. The fact that she was a coal merchant's wife exacerbated her anxieties. As Karl Ove Knausgaard, the autobiographical Norwegian novelist, has written: 'It is not the case that we are born equal and that the conditions of life make our lives unequal, it is the opposite, we are born unequal, and the conditions of life make our lives more equal.'[12] At the time, this colonial world, obsessed by class and based on a racist paradigm, seemed fixed and powerful, amplified as it was by a global empire at its zenith. Now it has all but vanished. Nearly every 'great house' in Hawke's Bay stands empty of its original occupants, turned into a boutique accommodation or similar. Ngāti Kahungunu have been given back lands and wealth stolen during this same colonial period. Everything has changed.

Grandma's very final letters were written just before she died in 1967. By then she was almost blind. She had to feel her way towards the paper, and her writing moves across the paper like an unstable mosaic, liable at any moment to fragment. She was in hospital and she had had to say goodbye to her garden. I was humbled by the pathos inherent in these letters: '*I do hope I can shop next year or else die one or the other I am so tired of everything. I have very great trouble seeing as well . . . It is giving myself Insulin I hate . . . I cannot eat the food . . . Mr Ellis* [a specialist] *cannot do anything more for my toes . . . Dad died in a room opposite . . . I feel very tired.*' In the final letter, she no longer writes the date but just the day, '*Wednesday*', and the words '*Royston Ward*': '*I will be glad to get home.*' This was the end of a paper trail that had begun when she was a nine-year-old in 1892 and had gone on, a forthright road of words, till 1967 when she was eighty-four and still trying to write letters as a way of staying in touch.

She had introduced me to the delight of language, pulled me into the world of words, soothed me into the very real pleasures of creating a self through letter writing. The fact I am a writer is due, at least partly, to her redoubtable example. The thought forms in my mind, delivered in her emphatic accent: *You ungrateful little shit.* She has given me so much, not least her love but also her example of a woman full of energy and brio, who expressed herself confidently in written language. It is not an inconsequential gift.

Oct 72 1948

Dear Chuck,
 I am pleased the house went through the Land Sale Court @ £1000.

You intend to put £500 of your own into the purchase & require £500 from me.

Well, I suggest term 5 years interest 3% with quarterly rests & right to pay any amount off the principal at any time, with corresponding reduction of interest on amounts so paid from next interest date.

If you like you could make regular monthly payments in this way it is surprising how the amount comes down.

I will post you a cheque for £500 early next week & you will have it ready then when the transfer is completed.

You could arrange with your Solicitor to make out the mortgage the above will give him sufficient information for that purpose.

 Your aff
 Dad
 E Wortley

The Business Letter

OPPOSITE

A letter from my grandfather to my mother in 1948: 'His spirit led me forward.'

Seventeen years after the Hawke's Bay earthquake, my grandfather Ern Northe lay dying. His three daughters and their offspring came back to Napier to say their goodbyes. It was Christmas 1948.

A PHOTO OF THE TIME shows Ern, clearly ailing, holding Russell in his arms. Russell, nine months old, looks curious, lively. Grandma looks nervy and wracked with anxiety. Grandpa's face is pinched with pain. The next time Bess saw her father, just before he died, she was pregnant with me, but in the custom of the time — suppressing emotion — she did not tell him. I was born seven months after he died. I grew up in an environment conspicuously lacking in male role models. Dad was diffident and not really interested. In the absence of anyone else, a grandfather I never knew took on this role. He was, anyway, so vividly alive in my mother's mind it was as if he had just stepped outside to have a cigarette.

My father, Gordon, never mentioned his own father. In fact, Dad's almost complete absence of commentary about his past — compared with Mum's ever-present evocation of hers — seemed to imply that he had none. Or that his past was immaterial and impoverished compared with Bess's richly detailed narratives, epiphanies and remembered sayings.

Bess's father's full name was Walter Ernest Northe, and he was born in Napier on 1 August 1879. He was the second of eight sons and known in the family as Ern. There was only one sister, Grace. I knew him via my mother's constant praise, as a kind man, a good provider, a hard worker, an intelligent man, a smoker of roll-your-owns, a book reader, a brooder in cemeteries where he often went for an evening walk. A wealthy man by his death, he still rode a bicycle. He maintained a modesty of profile that stood in contrast to his material accomplishments and his widow's more showy presence.

My grandfather, my mother told me, had worn himself out running the Northe family business, R. Northe & Sons, Coal and Wood Merchants. This was a thankless task, since Robert Northe, the father, had decreed that all the eight sons were to work in the family business and get exactly the same wages, regardless of the work they did. It was the recognition that he would never 'get ahead' in the firm that spurred my grandfather to branch out and create his own wealth from rental property.

Two remarks illustrate my problem in trying to adjust to his reality. His funeral, my mother told me, was '*one of the largest funerals ever seen in Napier*'. By contrast she also reported to me a comment my father had heard in the pub the evening of the funeral: '*There died one of the meanest men in Napier.*'

How could this be? The disparity between someone apparently liked and honoured, and one who was miserable, penny-pinching — worst of all, *mean*. At the same time, I knew the answer. My mother shared some of these characteristics. She showed a caution this side of obsession about saving money, and a slightly masochistic denial of spending money on herself. But alongside this was a generosity of spirit which saw her giving money to her children when required, when it was important to advance their careers.

What, too, was the reality of the woman who said at Ern's funeral, '*The poor of Napier would miss Mr Northe*', as reported by my mother. (Bess always pronounced poor with two syllables — poo-ar — as if to emphasise how far she was from this detested state.) Was this arse-licking by a crafty person (note the curtsey dropped before *Mr* Northe), or was the woman saying something genuinely felt? Was my grandfather a slum landlord, or did he provide low-cost housing for the needy? Who was he, this mysterious man who shone a benevolent light over my boyhood, seemingly kind and generous, never making me feel diminished, as my father did, so that my own feelings seemed strange to me, false and frightening? He was as unreal as a plaster saint in some senses, a man whose example I tried to live up to. But a man, for all that, whom I never touched, never talked to, never knew.

Here's a story about Ern's modesty — and pride. When he goes into the post office to fill in papers to do with ownership of property, the clerk, who is new to Napier and doesn't know who he is, reprimands him for using post office paper as scrap paper. Ern takes all the filled-in documents up to the clerk for him to register that he is actually the owner of a large amount of property. The clerk falls silent.

When I look at photographs of him taken right up to his death I am not sure that he isn't wearing the suit he wore in his wedding photograph in 1910. Even in the late 1930s he seems to be wearing the same suit. It has ridden up his arms over time, and appears to be too short in the sleeves. *Mean*? 'Economical,' as Bessie would say.

I HAD IN MY HANDS a book that was as close, in one way, as I would ever get to him. It wasn't a diary, full of personal feelings. There was nothing like that among his papers. (His letters, as we shall see, express his character in pithy, unselfconscious ways.) The book I was looking at was the minute book of R. Northe & Sons. My grandfather was the company secretary as well as managing director, and it had been his job to write the minutes from 22 May 1911 (the year of his father's shocking death), through the 1931 earthquake when the family business faced a crisis of almost unparalleled proportion, to the tensions of the Second World War, until 1949, when he died, worn out, according to my mother, by the trials of looking after his extended family.

I hesitated before opening the book. First of all, its modesty struck me. It was small, not much larger than a hard-backed school exercise book. Typical of the family firm, it was not fancy. Just like the registered sign for the company itself: you would be hard put to find plainer lettering, or a sign more lacking in flourish, gilt, panache. It was what it was. A sign. But then their business was modest in scale and nature. Wood and coal are very basic materials, grubby and utilitarian. In the nineteenth century they were also necessities. When the firm was set up in 1894, all houses were heated by wood and coal and, as importantly, food was cooked on a coal range. (Gas was used for lighting, but gas ovens were a novelty.)

Robert Northe's idea was that, having founded the business, his ability to sire eight sons could be put to good use. The sons would become tradesmen in the family firm. One was a carpenter, another a builder, another a yard hand; another walked around Napier collecting rents and looked after the horses; and my grandfather, because of his educational qualifications (two years at Napier Boys' High School on a scholarship), was company secretary and managed the office.[1] My cousin Philippa said he was to be the plumber of the firm, but this did not happen.[2] Crawling around under buildings to deal with sewerage was not, I think, his idea of a job. He dreamt of being an architect, according to Bess. But the notional word here is *dreamt*. I could add in here Joan Didion's understanding of colonial character: you did things you didn't particularly want to do because that is what you did. The area for manoeuvre was as pinched and narrow as a tunnel.

There were other employees who were not family — eight drivers, quarrymen at the firm's two quarries, and 'powder men', who extracted clay for bricks. An elderly crippled man worked as the office clerk.

The coal, coke, firewood and timber depot was in Raffles Street. The yard took up an entire city block on the urban fringes. There was a large corrugated-iron two-storey warehouse, typical of the pragmatic colonial period, with the pretence of a wooden front facing Raffles Street. The advertising on the front read: 'Wood, Coal & Grain Depot. R. NORTHE & SONS LTD. Contracts Of All Kinds Undertaken — Estimates Given. Stocks on Hand — Oats, Chaff, Wheat, Maize, Barley, Drain Pipes, Bricks'. The front was the office where my grandfather worked. The back was used to store the wheat, corn, bran and hay, as well as oats, potatoes and swedes imported from the South Island.

Upstairs, up to 3000 sacks of chaff were stored. Along with grain, the company sold coal (from Newcastle in Australia and Westport in the South Island), coke, charcoal, firewood, cement, shingle, sand, brick and drainpipes. They made the pipes and bricks themselves, all signed with an 'N'. As builders they had a large supply of timber — 'Best Matai' — stacked in the yard.

There was another large two-storey wooden building on the site facing Raffles Street. This carried the legend 'BUILDERS, CONTRACTORS & GENERAL CARRIERS'. Inside this building was a swing sawbench and a gas engine. The gas engine was used to smash wheat into meal for bakers, maize into meal for poultry, and oats into horse feed. At the back of the building and extending to Vautier Street were twenty stables and a feed room. The company also leased a large area on Hospital Hill for their horses. A dray and horses was in perpetual motion between the seafront and the yard, collecting stone and sand used for building materials.

I have a panorama 'landscape' photograph of the kind popular with Edwardians that displays the family business. I found it at Grandma's, stored (or hidden?) on top of a wardrobe where it gathered dust. It was definitely not on display. It shows the yard, the buildings, and nine carts lined up with their drivers, two carts with two Clydesdale horses, seven with single shire horses. There is some horse shit on the ground, not cleared away for the photograph, and the drivers all look grimy with coal dust. Ern can be seen standing outside the office, wearing a white shirt, his sleeves rolled up, a gold watch chain across his waistcoat. He is also wearing a strange, almost comical hat. He looks work-ready and relaxed. But alongside him is the contrast that blighted his whole life. His older brother Alf ('Darky'), who worked in the yard, is in black workman's clothes. Alf has a rough, challenging look in his face, as if he's been interrupted in his work and is there unwillingly. He lives rent-free in a house right by the yard, and though he is the eldest it is his younger brother who runs the firm. Alf is like a brooding manual labourer. Sardonic.

Whatever sense of achievement is shown in the display of horses and vehicles and staff is somewhat undercut by the broken windows in one of the warehouses: it looks as if street kids have aimed rocks at the glass and it hasn't been replaced. The horse shit makes it all seem very down home. Nevertheless, the panorama photo is a statement of pride in the family firm. It was taken after Robert Northe had died in an industrial accident in 1911. The surviving Northes are essentially a fatherless family. Or rather, my grandfather acts as father *in loco parentis*. At age thirty-two, it had fallen to him to steer the company on which his siblings — and four families — depended. So too did his widowed mother, Polly Northe, who had been left in difficult financial straits by her husband.

It's hard to get a sense of the scale of the firm. (There were at least two other competing wood and coal companies in Napier.) People ordered fuel for their stoves and fireplaces on account, and the nine horse-led carts (and, by the 1920s, lorries) delivered around Napier. A phone was installed relatively early, in 1894: 'Telephone 195'. There was also contract work on offer. For example, the company contracted to supply 200,000 bricks in Lyttelton in 1913. It also provided coal on contract to the major infrastructural bodies in Napier, like the pumping station, Port Ahuriri and the breakwater, as well as to visiting ships. It was very much a going concern.

All this was backed up by a careful deployment of capital. Rental properties were owned all over Napier, including several inner-city shops. There were acres of land in outlying suburban areas (five acres by Taradale Road) that would eventually be subdivided into sections. And surplus capital was lent out on mortgages — often second mortgages at relatively high interest rates. The company lent to people who were having trouble finding finance to build houses, as well as to farmers wanting to increase their stock. This was the reality that undercut the hoity-toity view that the Northes dealt in grubby coal and weren't the equals of white-collar folk. Recession, depression and quake tended to destabilise where people belonged in a hierarchy of class: in the end, it was whoever had cash in desperate situations who came out on top.

TO READ THE MINUTE BOOK is to get a feeling of how small-scale R. Northe & Sons was. At the very back of the book is a list of the company's

ABOVE

The family firm occupied a city block in Napier.

LEFT

The Almighty Northes in 1917. My grandfather Ern (seated far left) became unofficial head of the family after his father's dramatic death in 1911.

BELOW

Ern, second from left, on a rare holiday in Rotorua.

RIGHT

An R. Northe & Sons advertisement displaying my grandfather's sense of humour.

CENTRE

The Northe boys' float in the annual Napier mardi gras.

BELOW

Ern looking frail, Jessie looking nervy, and baby Russell, 1948.

Here, don't chop the old girl's wooden leg up!

Buy some Wood or Coal from Northe's.

THE LEADING WOOD & COAL MERCHANTS.

Oats, Chaff, and all kinds of Grain, etc., in stock.

R. NORTHE & SON, LTD.,
RAFFLES STREET, NAPIER.
'Phone 159.

Clydesdale horses: Guv'nor, Massey (after Massey's Cossacks in 1913, which gives some sense of where the Northes lay in the political spectrum), Floss, Dolly, Trooper (after 1914). In one sense the firm never outgrew its Victorian and Edwardian origins as a horse-drawn, family-owned company. Draught horses were valuable commodities; the cost of each was approximately ten times the weekly wage of a labourer. The firm bought its first lorry in 1915. Ern, as the brains of the family, sought to diversify, buy property, consolidate, lend at advantageous rates and generally leverage the business so it looked to the future with confidence.

I spent a day or so looking through the minute book, and when I closed it at its end — the company was liquidated in 1968 — a feeling of sadness washed over me. It was partly seeing the evidence of a man in his prime, working with agility for a large and seemingly inert family. In the 1920s Ern was in his forties and at the peak of his career and the amount of detail about the deals he was doing — lending and borrowing, developing land deals, buying and selling, calling in book debts — is notable. In the early 1920s the firm recorded record levels of profit. He promptly bought a block of shops in the main commercial street. It was by a tram stop, and went right through to the Parade. There's a sense of gusto here, an appetite — not exactly for risk, but for the excitement of opportunity. You sense he is enjoying the possibilities. But all the time he is chained to his brothers, the elder three of whom did manual work around the yard and probably resented his abilities even as they depended on him for a good yearly profit (which he always misspelt 'proffit'). It's not a neutral statement that Ern encouraged his three younger brothers to find employment outside the drudgery of the firm. He pushed them out into the world towards white-collar work.

By 1929 the company started feeling the headwinds of the Depression. Rents could not be paid, mortgages were foreclosed. Profits fell. Men had to be laid off. I remember Bess telling me it was 'the worst day in his life' when Ern had to 'let go' the elderly crippled clerk who had been with them all along. Then two years into the worst Depression of the twentieth century came the 1931 earthquake.

The annual meeting of the company's board did not take place until eighteen months later, such was the personal disarray of the family, the city, the province. It is, too, probably a statement of enduring shock that Ern, this man for whom numbers were key, put the wrong year when he wrote that 'the disasturous [sic] earthquake of Feb 3 1932 destroyed all buildings in the Firm's Hasting Street property all the wooden Building on the Emerson St property & did severe damage to all rented Cottages owned by the Company'. The company went from a much-diminished Depression-period profit into a loss of almost £6000.

Yet the effect of the earthquake, once conditions stabilised and rebuilding began, was to provide work and opportunity. Each house in Napier received a £200 subsidy to replace drains and rebuild chimneys. With the Northes as one of the few suppliers of bricks and pipes, business was brisk. Their work teams built banks around the river which surrounded the old Napier racecourse. It had been turned into an open-air hospital and camping ground during the emergency.

By May 1932 'all the rented houses have now been repaired & substantial assistance granted by Earthquake Relief reduced the cost very considerably,' Ern wrote. A tender had been accepted to rebuild one of the destroyed shopping blocks in concrete; the shops had been re-let and the flats above tenanted. The Rehabilitation Commission offered to lend the firm '£3500 at 5% repayable principal and interest in fifteen years with half yearly payments of £334/8/10'.

The company endured and slowly returned to health. The same could not be said for Ern, who was visibly aged by the trauma. His hair reputedly went white with shock after the quake. His wife and daughters were evacuated, but he stayed on in Napier. He just went on working. And working.

Certainly, after 1931 the minute book no longer indicates his almost playful sense of enjoyment in the adventure of small-town capitalism. He had needed not only to take care of his own family's physical survival, but also to take responsibility for the wider family's economic survival at a time when the city's existence as a mercantile entity seemed in doubt. Everything the family owned was in Napier. The quake provoked other, more subtle, changes that would put the firm on the back foot, too. When kitchens were rebuilt, homeowners usually chose a gas oven as a 'clean, modern alternative' to a coal range. The writing was on the wall for the coal business.

If the minute book is to be relied on, there is an almost palpable loss of energy in the yearly records after 1931. Ern's minutes are more sporadic and elliptical. He was having to run faster just to stand still. There is almost no evidence of future investment or creative attempts to increase capital. Perhaps this is a reflection of a change in perspective. Ern was looking elsewhere: he realised he had to construct his own financial future, separate from the family firm, if he wasn't always to be pulled backwards by yanking his large family along. He began creating his own personal fortune.

Then on 18 July 1949 he died. A Labour government was in power and had instituted high death duties. The meeting of R. Northe & Sons after Ern died was an explosion of family tensions. There was an immediate call to sell the firm they had, to varying degrees, depended on all their lives. There was criticism of Ern for not separating the wood and coal arm of the firm from its mortgage lending/property arm so that they operated independently. One of the brothers who wanted to become the new company secretary said he couldn't possibly run the firm on the wage that Ern had accepted all his life. Everyone wanted more money. By 1949, most of them were old men, so in one sense this was understandable. More controversially, given the family nature of the firm and the fact that most of its members did manual work, the new company secretary asserted that clerical work should be paid more than manual.

It was a tinderbox of emotions — perhaps not unusual after the death of a patriarch. But there's something sad about it all — the decay of a family firm that drifted on until its extinction in 1968. You get the sense of a man who had worked hard all his life for the betterment of the company but was never greatly recognised or acknowledged. The wider family wanted to get their hands on the capital and couldn't wait, in a way, to dismember the corpse. But this is his grandson talking, and I am not an impartial witness.

I understand now why Ern's family was regarded as snobs. They needed to separate themselves from the rest of the family for survival. To 'get ahead'. If you didn't assert this, you'd be pulled back to the family mat. I can see now why my grandmother used to shepherd her husband and children away when their visits to their grandmother, Polly, coincided with those of other Northe family members: 'Your father sees enough of his brothers during the week. He doesn't need to see them on the weekends.'

Bessie told me how her elder sister Jean, who had always regarded her as spoilt, once indulged in a subtle piece of sideswiping. In front of Bessie's Point Chevalier friends — to whom Bessie gave the impression she was a Hawke's Bay aristocrat — Aunty Jean took pleasure in announcing that

Ern was 'just an ordinary working man'. This touched Bessie on a really sore point. Bessie, presenting her case to me as if I were a member of a jury, ran her finger down the index of her father's accomplishments: he was *a managing director*, he owned *property*, he was *a wealthy man*. The fact is, he was probably all those things — *and* an ordinary working man who spent his life creating financial security for his wife and children. He was possibly a man without any snobbery at all. Unlike his wife and daughter.

THIS IS AS GOOD A time as any to look more closely at the few surviving letters Ern sent to Bessie. In them we can catch the flavour of his voice, especially his humour. It's probably also fitting that three of the four letters that survive are about money — or, to be more specific, Ern giving his daughter advice on property and how best to acquire a house. (This is most likely why these letters survived. They were important documents.)

He also models behaviour that Bessie in her turn modelled for Russell: lending money to a family member to purchase property by offering a lower rate of interest than that offered by banks. In other words, it was not an outright gift that would encourage profligacy. Ern was encouraging caution as well as emphasising the importance of property for a family's stability. Unknowingly, he was also seeding a dispute between my parents that continued to rankle with my father all his life.

The transaction is captured in this sentence: '*I note you have £600 of your own so would suggest you take the house in your own name & I will find the balance required.*' Bessie did just that, and her name was on the purchase agreement of the first house my parents owned.[3] In truth, the £600 she had was money from Dad's army pay which she had set aside while he was overseas. (She lived off her own earnings as a clerk.) In one way this strongly implies she was always going to go back to Dad when he returned. She was preparing for the future, and for the children she assumed she would have. At the same time it is possible to live, and function, holding two diametrically opposed possibilities in mind. One might be a fantasy, the other a reality; but just holding on to a fantasy at a time of an unacceptable reality gives comfort.

But the fact was the purchase of our first family home was made in Bess's name, and when she said airily, in Dad's hearing, 'When I bought the first house at the Point,' his face would pincer shut, his lips vanish and his eyes grow bitter. She was diminishing him in public — a shadow play, I see now, of what she did during the war. It also implied that she was, if not a woman of wealth, from a family of substance. Beside this, Dad was almost see-through. Was my grandfather unaware of the implications of his actions in lending Bessie money to buy a house, or was there an element of cool assessment of his son-in-law's ability to do what a son-in-law should do: aggregate wealth and property, provide security? I do not know.

The three letters about purchasing the property are relatively straightforward, as befits the important business of cash and property. This was Ern's area of expertise, you could say, and the advice he gives Bessie is practical. The house '*should be sound if only built 27 years of good materials. When you go through jump on the floors & see if the foundation are sound if they are not the floors will shake.*' He laid out clearly how an offer on the property had to go through the Byzantine land court procedure set up to stop profiteering during a time of property shortages. (The market was flooded by returned servicemen and the housing stock was static as a result of wartime shortages and, before that, the Depression.)

Ern's second letter is set out just as he would have a letter to any business partner: '*You intend to put £500 of your own into the purchase & require £500 from me. Well I suggest term 5 years interest 3% with quarterly . . . & right to pay any amount off the principal at any time, with corresponding reduction of interest on amounts . . . paid from next interest date.*' He would have written out sums like this all his life. '*If you like you could make regular monthly payments in this way it is surprising how the amount comes down.*' The rest is similarly business-like. It is signed, '*Yours aff[ectionately] Dad*'.

But Ern added a note along the side explaining why the letter is all about business: '*Mother writes all the news. She is like Rusty has a damn bad cold. I told her she would have to give up bridge if she allows all windows at the club to be open & then sits in a draught.*' This captures a little more of his character: he was always making fun of his wife's obsession with bridge, her race over the steeplechase of class. 'Rusty' refers to my brother — the first male grandchild, a potential heir to Ern's knowledge of the world, of finance, of property (which Russell seemed to inherit almost by osmosis, since he was only one when his grandfather died). Was this Bessie's role, however? To transmit some essential knowledge, to pass a torch from one generation to the next?

The final letter to do with finances was written just three months before Ern died. It was written on different paper from the others, a cheap lined pad which perhaps adds to the letter's immediacy. (Whatever lay at hand?) It shows surprisingly high spirits, opening with: '*It is just as well you broke that mirror your luck is right out (of the box). Last night you drew £800 free of interest on your Starr-Bowkett shares.*' (Starr-Bowkett was a co-operative non-profit financial institution that provided interest-free loans to its members. It operated by having lotteries. Ern was director and chairman of the company. The fact that Bessie won a lottery so close to Ern's death seems a remarkable piece of timing — or one could perhaps look at it in a more critical light.)

Ern then lays down various schemes for how Bessie could best utilise this stroke of luck. The information is detailed down to the last penny. In one way it is a further illustration of Ern's financial skills, with various alternatives clearly offered. He plumps down on one in particular: in twelve and a half years' time '*your position would be 1/house free of encumbrance 2/fully paid up Gov Stock £300 bringing 3% 3/Credit with StarrBockett in shares*'.

The glance into a future twelve and a half years distant is typical of a period when people thought in terms of decades. This was not a world for the quick fix. At the same time, Ern knew he had little time left: '*Make up your mind what you want done . . . & let me know immediately. I will not [bother] you with any news I will leave that to Mother.*' Then he edges out of the letter with another piece of high-spirited nonsense: '*I am sorry Gordie has a stiff neck no doubt he got this trying to beat the new Look dresses. Your aff-father, WE Northe.*'[4]

THE ONLY NON-FINANCIAL LETTER THAT Bessie saved was written two years before Ern died of cancer of the throat. (He smoked roll-your-owns — 'the meanest man in Napier'?)[5] It's probable that Bess already knew that her father was ailing, and she may have subconsciously selected the letter to keep as a memory of the sound not so much of his voice, perhaps, as of the way he thought, joked, made sense of the conundrum of life.

It was April 1947 and he had been on a very rare holiday to Wellington, visiting his two older daughters, Jean and Patti. Jean already had a daughter aged three — Suzanne, Ern's only grandchild at this point. But there is a ghost of mortality about this letter which, towards its close, indeed deals with sudden death.

His illness can be read almost in reverse in the letter: first in the fact he had even taken a holiday, and second that he records lying in bed in the mornings. Even his mention to Bess that 'Mrs Kutz' — his nickname for Jessie — is nervy could be read as a comment on the dread she felt at seeing her husband ail and begin to falter. Nobody knew what lay ahead.

Looking back on his holiday in Wellington before this, Ern reflected on a period of unaccustomed rest and recuperation. He stayed in bed most mornings until ten or eleven o'clock '*& one day stayed in bed until lunch time & had breakfast & lunch together. Patti had the car & we went somewhere every afternoon.*' He was in that space of knowing he would die sooner rather than later, and he was spending what came to be called 'quality time' with his children and one grandchild. There is of course not a single direct mention of any of this in the letter. Rather he concentrated on a wry sense of humour and the pleasure he took in three-year-old Suzanne.

'*One afternoon I took Jean, Tuppence* [Suzanne] *& Patti to a vaudeville show it was excellent a Kerridge Odeon* [a theatrical and cinema distributor]. *My word didn't Tuppeny enjoy it. There was a funny man trick riding on a byke* [sic] *& it fell to pieces & he fell off on the stage & Tuppeny roared with laughter ... There was a lot of gaggs* [sic] *put over but I failed to hear them. In the evening when George came home he said "I hope you have been a good girl" & Tuppence said to him "do you know what happens to good girls?" & George said no but as quick as you like Tuppence said "nothing" not bad for a 3 year old.*'

This had obviously tickled his fancy. But he moved on quickly. '*Maggie Northey* [his cousin Jack's wife, and approximately his own age] *died Sunday she did not live long after Jack did she.*' He went into considerable detail about the rather surreal death scene. Maggie was in ill health but '*insisted*' on going for a drive. '*Young Jack*', her son, rang the doctor who said '*it would do her good*'. Maggie's daughter arrived and tried to put a coat over her mother's dressing gown but '*Mag she insisted on being fully dressed.*' They got her into the car, propped her up with pillows '*& she said she was very comfortable. Jack got in to start the car & before he could do so Maggie threw back her head & expired without another word. It was a terrible shock to them all. It only goes to show,*' Ern wrote to his daughter, '*you never know when your number is up.*'

The letter has something of the quality of a stream of consciousness, because Ern suddenly changes back into humorous mode by writing: '*I sent mother a cheque for 30 pounds for her teeth I suppose she got it allright [sic] I made it payable to Mrs Kutz I hope she was not offended.*' This was typical of the sly deflating wit that he used against his wife's attempts at social pretension, a little in the modus of the Marx Brothers kidding Margaret Dumond. It would have also, incidentally, invalidated the cheque. I am sure 'Mrs Kutz' was not amused.

But then he moves on to what was probably a confidential part of the letter — his concern about his wife's health. Jessie and Ern were married in 1910, so by 1949 they had lived together for nearly forty years. Jessie's Type 1 diabetes had had a serious impact on her overall health. She had written to Jean saying she was '*not too well & was going to see a doctor*' — this is the private business of letters — but Jean then told Ern, and Ern now took the matter up with Bessie: '*I do hope he give [sic] her something to strengthen her up a bit she was very nervy before she left Napier. The trouble is she tries to do too much if she took things easy & let some of the work go it would be much better for her.*' This was not going to happen.

The final part of the letter is a patchwork of thoughts. The lawns at 4 Lawrence Road had grown long in his absence and required mowing. Ern would struggle to do this himself.[6] It was part of his make-up — a belief in thrift and caution — that he did not pay someone else to mow the lawns, just as he kept to a bicycle all his life although he could well have afforded a car. It was not his style.[7] He stayed a cautious, economical man, taking pleasure in providing for the financial security of his family — even when he would no longer be there. ('*You never know when your number is up.*')

His final thoughts reflect back on how much he enjoyed seeing his second daughter's vitality and health: '*By Jove Pattie [sic] look well and gets about like a 2 year old you would not think she was expecting in a week or two she seems even better than Jean is.*' This was positive news — the prospect of another child. (Geraldine was born in May 1947.)

The letter ends: '*I think this is all the news with love to your self Mum & Gordon & the cat.*' (The cat was a typical wry touch.) It was signed '*Your aff[ectionate] Father, E Northe*', a surprisingly formal wording for a family letter. Perhaps he thought so himself, for he followed this up with a further note: '*I am writing this to you because Mother might be on her way home before this letter reaches you.*' This was signed more informally, but still with considerable panache in his penmanship, '*Dad*'.

It is a simple almost demotic letter, with nothing self-conscious or posed about it. It gives me glimpses of the man I never knew: his delight at his granddaughter's quick uptake with a piece of saucy vaudeville wit ('*what happens to good girls*'); his awareness of death in the way he circles round the subject without ever acknowledging its presence; the misuse of verbs which infers his speech patterns were ungrammatical ('*By Jove Pattie look well*'). This seems to point to the kind of man he was. He himself had no anxieties about social class. He was not a snob. He was better than that. He was himself.

It is the letter of an affectionate father to a daughter within a close family of the sort I never really knew. Possibly this sense of a missing happy family life is what drew me to imagining what their lives were like in the first place. This man was dead long before I was born, but he lived on in my mother's stories. She conjured him up constantly. He was her moral touchstone. A man of honour.

I'VE ALWAYS HELD MY GRANDFATHER up as a thoughtful man who tried to do the best of all possible things in the circumstances. One action of his, however, provided a model that in effect changed my life.

Right after the quake and the city had caught fire, Ern made a snap decision. The city was ablaze, and he saw that nothing could be done to stop it. But there was a grocery shop (the Northes owned the building but not the business is my understanding) and he directed one of the firm's lorries be backed up to it, and the shop gutted of all food supplies. Tinned food, tinned milk, biscuits, cheese, anything you could eat. This was by way of looting during a disaster, one could say. Or, alternatively, it was a far-sighted way of saving much-needed food that was about to be destroyed.

Current thinking is that you need to have emergency supplies for up to three days after a natural disaster — the time it takes for any sort of relief to arrive. You are, meantime, essentially on your own. In the days following the Hawke's Bay earthquake of 1931, 4 Lawrence Road became a sort of informal food depot, dispensing food to those who needed it in the immediate environs of Hospital Hill.

Something about the individuality of this action — in a moment of extremity, a clear-sighted action — haunted my imagination. It was more than this. It taught me by example: always think outside the square. Make your own assessment of what needs to be done. Don't follow the crowd. It is an approach that guided me throughout my younger life, and has continued to give my life meaning.

During the 1980s, the demolition of Auckland and other New Zealand cities went into overdrive. 'The greed is good' decade had arrived. The intricate urban fabric — a horseshoe theatre, a glass arcade, old warehouses, tiny lanes — was cleared away for glass-sheathed office blocks that, theoretically, allowed maximum exploitation of the site. (Post-stockmarket crash, Auckland had more empty office space per capita than any other city in the world.) I decided that history — the pulse of the past, the stories of the ancestors — was important. I made a film in 1985 that provided a vision of the architectural beauty of Art Deco Napier — shabby at the time, and under threat of demolition — so that people could see its potential. It led to the conservation movement that today exists in Napier. In 1989 I went on to help save the Civic Theatre in Auckland, a beautiful, much-loved, atmospheric picture palace, when it too faced demolition.

My grandfather helped me in other ways, too. When I was setting up the Auckland Writers Festival in 1999 with a close writer friend, Stephanie Johnson, we were told by Wellington funders that Auckland could not sustain serious cultural activity. I thought of my grandfather: make your own assessment and act on it. Don't follow the crowd. Follow your instinct. Indeed, even working for sexual equality and homosexual rights (something a conservative man like him would certainly not have approved of) or fighting the stigma around HIV-AIDS in the 1980s, I was influenced by his example of thinking for yourself. Be independent in your analysis of what is happening. Do what needs to be done. And act.

It was as if, in my dreams and reveries, this man I never knew was always ahead of me, just around the corner. His spirit led me forward, at times fearlessly and against great opposition — and this was unusual, as I saw myself as timid and shy. I felt his (and my grandmother's) presence palpably when I was in Napier making the documentary to rally support for the city's at-risk architecture. Their footsteps echoed ahead, leading me forward.

People so often say Māori are spiritual, Pākehā are materialist. My view is that it is not a matter of race, it is all about listening. Anyone can listen. You just have to train your ears to hear.

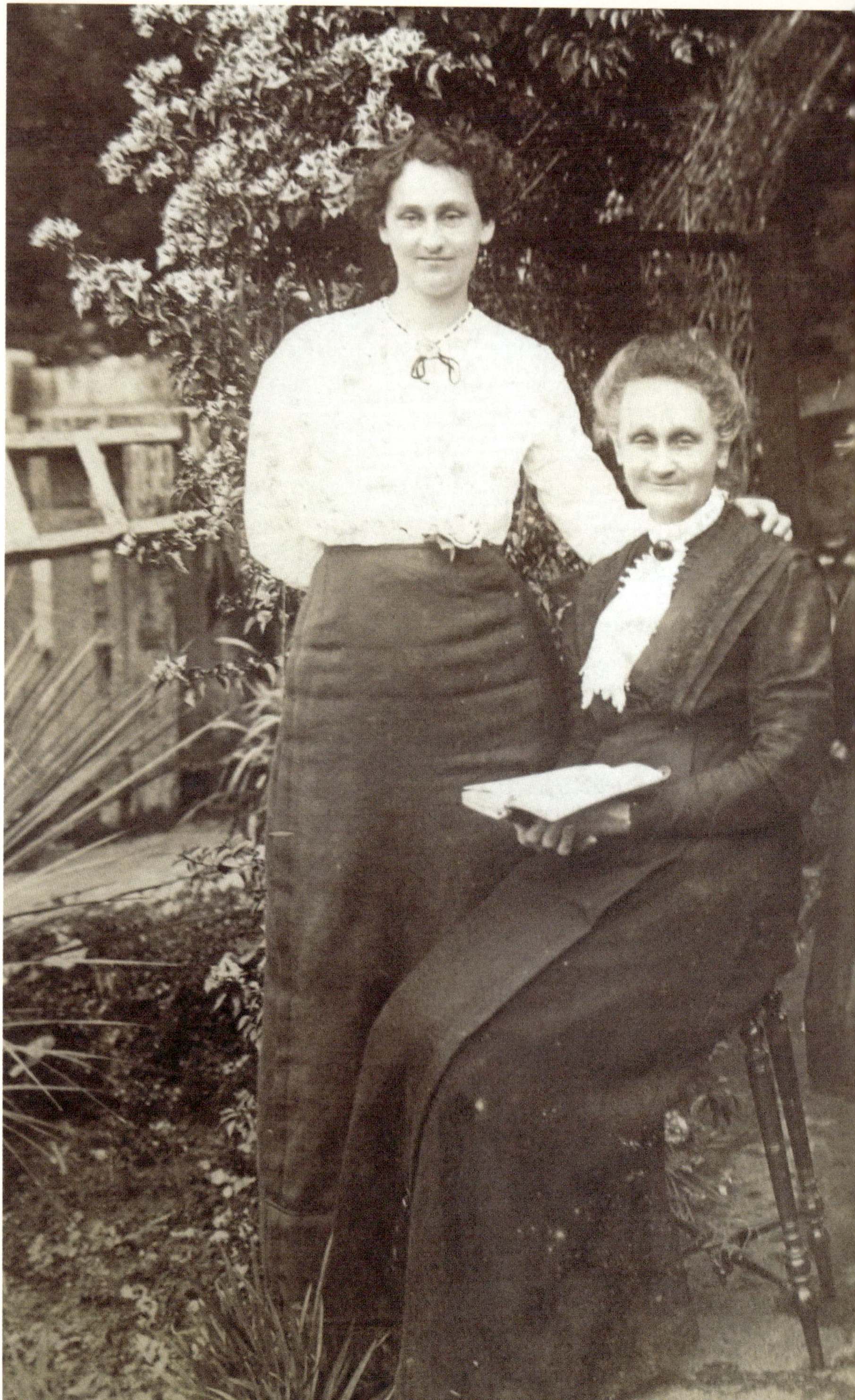

Polly

OPPOSITE

Grace and Polly Northe, around 1917: 'A vanishing is really a signpost to a story.'

Who was Polly Northe? Her 1942 obituary in Napier's *Daily Telegraph* struggled with the dilemma. While she was 'one of the most highly respected residents of Napier', she appeared to have done nothing more than be born, marry, have children and die.

'THE LATE MRS NORTHE DID not take any active part in public life but was well known and esteemed for her kindness and generosity to all deserving cases.' The obituary went on, as if struggling to find some further redeeming quality or achievement: 'Her many friends and relatives were always certain of a hearty welcome at her home.'

So she was kind, a 'hearty' hostess and helped people in need — so long as they were deserving. This hardly amounted to much, considering her lifespan of eighty-two years. What had she seen, felt, understood — misunderstood?

Like so many colonial women, her life was subsumed in her husband's biography. Even in her obituary he takes up more elbowroom. She was the 'widow of the late Mr Robert Northe, founder of the well-known firm of R. Northe and Sons, merchants'. She had accompanied him to Clive 'when her husband took up farming'. She had had eight sons, and a daughter who predeceased her. She had twenty-one grandchildren and ten great-grandchildren. In its own way, it was some sort of accomplishment. As a heterosexual woman she had fulfilled her function. But was that all?

I ask this question because her apparent lack of accomplishment — she took no 'active part in public life' — meant her life, like those of so many colonial women, was routinely underestimated. Even in the graveyard, the most these women got was a single line, in second place, below their husband who in death, in granite or marble, still got further space, a bigger headline.

In the absence of any other information, I wondered how I could evoke this woman who featured in Bess's conversations as if she were still very much alive. Polly, or Grandma Northe, as Bessie called her, was a kind of emotional touchstone. She lived just around the corner, and Bessie went with her parents and sisters to visit her on a Sunday. (All Polly's sons lived 'around the corner', like planets orbiting round their sun.) Ern 'was always very good to his mother', Bessie told me. 'He loved his mother.' In one way his relationship with his mother stood as a model for mine. But when I asked Mum about Polly, hoping to find some historical romance, all I ever got was: 'She was very kind' — which was pleasing news but it hardly qualified or *quantified* her.

No letters of hers survive — well, she lived 'around the corner', so letters were unlikely. And there were no objects that expressed Polly's personality: no jewellery, gloves, even any stories. There was nothing, apart from the rather stilted photographs of her as a matriarch surrounded by her family, much as a convict might be surrounded by arresting officers. It took me a long time to realise there was not a single photograph of her as a young woman or a bride. There was a reason for this, but like most absences in family stories (or any story), it takes a while to recognise what is missing. A silence usually indicates a story.

The obituary had dutifully sketched in her origins. She was born at 'Onepoto Valley' in 1859, 'the daughter of the late Mrs Thos. Campbell and the late Mr John Summers, of the 65th Regiment of the Imperial Army, who was lost in the Maori war in the Waikato, in 1862'. Now we edge a little closer to a story. 'He was eaten by the Maoris,' Bess said to me when I asked about this vanishing. He was 'lost', as the obituary said. He leaves the story neatly at this point, never to be referred to again.

When I became old enough to undertake independent genealogical research — that is, I was old enough to write letters, address them to government authorities and ask for information — I sent away for the marriage certificate of Polly's mother and the man I thought was Polly's stepfather, Thomas Campbell.

To tell the truth, I was lured by a single word in the drumroll of Polly's birth name: Mary Ann Alice Earl Summers. What was the origin of *Earl*, I wondered. Was this a hint of fabulous aristocratic ancestry hidden like a gilded thread in the rather dull and threadbare family tapestry? What I received was the equivalent of an electric shock. The marriage certificate listed Polly's mother Agnes as 'laundress' and Thomas Campbell as 'labourer'. When I asked Bess, the gentrifier, what was the meaning of this strange information, she was uncharacteristically terse. 'Life wasn't always like it is now,' she said. 'It was tough back then.' When John Summers was 'eaten by the Maoris', she explained, his wife was left with two daughters to bring up. Taking in laundry was one of the few things an uneducated but respectable working woman could do.

John Summers was Irish by birth. He had managed to get away from the death machine that was famine-struck Ireland and had washed up in Tasmania. He was a twenty-year-old labourer when he enlisted in the British Army in 1852. He then moved with the army to Wellington, and married Agnes Earl, a Devonshire lass the same age as himself. She was an assisted immigrant, part of the Wakefield scheme. The army moved to Napier in 1858, at a time of tensions among Hawke's Bay Māori, and it was here that Polly and her sister Elizabeth (Lizzie) were born. Neither of the daughters was registered at birth, which gives some sense of the obscurity and modesty of their lives. But Polly, or Mary Anne, or variously Marianne, was baptised on 18 April 1860 in the Anglican Church.

Some two years later, whatever shreds of respectability Agnes had been able to gather around herself vanished. To be a soldier, as her husband John was, was to be moved like lumber to wherever points of tension were. In 1862, this meant the Waikato. Governor Grey had instructed that Auckland's Great South Road be built, pointing like a dagger straight at the heart of the King Movement in the Waikato. It was the beginning of another war over land.

Waikato Māori began picking off by sniper-fire soldiers labouring as road builders. On the night before an attack on 8 June 1862, when the situation seemed especially threatening and Summers' unit had been ordered forward into terrifying enemy territory, Private John Summers vanished. He was listed as five feet, eight-and-a-half inches tall, of 'Irish complexion' (meaning fresh), with brown hair and grey eyes. He was last seen wearing a 'blue serge' jacket.

He was a deserter. This made sense of the 'he-was-eaten-by-Maoris' story. His abandonment of a wife and two tiny girls (Polly was three) precipitated a crisis. Agnes, aged thirty-two, had no capital and now no income. She had no skills. She became a laundress, working in what was called 'Soap Suds Gully', an open well in what is now the Napier Botanic Gardens. It is difficult to think of a harder job. But the benefit of being a laundress was that she could keep her children; they were not sent off to an orphanage. In a very small way, then, she operated as a contractor selling her labour. But it was backbreaking work for a pittance.[1] Within six months of being abandoned, Agnes had married Eugene Hibbens, twenty-two years older than she was. This could only have occurred if her first husband was dead. The story of John Summers being eaten by Māori was a ruse for a hard-pressed woman who was prepared to marry a much older man, bigamously, in order to give her daughters a roof over their heads and to put food on the table. It is not a pretty story.

Hibbens, husband number two, was the son of an Eton-educated judge advocate who had retired in disgrace. The marriage lasted three years. The wedding certificate listed him as 'a settler', but when Eugene Hibbens died in June 1865 he was described as 'a shepherd'.

Once again Agnes was thrown onto the merciless open market. Once again she turned to the only thing she could do: laundering other people's soiled clothes. Then on 18 December 1866, thirty-six-year-old Agnes married Thomas Campbell, a Scotsman of the same age, in a registry office on Milton Road, Napier. Her daughter Polly, who was now seven years old, had already had three 'fathers'.

If this was a contemporary story, this narrative might have been advanced as an explanation for addiction or dysfunction. Agnes could have taken to the bottle or prostitution and abandoned her children. She did not. Agnes held staunch through all the changes, inculcating love and loyalty into her daughters as well as the example of the honesty of hard work. Perhaps people expected less and took what they could within the narrow margins of their lives. Besides, what lay outside that narrow corridor was frightening: children were often abandoned as unwanted encumbrances or even became prostitutes themselves. Indigent men and women sometimes committed a minor crime so they could spend a night out of the cold in the cells. The myth of egalitarian New Zealand had not yet been born. There was of course no social security, only charity. If Polly was remembered in her obituary as being responsive to 'deserving cases' of charity, it was perhaps that she understood only too well the terror of need.

On 9 November 1876, at the age of seventeen, Polly married my great-grandfather Robert Northe, who was twenty-six. He was already a man of business. (And interestingly, Polly's blend of Irish and Devonshire genes was the exact same mixture of Robert Northe's own mother, Nancy O'Donnell.) The marriage took place at the home of Polly's mother, Agnes, who had now scrambled back to respectability. Her husband Thomas Campbell was no longer a labourer but a cab driver. He also owned several sections in Main Street, Onepoto Gully, as it was known (rather than the elevated 'Onepoto Valley' of the obituary).

Both Robert and Polly were New Zealand-born, and both had grown up in the steep, dark Onepoto Gully, where Polly's father, Private John Summers, and Robert's father, Sergeant John Northe, had converged in February 1858 when the British Army arrived in Napier. The Gully was where the 'other ranks' (the non-officer class) dwelt. When, almost twenty years later, Robert Northe and Polly Campbell met and married in the same gully it was a demonstration of what historian James Belich calls 'ethnic persistence'.[2] Both Robert and Polly were army brats — descendants of other-ranks soldiers, a close, rather tight and inward-looking caste, never shifting far from where they had come. Given the fluidity of much colonial life, one might ask why neither Robert nor Polly married 'out'.

Ethnic persistence argues for a consciousness of race and caste, but perhaps in this case the distinctiveness came from the army's other ranks creating their own small microcosm of a world, slightly separate from the rest of colonial Pākehā society. Like kept to like. If one looks closely, not only had Polly's mother been married to an other-ranks soldier, but two of Robert's sisters also married men who started out as other-ranks (non-commissioned officers, like their father). Moreover, the Northe sons mostly kept living on a hill closely associated with the barracks that their father, Sergeant Northe, had managed. It was indeed 'residential clustering' and almost fiercely inward-looking.

In fact, the connection between Robert and Polly was even tighter than this. Robert Northe grew up on the other side of Main Street from Polly and could remember her arrival as a baby. It was he who as a boy had run to call the midwife.

It was a love match. I am tempted to say, 'It began as a love match', a subtext to many a marriage, I suspect. There is a report in the *Hawke's Bay Herald* of 11 November 1876 of high-spirited shenanigans on the night of the wedding. A group of six men, playing piccolo and banging tin drums, went to serenade the newly married couple outside their house but had the wrong night. 'Northe knew we were coming, and said it was alright.'

Robert eventually took his wife to a house he had built in Havelock Road; Polly would spend the rest of her life there. The house and stables were set in half an acre on the top of Hospital Hill, and overlooked the Onepoto Gully, as if to demonstrate how far Robert Northe and his bride, in one generation, had travelled.

They began in high style: 1876 was the last year of a six-year boom which had followed the successful war of attrition against Kingite Māori. (Successful for colonists, that is. Disastrous for most Māori, who now faced unrelenting pressure to either sell land or have it taken from them in outright confiscation.) The colonial government had borrowed heavily in London and an artificial boom blossomed across the 'peaceful' land. The colonial state expanded rapidly, and Robert Northe as a carpenter and contractor was well placed to take advantage of the changed conditions. He had obtained a contract to help clear the area around Takapau and the

Seventy Mile Bush. The spec was to clear a 'roadway, 33 feet wide, of all timber and roots, so as to form a perfectly even surface. The timber and scrub, 16 and half feet on either side of the roadway, has to be cut down to within 15 inches of the surface, and to be removed, together with all fallen timber, so as to leave 66 feet in width clear of all timber or scrub'.[3]

Now that the wars were over, what was once Māori land was being 'opened up' and 'cleared', in colonial parlance. Deforestation was integral to the infrastructure that created contemporary New Zealand. As citizens of Aotearoa we weep for the loss of the primeval forests; however, we also enjoyed good roads and efficient rail travel throughout the twentieth century, and suburbs full of elegant villas built of kauri and rimu. This is part of the ambiguity of all New Zealanders' inheritance. The creation of this infrastructure, as well as the decimation of the primeval forest, was part and parcel of how Robert Northe, like many others, progressed from being the son of an indigent migrant into a small-scale capitalist. In the 1870s contractor Robert Northe was earning £20 a week when the average working man was earning less than £5. He was on his way.

There is a sense that he was a square peg in a round hole. His cautious father had wanted him articled to a trade. Sergeant Northe, as patriarch, chose printing. But Robert was not a suitable candidate for patient, intricate and attentive work. There was something of the wild colonial boy about him, some fiery spirit that pushed him away from the cautious and circumscribed world of his father towards something riskier, more entrepreneurial. He was born in New Zealand after all.[4] It was not foreign territory — it was all he knew, and he was anxious to take advantage of this local knowledge.

His Cornish father had worked hard all his life to pay for four small town sections (and a family plot in the cemetery) but Robert was more interested in exploring a rambunctious free market. He worked for Robert Holt, who owned a timber mill and was an entrepreneur, perhaps something of a role model. In the following years, Robert Northe set himself up as a carpenter, a builder, a contractor. He appears in the newspaper in a variety of guises, as if trying on clothes to see what fitted him best. In 1871 he was a contractor; in 1877 he had a timber yard in the Spit; in 1878 he was listed as a carpenter in Hardinge Road, with a yard going through to Waghorne Street; in 1891 he joined A. H. Wilson in an ironmongery that sold a variety of items from spades and bedsteads through to trusses. He also had a contract team with

THIS PAGE

Robert Northe, self-made man, tough and wilful. He disappeared to Australia whenever he wanted.

a steam-thrashing machine that mowed grass and stacked bushels of grass seed, Robert Northe 'working the same as the rest, sometimes helping on the stack. He appeared satisfied when the work was done, and gave the men some beer'.[5] He had a brick yard with quarries in Faraday Street and lower Burns Road in Napier; was a Land and Commission Agent and dealer in general stock at Whetukura near Ormandville. He expanded the business so it incorporated potatoes, beans, bran, pollard. He gave estimates on building and filling in sections. He bought five acres alongside Taradale Road in 1898. He had a company supplying manure. There was a sense of a restless, volatile energy, seeking profit wherever he could.

He lived off rents and investments for a while, a kind of imitation gentry. But he was still a rough, wild character, a colonial larrikin with a booming voice and bristling beard. He was tall and almost cadaverously thin, with big raw sticking-out ears. It was not unusual for him to vanish with a carpetbag on a ship going to Australia, leaving behind his wife and children without any explanation. (His mother had family in Australia, the O'Donnells.) Even as a forty-one-year-old (weighing nine stone one pound), he was competing as a rower and winning races, speaking at rowdy dinners following the all-male regattas.[6] He took part in local politics and was a prominent member of the Harbour Board League which advocated for a port placed in the inner harbour. He was restless, energetic and irascible.

But what of his wife? One can trace a man through his ownership of property, the jobs he had; nineteenth-century women are more difficult to trace. A woman was meant to be sexually compliant to the man who provided the roof over her head. There was no contraception; the concept of rape within marriage did not exist. Hence a nineteenth-century colonial woman is chronicled through the children she bore, often in appallingly quick succession. (This coincidentally also set the pace for the expansion of the colonial state: fecund young Pākehā women were as much a part of the creation of colonial New Zealand as the march of armies and the clatter of guns or the cutting down of trees.) James Belich argues that Māori society in the 1880s juddered to a halt partly because Pākehā birth rates were so high they swamped those of Māori, whose birth rate was, if not declining, not at all robust.[7] Societies work in complex ways. Polly gave birth to four sons in quick succession and more children were to follow.

Robert Northe decided to dabble in farming in Clive in the 1870s, but this ended in disaster when the deforested landscape provided no absorption during an epic downpour and the Clive River rose and flooded the low-lying paddocks. Like so many settler Pākehā, he was really a townsman at heart. He returned to Napier, and in 1894 set up the wood and coal company that would later employ his sons just as the 'Long Depression' of 1876–1895 eased and conditions changed for the better. Like all things, it was a matter of timing. He started the company just as the economy began to improve.

NOW WE FAST-FORWARD TO Robert Northe's shocking death a decade later. On Thursday, 23 March 1911 he was at his quarry in Faraday Street. The mode of obtaining clay for bricks was to insert gelignite into a cliff, light it, stand back and take it from there. On this occasion, one of his quarrymen lit the fuse but there was no explosion. Robert Northe was impatient, irascible — and when he went forward to re-light it, the gelignite exploded. He had first-degree burns all over his chest, face and head. He recuperated, then complications set in, and he died in agony several days later. The bold entrepreneur had lived by risk and taken one risk too many.

There was no inquest, no newspaper report. (Did the family exert pressure? At a time when the smallest incident in town life was eagerly covered, there is nothing.) An odd silence seemed to fall — apart from his screams, which had sounded all over Hospital Hill when the nurse undid his bandages, ripping away his skin. My grandfather Ern elected to sit by him in his death throes. Where was Polly? you may ask. A woman missing from her expected place also indicates a story.

Robert Northe's obituary (this was a time when almost anyone merited an obituary in a small-town newspaper — it helped sell newspapers, after all) listed his sporting achievements and business prowess: he was 'a noted oarsman and represented the Union Club in many a hard fought race ... Of sterling character, honest and upright, deceased gained the personal regard of scores of friends and the news of his death will be learned by them with genuine regret. Deceased leaves a widow, eight sons and one daughter to mourn their loss.'[8] As was the custom, Polly was not mentioned by name. After thirty-five years of marriage, nine children and ten births — one child had died soon after birth — she was now the 'widow'.

What of Polly's life after Robert? Once again there is an official silence. We find her, in silhouette as it were, in the minute book of R. Northe & Sons on 10 December 1912 in the oddly formal attire of 'Widow of late General Director', even though it is her son Ern writing up the minute: 'Resolved that as the company use stabling & paddocking at the property of Mrs R Northe the Company Pay all rates & taxes on the property & allow firing not to exceed £1 10 shillings per month.' This was by way of the filial duty of sons to make the Widow Northe's life slightly more comfortable. The company would pay her rates and taxes on the Havelock Road property, a considerable help. Note the caution, though, of that 'not more than £1 10 shillings' a month of coal and coke and wood to keep warm. There are no extravagant gestures. Each Christmas she got a present of five guineas; for the rest of the year she had to eke out the small annuity Robert Northe had left to her.

Robert Northe left a tidy estate of more than £9000 — not bad for a man who had started off with nothing. Of this he left his wife £150 a year. She would not starve, but she would not prosper. It was the equivalent of a very short leash. Everything else was to go to his offspring. The catch was that nobody could inherit until the *youngest* was twenty-one, a tough caveat in a family that ranged from middle-aged men to boys in short pants.

It was as if Polly was a mere conduit through which the children had emerged, each male carrying the proud imprint of his surname, each son to a degree indentured to the family firm, forever part of R. Northe & Sons, and each less an individual than part of something Robert Northe himself had created. They had to bear the weight of expectations he placed on them just as, to a degree, he both offered them a future and imprisoned them in the past. It was patriarchy as gift, patriarchy as imprisonment.

Or this may just be a twenty-first-century misreading of the situation. How about: Your father offered you work and eventually part-ownership of the business? You weren't on easy street, but you had the pride of being part of a family business — a family business that did well, too. Remember that encomium: 'honest, upright and of sterling character'. It was an assured future, which was something when circumstances can always change for the worse and there are a great many desperately poor people around you.

There is plenty of evidence that the sons were proud of the family firm. Each Mardi Gras they entered floats in the procession: pastiche houses made of bricks with a flue; an imitation whare with the Northe boys in grass skirts (actually sheep skins). It was a time of unconscious appropriation of

Māori motifs — less a celebration than a sign of Māori defeat and loss of control of their own imagery. The Northes were colonials made good. But still the boys, or now married men, were imprisoned by the yoke Robert Northe had placed on their backs.

But why would his will so overlook his wife of so many decades, who had stuck with him through thick and thin, through flood and the birth of ten children and the harrowing death of a child? Marriages wear thin. What begins as a love match between a young man and his very young bride becomes, over the years, something different? Perhaps self-made men, with their bristling egos, their sense of having created the world through sheer brute force and street smarts, make impossible husbands? He was a contractor, used to assessing and pricing labour against profit. Did he think he could have got a better bargain than a wife who was the daughter of a laundress and a deserter? Or was he just a bastard? Or is this again an ahistorical misunderstanding?

In 1918, long enough for the rawness of Robert Northe's death to have faded away, his sons decided to file a case in the Supreme Court challenging his will. Polly is the silent witness in all this, though we find her again appearing like a phantom in the minute book of R. Northe & Sons as 'Mrs R Northe'. As always, it was left to Ern as the brains of the firm to undertake the task. He went to Wellington and, by way of doing a tidy little bit of business on the way, sold some R. Northe & Sons land in Pahīatua. It was not until March 1920 that the Supreme Court judgment was received: 'trustees after providing £3600 in war bonds to secure Mrs R Northe [an] annuity' could subdivide the estate. Polly at last could be comfortable, with a reasonable annuity. His children could get on with their lives.

The eight fond sons and one loving daughter had all championed their mother. The daughter, Grace, who had a tubercular hip which limited her chances of marriage, had shared her bedroom with Polly. Despite what could only be described as a rough beginning, Polly was indeed, as the obituary observed, kind, warm-hearted and beloved. Is that not something to place on the historical scales beside the absence of a career or ownership of property as indicators of character and achievement? I dare to suggest that Robert Northe, the founder of a small family fortune, was not loved. He was certainly someone of whom you could be frightened. He may even have been hated.

Here's a family story that explains this. At Polly's fiftieth birthday party

— the only birthday party she had ever had (what does that tell us of her life?) — Robert Northe decided to disrupt the proceedings. He made a public announcement that when he died he intended to leave her a pauper.

Here is another family story. She shifted out of the marital bedroom. She never spoke to him again.

Here is another family story. When he lay on his death bed, shrieking with pain, she simply walked out of the house. She refused to talk to him as he lay dying. There was no reconciliation. She did not forgive. I do not know if she walked in his funeral procession. Probably she did, since to not do so would invite the public into private discord. But the only time she ever visited his grave was when she had to lay her one daughter, Grace, beside him twenty years later.

Here is another family story. All her life she wrote a diary. Bessie told me, 'If ever there was a question of when something happened, Grandma would run away to her room and look at her diary.' This implies the diaries were factual, lists of events rather than introspective maunderings. But let's take this another step. A diary presumes privacy. The fact she 'ran away to her room' gives the sense of someone who went out, perhaps even opened a locked drawer, consulted the oracle in private, then came back and passed on the information. There is no suggestion that she would bring the diary into a crowded room and point out a line or a date.

What happened to these life-long diaries? Here is another family story, Bess's version: 'Dad was so furious when he found out Queen [a sister-in-law resident in Polly's home when she died] burnt the diaries. They were full of the history of Hawke's Bay.'

Another family story: 'The diaries were buried with her, placed inside her coffin . . . The coffin was so heavy the boys struggled to lift it.'

Whatever the method, the diaries vanished. And a vanishing is really a signpost to a story. Why were they destroyed? My theory is that Queen, Polly's daughter-in-law, read them and realised they were the record of an unhappy marriage. Unhappiness is an uncomfortable vision, especially in the context of a grieving family.

Why do I think Polly recorded the unhappiness of her married life? We might read it in reverse, as it were, in the stoicism Polly practised — perhaps even a stoicism she learnt in that hectic period when she had three 'fathers' in seven years: a mode of endurance, a practised silence, an inward turning towards the solicitude of recording your own impressions of things in private. Given that women had such a severely restricted area in which to express themselves in public life, diaries were often a place where the self could be set free. The self could talk to the self.

Yet I can add a heartening footnote to this tale of silences, omissions, destruction of a written voice. It reveals something else about Polly, something she could never say out loud. She left behind four words that say everything.

They can be found on Sheet 428 of the 1893 Women's Suffrage Petition, the petition that led to New Zealand women being the first in the world to get the vote. In a larger sense it was the beginning of an assertive demand for women's rights. The four words on Sheet 428 are: *Mary North [sic] Havelock Road*.[9]

But look at the misspelling of the family surname. Her husband's name was everywhere: on his company's advertising on the buildings in White Road and Raffles Street, and in newspapers. There is no way Polly did not know the correct spelling of her husband's surname. Like all women, she was born into a man's surname and exchanged it for another man's surname on marriage. Was this misspelling a sleight of hand, a duck under the cover of illiteracy in the hope that her husband might not find out she had signed it?

These are questions no one can answer. Perhaps she really did accidentally misspell her surname, such a key part of her husband's identity. Or did she deliberately misspell it as a way of giving him the fingers and asserting her own private identity? She needed it to be recognisable for it to count in the petition as legal. Yet the small variance in the surname, by effectively castrating that dangling 'e', made it her own.

And what happened to Agnes, the hard-working laundress? In old age she lived with Polly and Robert Northe, as was common in those more communal times. This is the good news. After she died, she was buried in the Northe family plot. Possibly a headstone was always going to be placed there. But it never happened. Like so many who came to a new country, worked hard, struggled and hoped for a better life, she lies in an unmarked grave.

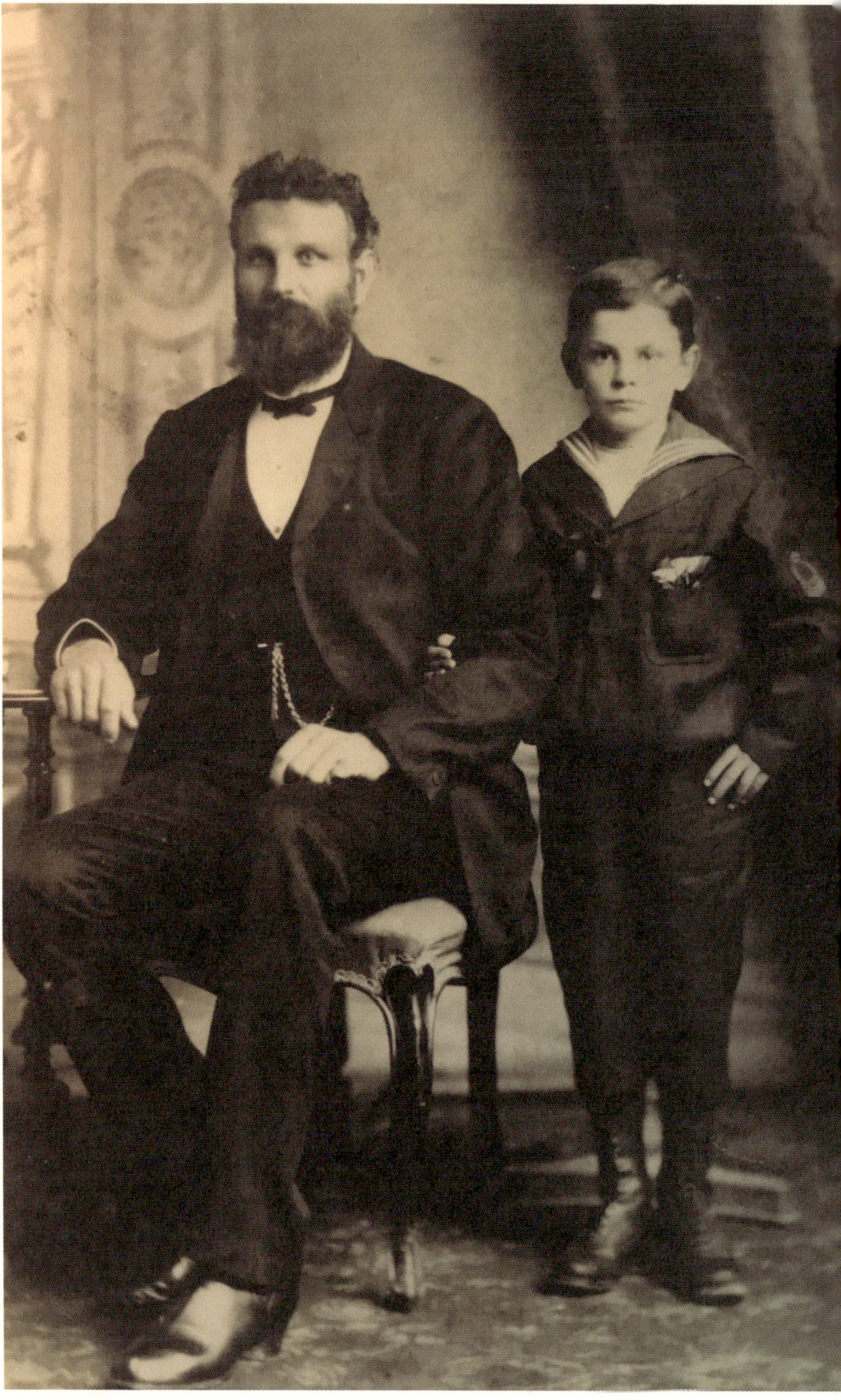

What's in a Name?

OPPOSITE

John James Northey and his son, Jack, some time in the 1880s: 'He became a New Zealander at a time there was probably little sense of such a hybrid being.'

I was sitting in the Hocken Library looking at hard copies of newspapers — a rare pleasure. A nineteenth-century newspaper is like a Dickens novel, full of pungent detail evoking the way people laboured, loved, fought one another or tried to scrape a living in whatever devious way they could.

IT'S LIKE LOOKING THROUGH A tiny keyhole at a tumultuous yet vividly alive world, frozen for a second and then broken down into print. For anyone interested in history, reading newspapers is nectar, opium and entertainment all in one.

I had looked through the *Hawke's Bay Herald*, then the *Hawke's Bay Times* for 1871. The latter was an advocate of abstinence from alcohol. It supported the Rechabite movement, whose followers took a pledge to abstain from liquor, drank tea and espoused the virtues of being a teetotaller. (In a way it was a forerunner of Alcoholics Anonymous.) I understood why nineteenth-century Napierites would be so passionate about providing an alternative to the allure of alcohol. Booze threatened the economic viability of working people's lives. It was often the difference between food on the table or hunger. Napier, like every colonial outpost throughout the Empire, was saturated in alcohol. By the 1870s there was one pub for every 287 people (including children) in New Zealand. Alcoholism was like a colonial disease.

Whether people drank purely for enjoyment is debatable. I asserted earlier that I felt drinking helped migrants who were profoundly affected by a series of psychological and spiritual losses. Everything around them reminded them they were not at home — would never be at home. Most lacked the ability to return to a homeland that, anyway, had effectively expelled them. Some people had the inner resources to cope. But many did not, and for them alcohol was a drug that eased the nagging sense of estrangement.

I turned to the *Daily Telegraph*, the third daily newspaper produced in the provincial capital of Napier. This in itself astonished me — the population of Napier in 1871 was a mere 2179. That it could sustain so many newspapers illuminated the fact that this was the maximum reach of both literacy and the printed word. Newspapers had been revolutionised by the invention of the steam-driven printing press. And while not all people could read, it was not unusual for a literate person to read newspapers, books and letters aloud to those who were unable to do so themselves. The presence of the three newspapers was also a salute to the hyperactivity of this small colonial town, which boasted a gentlemen's club, artillery dances, a reading club, plays, lectures, penny readings, and an acclimisation society which in 1871 was importing 'insectiverous birds' and grapevine cuttings from Auckland and Melbourne.

In the *Daily Telegraph* of June 1871 I came across a very small item with the headline 'Days & Northy'. Since this was not what I was researching I read the report quickly: it was a rather dry account of a court case involving a failed contract to do with building a bridge. I took note of the date and went on with my work. It was only much later, when I was beached at the National Archives in Wellington, awaiting documents, that I came across a further reference to the Days & Northy case. My interest was piqued. A cache of letters relating to the court case was in the archives. On the spot I decided to ask for them.

A bundle arrived on my desk.[1] There is always something potent about handling historic documents. You can't help but feel the shock of reality in encountering these dispatches from the past. It's there in the nut-like reek that hovers about the paper. (The ghost of a smell from coal, wood smoke, sweat, dried tears, damp wool, dirty personal linen, whatever rags went into making the paper itself, the tannic acid and gall that was ink.) Paper is almost a blotting paper soaking up the stink of the past. Then there is the language of handwriting itself: each individual shaping of a word is a pen-portrait of the person who wrote it — quick, crabbed, a stab with the sharp end of a nib, or scratchy and nervous, each letter arduously formed, tongue clamped on lower lip.

As I looked through the letters, some with notes scrawled across the back, I realised they were so complete they provided, as it were, a 3D picture of the case and, simultaneously, of the power structure of Napier. There were handwritten letters from a variety of people, including Charles Days, who was in partnership with John James Northey, a brother of my great-grandfather Robert Northe. There were also letters from major historical Hawke's Bay figures: J. D. Ormond, the superintendent of the province, and James Rochfort, Napier's principal engineer and the brother of John Rochfort, surveyor of much of the North Island. What is, on one level, a matter-of-fact judicial case gives a good sense of where John James Northey — and the Northe family itself — fitted within the surprisingly stratified society that was evolving at this time in Napier.

JOHN JAMES NORTHEY WAS BORN one year after the signing of the Treaty of Waitangi, on 7 August 1841 in Bathurst, Australia, the first-born son of Sergeant John Northe and his wife, Nancy. (Sergeant John Northe and Nancy are the start of the Northe family in New Zealand.) Birth order is often key to personality, and to be a first-born son is to carry all the hopes, all the obligations and often some of the harshness that goes with parents' high expectations of — and unfamiliarity with — the incorrigible nature of a growing child. At the age of eight John James shifted to New Zealand with his family. He became a New Zealander at a time when there was probably very little concept of such a hybrid being.

John James was both an army brat, a child of an itinerant soldier, and the son of a non-commissioned officer serving in a force whose emphasis was on conformity and hierarchy. The family moved with the army from Auckland to Wahepu, near Russell, a base created following the 1844 attack by Hone Heke on the flagstaff at Kororākeka. By the time the family came with the army to Napier in 1858, he was a young man of seventeen.

Understandably, he was restless. He had never had a fixed home and he seemed to have a love affair with the sea. But a key part of his identity was that he, of all Sergeant Northe's children, changed his surname.

There was an instability about the surname anyway. Partly this related to illiteracy: people who are not confident about writing their names cannot be expected to possess it in terms of its spelling. It may have been that the illiterate members of the family relied on saying their name out loud and other people writing it down, making it up as they went along. (Hence the family name appears at different times in newspapers and documents as North, Northe, Northey and, here, Northy.) Northe may have been a transliteration of Northey, in any case — the single 'e' having to express the characteristic Cornish 'errrrr' sound at the end of the name. But there is another theory about the name change that has to do with the antagonism that sometimes occurs between fathers and first-born sons.

A family story goes that John James Northe chose to add a 'y' to the name as a way to differentiate himself from his father, Sergeant John Northe. There were no longer two 'John Northes' in Napier. There appears to be some credence to this story. When he was a young man, John James left Napier for Auckland. The certificate for his marriage to Jane Scott (the daughter of a shoemaker) on 29 July 1869 in High Street, Auckland, notes his surname as Northey and his occupation as shipwright.

In 1870 John James was the second mate aboard *The Star of the South*, a seven-year-old schooner that traded cattle between Auckland and Napier. The ship had left Auckland on 21 June 1870 and was out off Napier — an area notorious for its huge swells and rough coastline — when the captain made a navigation error. John James was on deck in the early hours of the morning while the captain, having set the determinants, was below decks asleep. There was dense mist, and the schooner was headed not towards the port but towards Awatoto, a bleak and stony shore just to the south of Napier. It rammed onto the rocks. John James Northey, a staunch colonial lad, swam through the crashing surf to raise the alarm.

'Immediately on information reaching town,' reported the *Hawke's Bay Herald Tribune*, 'assistance was promptly sent.'[2] The wreck was not a complete disaster: no lives were lost and the cargo was landed safely before the vessel broke up in the surf.

John James's father, Sergeant John Northe, wrote to his daughter Eleanor Evinson about the drama three days later, on 24 June 1870: '*The Star of the South whent on Shore last night on the long Beach, high and drie. She is laying facing the road leading up to the Meaney. It was very dark and the sea running high . . . John swam on shore this morning at 3 o'clock and came up to Town to give the alarm.*'

Interestingly, in the *Hawke's Bay Herald*'s account of the inquest into the shipwreck held at a tavern eight days later, John James is described as 'John Northe, second mate'. This may have been part of his current Napier identity. In the same letter to his daughter, Sergeant John Northe adds a fascinating insight into the next step in his twenty-nine-year-old son's life: '*As far as I can learn John is about to settle on the Spits, he is about to go into partnership with a young man named Charles Days — Boat Builders, and I think with care they will do very well.*'

'As far as I can learn' implies that the patriarch was not in close contact with his son. In fact, the two were estranged. But the information Sergeant Northe had on hearsay was correct and leads us into the main stem of our story.

BY 1871 PĀKEHĀ IN THE North Island were just starting to recover from the nightmare of the land wars. For too long it had looked as if New Zealand was a failed colonial experiment, a place of never-ending war and financial ruin. Migrants had been pouring out of the country for years, and those left behind had the sour feeling they had to stay simply because they had so much invested in it, personally if not financially. But as 1871 progressed, there was a feeling that a corner had been turned. The war in Waikato was over: the warrior prophet Te Kooti Arikirangi was in retreat. The capture and bringing to trial of Kereopa Te Rau for the sensational utu killing of the Protestant minister Carl Völkner underlined the fact that the war on the part of Māori rebels, as they were called, had been a failure. 'I am constrained — to admit somewhat unwillingly,' a Napier newspaper commentator wrote, 'to recognise that a revolution — and indeed a very great revolution — in Maori affairs is at this time being accomplished.'[3]

Iwi began to treat for peace. Part of this dawning sense of sea change was that roads could now be put through what was previously hostile enemy territory. 'No one will be much surprised, we imagine, if by the end of 1872, we have almost forgotten that we ever had a native difficulty in New Zealand,' the *Hawke's Bay Herald* noted airily at the end of the year.[4]

Added to this almost surreal premise was a surprise bonus: the American civil war and the Franco–German war in Europe had knocked out powerful competitors for wool. New Zealand wool was in demand. This had a flow-on effect in a small port town like Napier. A building boom commenced: a splendid new neo-classical Australasian bank was built; Large & Townley, a general store, made extensive additions; new buildings went up all over town. 'So far from employment being scarce in Hawke's Bay at present, labour is so scarce that we hear, in many parts of the country, it is hardly possible even to get a man to cut firewood,' the *Herald* commented on 5 June 1871. The whole colonial economy was expanding, and infrastructure like roads and bridges needed to be built.

In 1871, Charles Days and John James Northey signed a contract with the provincial government of Napier to repair and enlarge the Ngaruroro bridge, which led into the burgeoning township of Clive to the south, and the Petane bridge to the north. It was a brave, if reckless, undertaking. The job had to be done in six days. One contractor had already turned it down as too risky. Days and Northey, two mates, were relatively inexperienced and had not factored in various contingencies. The whole project soon went awry, and they failed to complete the job within the very tight timeline mandated in the contract.

The best place to enter this quagmire is via the humble but grizzlingly defiant letter written by Charles Days to 'His Honor, the Superintendent of Hawke's Bay', J. D. Ormond, a Scotsman who was a stickler for detail. Since Hawke's Bay had broken away from Wellington to form its own separate province in 1858, the Superintendent was the unofficial governor of a tiny micro-state.[5] Ormond was exceedingly powerful within Hawke's Bay, the distributor of contracts and the arbiter of disputes such as this.

Days' letter is dated 19 June 1871 and from the first sentence we get the tone. It also suggests the steep incline working men had to walk when they sought to address their 'betters': *'We the undersigned beg to lay the following Statement of work Executed at Ngaruroro Bridge and we are prepared to prove the Same to be correct.'* There is an odd mixture here of nineteenth-century obsequiousness ('lessers' deferred to 'betters'; we 'beg' to lay information) and a plainer, more workmanlike challenge: 'we are prepared to prove the Same to be correct.' (The handwriting is sketchy and awkward, as if Days' hand was not used to holding a steel-nibbed pen. And, in a style that harkened back to the eighteenth century, Days used capitals as a way of adding emphasis to words. Nor did he match subject with verb, as in 'we done'. It's more of a spoken language, written down arduously on paper, than a fully fluent script.)

Days then goes on to say that *'the pile driving plant not being ready and at the Bridge as specified we were directed by the Overseer and Provincial Engineer* [James Rochfort], *to get the pile driving machine to the Bridge and Strength it, and charge for our time & the Hands we employed by the day.'* This is the beginning of one long continuous sentence of complaint: *'I was 11 hours at work on that day on the 28th we worked 10 hours at the same, on the 29th we worked half a day at the same. On the 29th in the afternoon we started driving but finding the pile was too long for the machine we were half a day trying to get the pile under it, we took it down to dark.'* Rochfort then arrived at the bridge and ordered the piles to be taken up. *'. . . [W]e done so as directed, on the 31st the weather came over bad. we also lost time in work, April 1st we were half a day Strengthening the pile driving plant as directed on Monday 3rd April weather had unfit for work to be carried on the 4th we worked Extra at night Trying to make up Time, on the 5th weather very bad, but done all we could on the 6th weather very bad . . .'* The river then rose, causing one of the stray piles to float away: *'. . . it took us considerable time to secure the piles and rebuild the stages on the following day'.*

It is a litany of disaster, and the long unpunctuated sentences suggest a man speaking at speed in heated and vehement complaint. It did not end there. The piles began to split and Rochfort came out in the evening and ordered the pile to be taken out. Then, a further disaster: the winch broke, so they had to wait for another one to be sent from Napier. And just when the contract appeared finished, *'the provincial Engineer pointed out some Extra work that required to be finished before my original contract could be completed'*. (Note how Days seems to be speaking entirely on his own behalf here; he does not mention his business partner.)

This opened up into his main complaint, what he described as 'Trafic', the constant use of the bridge under repair by people passing over. This meant that the two contractors and their labourers had to stop working. Rochfort saw the situation was bad and told Charles Days that he *'would See the Superintendant about Sending a Constable out, No Constable ever came and we had no means ourselves of stopping the Trafic, the Engineer himself in one or Two Instances asked me to stop the works in order that a carriage might pass with Ladies in it.'* These delays caused *'Expense for which we get no return. Another instance a native cart loaded with Firewood got Jammed with the piledriving Machine, the Horse took Fright & Fell on the Bridge, we had partly to unload the Cart File some of the Chains to get the horse clear and was obliged to Pull the cart off the Bridge ourselves . . . We had also to knock off work Twice a day to Make room for the Mail Coach passing we might say that the Stopages were hourly and that it was not in our power to prevent it . . . We are Sir your obet Servts, Days & Northy.'*

I have reproduced so much of the groaning burden of this letter because of its use of language and the images it creates. There are workmen stopping under the direction of the engineer so a carriage with 'Ladies' in it can pass by, the implication being that the ladies were Rochfort's acquaintances or that he wished to impress them with his gallantry (workmen be damned). There is the 'native' cart loaded with firewood which jammed on the bridge and had to be unloaded; the panicking horse lifted out of the space into which it had fallen. (There is no sense that a Māori-owned cart was treated any differently from the way a Pākehā-owned one might be.) Then there is the all-important progress of the mail coach, at a time when mail was the sole means of communication — apart from telegraph which was expensive and hence used only in emergencies. The workmen had had 'to knock off'. In one way, it was as if all the northern traffic into Napier passed by and obstructed the men's progress. Their imagining of the cause of the delays was visceral, and not without its pathos. Even the letter's poor spelling and rat-a-tat rhythm summon up the sense of a genuine person who does not know or understand persiflage.

Letters like this from the past tend to be rarities, given that the well-educated generally dominate conversation about what the past looked and felt like.[6] The oversupply of documents from the prattling genteel and literate class leads to a distorted view of what the majority of people thought and felt, let alone what they wrote. Most working people felt ill at ease with writing; arcane rules of grammar would slyly catch them out. It was not their natural mode.

The clear implication of this letter is that not only were Days and Northey fighting for their financial lives but they were also demanding to be treated fairly, 'as is an Englishman's right'. John James Northey and Charles Days were backing into public notice by claiming costs against the most powerful unit of government in Hawke's Bay, the provincial council. If this amounts to a rare mention of the Northes in public discourse, it also reflects a nascent sense of power.

The *Hawke's Bay Herald* would later comment superciliously that the 'yeoman' type of Englishman of which 'we hear so much' did not seem to exist in the colony. (A yeoman was an honest free Englishman of integrity.) There was much more evidence of rampant alcoholism, trickery and theft. Newspapers in 1871 reported an epidemic of shifty male settlers horse-stealing, house-breaking, committing assault and forging false cheques. Female migrants got drunk and disorderly. (Abortion and prostitution, however, seemed to pass under the radar if the newspaper reports are anything to go by.)

In fact, Days' complaint seems to represent a kind of plain honesty which was part of the fable of the sturdy English yeoman. Here he is advocating for his 'rights' — the rights of honest dealing in an appalling situation, part of which involved working under an autocratic superior, James Rochfort, Provincial Engineer.

Ormond, ever the micro-manager, read Days' letter of complaint, and two days later, on 23 July 1871, wrote a memo, passing the information on to Rochfort for comment: '*For the Prov Enginner's report. Messrs Day & Northy make no specific claim but ask for . . . consideration on ground set forth; the main points urged are that the material was not on the ground at time appointed — that their work was obstructed by passers by.*' (Note the misspelling of Days' name, which implies that Ormond did not know either man and did not consider it important to get this basic fact correct.)

James Rochfort did not reply for two weeks. When he did, he made it clear he would not give an inch. His response breathes entitlement. On 11 July 1871 he wrote: '*This statement is in several instances incorrect. The contractors were not kept waiting for material or plant — But have been allowed both in time and money for putting plant together and for any delays which they could fairly claim although strict reading of the contract would include the putting of this plant together in contract time . . . The contractors agreed to keep the bridge open for traffic. James Rochfort.*'

Days and Northey now had to obtain the help of a lawyer to advance their case. They chose Gerald Lee, a duty solicitor in the Napier courts. He was a Londoner by birth, relatively young and probably restricted from going further by the fact his legal qualification was 'colonial' — he had trained in Auckland rather than Temple Bar, London, where so many of the colonial lawyers who became judges did their training. Lee had been in practice for fourteen years. He was also a passionate Catholic, and to be Catholic in colonial New Zealand placed you on the back foot. But he was used to arguing small-scale cases on a daily basis, and would have been an inexpensive choice for young working men. (In the near future, Lee would be called to an impossible task: defending Kereopa Te Rau on a charge of murdering Carl Völkner. Perhaps this was a deliberate assessment of his talents on the part of the government. But as we shall see, he had a sly intelligence.)

Lee begins his letter with a little kow-towing to Ormond: '*Days & Northy are very reluctant to take any proceedings in this matter as you will be the defendant.*' He then presents his argument that the case could be held before a resident magistrate. This meant it could be heard soon, essentially while Rochfort was still the engineer. (Rochfort was leaving his job.) A resident magistrate was always a local, while trial before a District Court judge (who would have to sail up from Wellington) would mean a delay. But the problem was that cases involving amounts above £20 were nearly always held before a higher court and a Wellington-based judge. '*By consent however the whole matter may be tried in one action before the Resident Magistrate . . . I write this that you may think over it & I will see [you] at eleven tomorrow.*' He then signed the letter with a startling informality, '*Yours truly, G Lee.*' Being local was everything in a colonial town.

Ormond now tried to spur Rochfort into taking a closer look at the merits of Days and Northey's case. '*W. Lee Solicitor has called on me acting*

Messrs Day & Northy . . . W. Lee has deferred any action in the matter until he hears from me but he informs me he will go to Court on behalf of his Clients if claim unsatisfied.' In other words, the Superintendent wanted a clear steer from Rochfort, otherwise the case would end up in court.

Rochfort dourly replied on 25 July, four days later: '*I have passed vouchers for Messrs Days & Northy for all the money that can be fairly claimed by them both for the (two) bridges and if they are not satisfied I cannot help it.*' Rochfort signed his name, but on re-reading the note he added a further sour note: '*To pay them more money would be giving a premium to contractors for not carrying out their contracts.*'

Rochfort may well have been feeling generally vindictive. He was exiting provincial government after a scheme he had spruiked — a railway from port to town — had been turned down flat. Small towns were full of fantastical improvement plans, coincidentally lining the pockets of their spruikers. Rochfort was on the way out. He was not feeling generous.

Four days later (29 July 1871) Ormond wrote to Wilson, the provincial government's lawyer: '*This note refers to an action to be taken by Messrs Days & Northy contractors to obtain payment of sums which Mr. Rochfort Prov. Engineer refuses to recommend. Mr R's memo is attached. I have no objection to Mr Lee's proposal* [for it to be held in a magistrate's court] *unless you think it will prejudice case. Be good enough to communicate to Mr Lee so that the case can come on at once as Mr Rochfort is leaving office.*' Ormond wanted the case heard while Rochfort was still engineer.

The political football — which court to hear it in, what sum to settle for, should the provincial government, as Rochfort advised, not settle at all — was kicked from one person to the next. In the end the case was heard on the morning of Saturday, 12 August 1871 before Resident Magistrate Henry Sealy, a Napierite. (The *Herald,* in an editorial noting the peculiarity of using a resident magistrate in a case involving more than £20, described the position as 'a sinecure': 'There must be some cause to make the litigants prefer the decision of an unprofessional gentleman to taking their cases before a Judge of long legal practice and experience,' the paper noted. In fact there was.)

All the Hawke's Bay newspapers reported on the case, and all gave John James's surname as his father's — Northe — despite the spelling in one headline as 'Northy', which was Charles Days' understanding of how to spell Northey.

Having the case heard in a magistrate's court turned out to be a shrewd move on Gerald Lee's part. Justice Johnson, who was the usual Wellington judge, was almost brutally severe and might have delivered an entirely different verdict. Lee must have calculated that a local magistrate would be more sympathetic to the cause of natural justice implicit in Days and Northey's case (and perhaps more critical of the unpopular and peremptory Rochfort). The magistrate said that 'the terms of the contract were so precise . . . that the Provincial Engineer's decision should be final'. However, he also went on to say that 'the delay was caused by the Government . . . and after that date the work was impeded by the passage of vehicles . . . The penalty against the contractors for the delays therefore could not be enforced'. Sealy judged that the substantial sum of £68 8s 6d was owed by the provincial government to the contractors, with court costs of £2 15s added.

It was a victory. But only of sorts. They had asked for £86 8s 4d and received rather less. They may well have still been in debt. And the experience of working together in unendurable conditions, probably also taking on a task that was beyond their capabilities during a boom, strained the relationship of these two men who started out as mates but ended up yoked together in a failed enterprise.

Somewhat surprisingly, they went on to form a firm which the newspapers advertised as 'Days & Northe shipbuilders and boat builders' — 'boats from twelve to 25 feet built at 18 shillings per foot' — but from 28 September 1871 they were no longer in partnership. Days even took an advertisement in the *Hawke's Bay Times* on that date to say 'the said John Northe having circulated reports detrimental to my character, I am prepared to prove, from books kept during our partnership, that John Northe has received over and above his share of all Monies received during the time we worked together.' The disputatious John James Northey would go it alone.

A court case like this is a prism illuminating a particular time and place. Nineteenth-century Napier was fiercely unequal in a great many ways. Rochfort used his literacy much as a man might use a horsewhip. Charles Days advanced his case bluntly, disregarding what might be regarded as his illiteracy when he saw his rights had been infringed. As it turned out, this was correct. But it could have gone another way entirely.

Looking through the papers of the provincial government of Hawke's

Bay, I came across a number of barely literate letters to Superintendent Ormond, petitioning for friends or family members to be brought out in the new immigrant scheme (by which migrants were assisted so long as they stayed in Hawke's Bay and worked, hence paying back part of the costs of transportation). What resonates most with these halting, almost genuflecting letters is the way illiteracy — the inability to write (and probably speak) a received form of English — worked against working-class people, making it difficult for them to articulate what was in their best interests.

Hawke's Bay has always been famous (or infamous) for its class structure in which a 'squirearchy' of 'sheepocrats' sat at the very top tier of Pākehā society. As Richard Halkett Lord, the London-educated editor of Napier's *Daily Telegraph*, commented in 1871, 'There is a growing tendency, upon the part of many run-holding families, to assume to themselves the lofty position that is accorded to county families in England. The assumption is, unfortunately, very one-sided.' He himself derided 'such presumptuous ambition', commenting that these self-elevated families offered little 'beyond a few invitations to eat badly cooked dinners, and to listen to inferior music played on ill-tuned pianos'. They were 'a mere handful of parvenus', in his view. The Hawke's Bay Club he pilloried as a 'Hospital for Decayed Sheepfarmers'.[7]

Toxic levels of colonial snobbery in Hawke's Bay were clearly visible in the 1870s, when wool was beginning its relatively long economic reign in the region. Yet this court case showed there was another world entirely alongside it. Working people sought opportunities for mobility. Townsmen and women, drapers, cabinet makers, shop owners, worked hard in drab jobs. When Halkett Lord covered a fire in what he described as a 'rookery' of squalid cottages in Shakespeare Road, he laid bare a life of deprivation. A widow owned the property but she survived by letting out her upper bedroom to a woman — a recovering alcoholic — with two sons, all of whom slept in the same bed. The widow herself shared her bed with a young girl escaping an abusive, drunk father.

There was a clear suspicion the fire had been deliberately lit to obtain the insurance. The widow was deeply in debt. There was no fire brigade, no source of water apart from tanks. The conjoined wooden cottages burnt to the ground. There was no safety net apart from charity, and charities themselves had a punitive edge to encourage the penitent (or failures) to move on and find some salvation in hard work. (As J. D. Ormond himself said: 'To the deserving poor he would render every assistance; but would have it rigidly withheld from the undeserving.'[8] It was a chilly world outside the drawing room — and probably even within.)

But in Charles Days' passionate diction we find another voice from the past: '*we took it down to dark*' (we worked until it was night); '*we done so as directed*'; '*the weather came over bad*'; '*we worked Extra at night Trying to make up Time, on the 5th weather very bad, but done all we could*'. It's hard not to think that these words would be spoken in a distinctive New Zealand accent, though the development of this crystallised a little later. I do not know about Charles Days, but John James Northey was antipodean-born and knew only this part of the world. Was this how he would have sounded? '*We had also to knock off work Twice a day to Make room for the Mail Coach passing we might say Stopages were hourly and it was not in our power to prevent it.*' If the letter ended up in the format of the time, '*We are Sir your Obet. Servts*,' there is a distinct feeling Days and Northey were saying they were prepared neither to be obedient nor to spend their lives as servants.

The case showed both doughty young men had failed at the first hurdle of capitalism. Yet in the way of a free-market economy, they were ready to try again in another form. Charles Days had his separate boat building company, and John James Northey, now resigned to living in the same town as his father, set up his own shipwright company on the slip at Westshore. In time this came to be known as 'Northey's slip', built on land he leased from the Harbour Board for a peppercorn rent. He and his wife, Jane, began to develop their own separate branch of the Northe family — they had twelve children — who forever after went under the surname of Northey.[9]

BIOGRAPHY TENDS TO CREATE A false persona in giving a uniform direction to a person's life, as if the end point of a shipwright company on Westshore in Napier was where John James would inevitably end up. Yet, as the *New Yorker* writer Adam Gopnik has commented, biography is 'inevitably double, and full of the tensions and contradictions that touch any real life'. He goes on: 'The narrating self doesn't replace sense with story; it makes a story that makes sense.'[10]

So who was John James Northey, outside of the story I have created to make sense of his life? A photograph of him as a young father shows a darkly handsome man, well built, bearded, and wearing shiny new American boots as if to advertise his prosperity. He looks proud of who he is, what he has achieved. He had some success as a shipwright. In October 1879 he built the first steamer ever to be constructed in Napier, 60 foot in length, weighing 23 tons and called *Maori*. (It traded between Wairoa and Napier.) He signed the building certificate in a clear and flowing hand, 'John Northey'.

It's impossible to say at this distance why he called the ship *Maori*. Was it part of the philo-Māori sentiment that came into popularity just at the point that Māori culture was being swarmed by a robust Pākehā culture? In other words, now that Māori as a people were no longer seen as a threat, they could be perceived more sentimentally? Or did he have respect for Māori? That unloading of the wood cart points to a feeling of democratic equality. Besides, Wairoa was a more profoundly Māori town than Napier. But *who was he*?

The building of *Maori* led to a dispute that is revealing. John James was charged with the assault of his shipwright partner, George McAuley. The case came to court in July 1880. McAuley alleged that 'John Northe' came up to him when he was working on the deck 'and used very foul language . . . Northe said to him "Now the money is all done you try to do as little as you can." . . . He accused witness of being lazy and struck him,' one witness said, with a hammer. 'They scuffled together and McAuley sang out "Murder!" Northe challenged witness to go on the beach.'

The beach was a place that was slightly beyond the purview of the law — a neutral, unpatrolled place where bareknuckle fights were often fought, sometimes with onlookers laying wagers. The crowd vanished the minute a copper appeared. 'Here John Northe said "Put up your props!"' and McAuley had to defend himself. They then had what John Northe described as 'a set-to'. When McAuley 'said "he had enough" they 'knocked off'.[11]

The language is as colloquial as Days' letter of complaint. The magistrate saw it in the same light: local lads having a bit of a scrap. He decided that though 'Northe had lost his temper the assault was not a very grievous one he thought a small fine would meet the case'.[12] Make of that what you will. It offers some sense of the doubleness of John James Northey, I think — the quick temper, rough language and the challenge on a beach to 'put up your props!' He was a man to take a grievance and go with it.

ABOVE

John James built the first steamer ever to be constructed in Napier.

RIGHT

Jane Northey, John James's long-suffering wife, was a teetotaller.

But there had been an incident three months earlier that offers some further insight. This was a case of indecent assault against a woman called Sarah Martin. 'The charge against Northe was the result of a drunken spree,' John James's lawyer asserted, without saying specifically what had happened. 'And . . . from what he had been told by the police,' his lawyer added, 'he did not think they would prosecute.' Contemporary attitudes to women infuse the *Hawke's Bay Herald*'s report, from the jokey headline ('A Curious Prosecutrix'), to the cavalier treatment of the offence (the collusion of Inspector Scully saying 'he did not think there was sufficient evidence to warrant a committal, and he would therefore decline to go on with the case'), to the judge saying he would 'decline to take any evidence, as he did not think Sarah Martin could be a respectable woman to offer to take £5 damages for an indecent assault'.[13] (She had gone outside the court to consult with an unknown person and had come back into the court asking for £5 damages.) The implication is that she was a prostitute operating at the port and her case lacked credibility.

But it was still an indecent assault. John James Northey was captain of the Union Rowing Club at the time, and it would be safe to assume he was a popular man, a friend or at least an acquaintance of all the other men involved in the case. It was a small town, after all. What is key here, though, are the words 'a drunken spree'. Was this part of John James's doubleness? Was it his way of coping with what a newspaper looking at the prevalence of alcoholism in Napier described as 'a narcotic to the overwrought and excited brain, a restorative to the tired and jaded body, and a calmative and soother to the distressed and troubled mind'.[14] Was his mind troubled? We know his wife Jane had taken the pledge and joined the Salvation Army — a move often prompted by personal acquaintance with the devastation alcohol could bring on a family. Was John James an alcoholic or just a heavy-drinking colonial dude? One of the boys? Often out on a spree?

John James Northey, his preferred name, was obviously feisty. All of Sergeant John Northe's sons were volatile men, ready to assert their rights, physically strong. This was part of the burden of masculinity. There were other burdens to do with masculinity, too, one of which was being emotionally inarticulate. A man did not emote, cry or talk about his feelings. John James, as we have seen in his business dealings, was also disputatious. This included writing letters to the newspaper on a variety of topics to do with the port. He was, it appears, literate in a way Charles Days was not. His letters to the paper were briskly opinionated pieces that displayed evidence of a strong ego: '*The plan adopted by the Harbor Board to "protect" the beach is so stupid and senseless that one would think that member of the Harbor Board had reached an advanced stage of senile decay...*'[15]

In fact his letter writing led him to being chief suspect in a sensational court case in 1903 in which A. E. Eagleton, a Napier borough councillor, sued the *Daily Telegraph* for libel. An anonymous letter had appeared in the newspaper suggesting that the councillor was behaving inappropriately. The letter was full of innuendo — '*Considering the reasons to which I refer, reasons which are well known to a large number, possibly the majority of citizens*'. As Cornford, Eagleton's lawyer, said, 'in a small community everyone knew all that went on'. As well as being a borough councillor, A. E. Eagleton was a tobacconist and hairdresser, and used his shop as an illegal betting shop. He was a bookie. Even the local vicar dropped in to lay the odd bet. Moreover, Eagleton was supported on the council by a variety of publicans. Coincidentally he sat on the licensing bench, which decided key questions to do with selling alcohol. In a way it was the familiar intertwining of alcohol and gambling interests, a nest of small-town corruption.

John Northey, finally named correctly after a lifetime of being 'John Northe', took the witness stand, the chief suspect as source of the anonymous letter. He was there 'to interpret' it. His responses were wilfully laconic.

'Mr Cornford: Do you sometimes write to the newspapers? — Yes; but I always sign my own name.

'On what subjects? — Mostly harbour subjects, the breakwater in particular.

'Not on literary subjects — literature? — No.'

The lawyer and judge constantly sought to catch him out as the letter writer, but John James parried their questions with obfuscation.

'Are you interested in the turf? — Sometimes I go to the races.'

'Might I call you a sportsman? — Well, not exactly; I don't bet very heavily.'

When the judge, irritated by John James's responses, which always managed to hint that he shared all the opinions expressed in the letter without ever admitting he had written it, challenged him to say whether he thought 'a man who violates the law is fit to be a member of the licensing bench and of the City Council', John James's response was a diffident, 'Well, I don't know.' He was stood down after this.[16]

What drove him to write such a controversial letter, if indeed it was he who wrote it? That 'everyone in a small town knows everything' hints that 'everyone' knew he was its author. (An earlier letter to the newspaper had stated 'The majority of your town readers know who Mr John Northe is.')[17] Possibly the editor of the *Daily Telegraph* recognised his handwriting. Moreover the letter writer had followed up his first salvo by doubling down with another letter hinting at further 'grave concerns'. Surely a drinker and a gambler, 'a sportsman' who a few years before had been vice-president of the Port Ahuriri Football Club, was the least likely person to object, on moral grounds, to a spot of illegal betting or a councillor in charge of licensing pubs being in cahoots with the sellers of alcohol? Or had the man who had assaulted a woman on a drunken spree become an advocate for sobriety and high morality in public life?

It's that doubleness I was talking of. Was this part 'of the tensions and contradictions that touch any real life'? The Northe sons were macho men. Drinking and running wild was part of the colonial ethos, and John James also carried the burden of being a first-born son. His stroke as an oarsman was described as 'relaxed and confident' when he won a widely watched race on the Waitematā in 1863.[18] This could have described his natural mien if something more volatile, something darker, was added in. On 17 May 1904, John James took his own life by eating arsenic.

The newspaper report of the inquest that followed ('Mr J. J. Northey's Death') said that the sixty-three-year-old was depressed by a bout of influenza which he had not been able to shake. But many people get depressed by influenza and do not kill themselves. There was something darker at work. Was one of the central agonies of his life, as is often the case with men, 'an inability to communicate an internal state'?[19] He had begun drinking whiskey and beer in the way of a determined and fatalistic drinker who drinks to oblivion. He had asked Jane to go and buy him some whiskey. When she refused, he had gone out to a shed to find arsenic. He took only one spoonful mixed with water. 'I have done it this time,' he said to Jane. 'He also said he had taken the arsenic because he wanted to get rid of himself, as he was tired of drinking and tired of life.'[20]

Anyone who has read Flaubert's masterly description of Emma Bovary's death knows how protracted and agonising death by arsenic would be.

(Flaubert took some arsenic to get an idea of the effect.) This included, the newspaper said of John James's death throes, 'violent vomiting and diarrhoea'. Jane could only stand by his side, helpless. A doctor was called, and for a while it seemed John would pull through. The doctor went out to dinner but was late calling back, and by 9 p.m. John James Northey was dead.

Suicide is always the deepest and most damaging of enigmas, the unsolvable conundrum that everyone left behind must wrestle with for the rest of their lives. He was reported to often say, 'I would like to get out of it' or 'It's time I was out of it.' His wife Jane denied he ever used the word 'suicide', but his son John Northey was more artlessly transparent. 'He did not drink to such an extent as to get drunk every day, but he was always in a muddled state. The liquor changed him greatly — made quite a different man of him. Prior to the last twelve months deceased had not touched any liquor at all for thirteen years.'[21]

If we count back, we head towards that period of both the fight on the beach at the time of the launch of *Maori* and the 'drunken spree' — the sexual assault — on the woman at the port. We can conjecture that the shame of the public exposure, especially in a small town in which 'everyone knows everything', led to his long spell of sobriety. What led to John James's breakdown so much later we shall never know, but we do know that his abstinence broke down under a degree of melancholy so intolerable he switched from whiskey to arsenic. 'I've done it now.' 'It's time I was out of it.' 'He was tired of life.'

Biography, too, is an enigma, and we have to leave John James Northey in the labyrinth, the son of a migrant to a new land, the man who swam ashore to announce a shipwreck, who built a ship called *Maori* and tried to shape his destiny by changing his name.

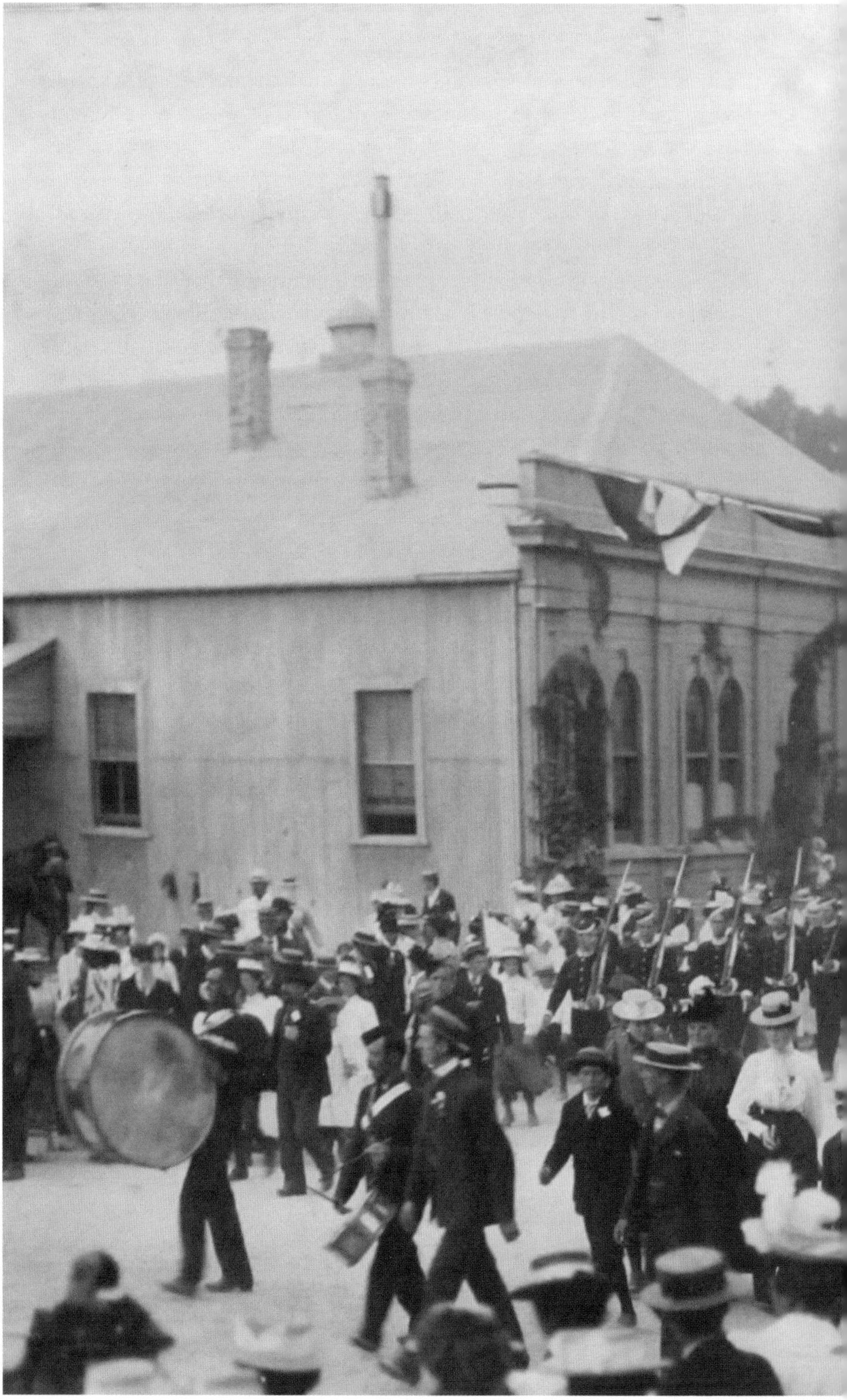

Local Hero

OPPOSITE

The Napier parade before Sidney Northe marched off to the war in South Africa: 'War was inseparable from New Zealand's sense of self, its concept of masculinity.'

'Trooper Sidney Northe comes from Hastings, Hawke's Bay, and was a member of the Hastings Rifles when he volunteered for active service with the First Contingent for South Africa. He was with the Contingent right up to Pretoria, when he joined the Mounted Police. He returned to New Zealand in December 1900, and returned to South Africa in 1901, and is in the Imperial Military Railways, Natal, South Africa.'[1]

HOW DOES AN INDIVIDUAL RELATE to a vast event like a war? How much can an individual carry the blame for actions taken in the name of the military authority under which he fought, in however small or unimportant a capacity? How is a human implicated in large events which might have perpetrated racism and other evils, and to what extent was that individual knowingly implicated? Or was he or she simply implicated through a kind of passivity, being a fellow-traveller as much as an active perpetrator? Or are they one and the same?

This question of historical guilt interested me as I interrogated the degree to which my mother's family, the Northes and the Northeys, had been implicated in the injustices of nineteenth-century Aotearoa New Zealand. They were essentially a military family — of a lesser sort, definitely not of the officer class. But what is an army without its loyal troops? They were also small-business people of the type who contributed to the creation of infrastructure of towns.

But how specifically did they contribute to, say, the land confiscations that so plagued Māori in the nineteenth century? Not one piece of land the Northes bought was purchased illegitimately or through improper channels. You cannot say the family contributed in any active way: no Northe or Northey sat on any official body which made the confiscating decisions. Rather, you could say they contributed a kind of opinion from which these unjust decisions arose: they held the tacit and sometimes vocal opinions that allowed these injustices to be created.

Or could you say the way two of the sons of Sergeant John Northe became Napier Rifle Volunteers at the time of the land wars indicated very clearly where their sympathies lay? William Henry Northe fought at Mōhaka against Te Kooti Arikirangi. He also fought at the Battle of Ōmaranui in 1866, in which twenty-two Māori and one Pākehā were killed. Today the Waitangi Tribunal presents 'the one-day war' as a trap skilfully laid by the *eminence gris* of colonialism, the ever-wily Donald McLean.

His master plan was to seduce the Pai Mārire (or Hauhau, as Pākehā tended to call them) into compliance, then eradicate them.[2] This was in preparation for confiscating their lands. Even my Northe ancestors are presented, in the Tribunal, as land confiscators dressed up in military uniform. If this was so, their presence at the battle led to spectacularly unsuccessful results. William Henry obtained the New Zealand War Medal, which he subsequently mislaid, and he was incorrectly listed in a gilded tome *The Defenders of New Zealand* as part of the militia.[3] Neither man directly obtained any land, confiscated or not, from these actions.

Or could one extrapolate and say that the peace which followed these small and bitter battles laid the groundwork for Robert Northe's financial success as a contractor and small-time businessman? In 1871 both brothers, Robert and William Henry, listed themselves in *Harding's Almanac*, a Hawke's Bay trade directory, as 'contractors and builders', yet only one brother went on to financial success. William Henry filed for bankruptcy in 1879 and lived a modest life thereafter, working as a carpenter. He was the first superintendent of the Sunday School for the Hastings Presbyterian Church. He believed in abstention from alcohol, and joined the Grand Templars Lodge which was open to women as well as 'all races'.

The individual comes into play within this broad schema of 'all Pākehā were racist land confiscators' and 'all Māori were noble fighters for indigenous justice' — even as we find, fighting alongside William Henry Northe, though in their own independent force, Karaitiana Tomoana and Renata Kawepo of Ngāti Kahungunu. Colonialism presents a complicated picture.

Hindsight, of course, is a great thing: a false thing, really. As humans we are all caught in the cage of the present, and we look at events through seemingly predestined portals which dictate, to a degree, how we foresee the outcome. As historian Michael King wrote: '. . . the past can only be understood in and on its own terms. People are limited always by the viewpoints of their own age, and by the amount of information and the degree of insight that has reached them.'[4]

This chapter is about a decision, made at a time of public celebration, which sped a human to his death. It arose in a tumult of patriotism that today seems inconceivable. (Though these days major sports events arouse a similar descent into unreality, as larger-than-life individuals take on seemingly heroic roles.) For one moment in time Trooper Sidney Northe, the first-born son of William Henry Northe, nephew of John James Northey and grandson of Sergeant John Northe, blended into this heroic figure: he became less himself and more a substitute for all the other military figures of yore. He became, in fact, that unstable being — 'a local hero'.

AS POLITICS CHANGE, SO TOO do names change. What was once called the 1857 Indian Mutiny (an event which provided so many of the place names in Hawke's Bay) is now called by some Indians 'The First War of Independence'. Pākehā New Zealanders once unselfconsciously called the land wars the 'Māori Wars' as if Māori had caused the wars by their acts of resistance. In a similar way, what was once called the Boer War (for a similar reason) is today rightly called the Anglo–Boer War.

Two series of events conditioned New Zealand's first rush into engagement in international affairs. One was Queen Victoria's Diamond Jubilee in 1897. This was a global spectacular, a highly managed media event in which the vastness of the multicultural empire preened itself on the world stage. Imperial fervour rose to hitherto unknown heights. New Zealand had sent troops to march in the procession, along with loyal Māori who rushed to be included in an apotheosis of British imperialism. Prime Minister Seddon appeared, his vast bulk draped in a gilded palace uniform. There was a sense of pride in being part of the largest empire the world had ever seen.

This was followed, in December 1899, by three devastating defeats, when Britain lost 2776 men killed, wounded or captured in a fight they had expected to win easily against the Boers in South Africa. Britain's essentially eighteenth-century understanding of warfare — formations, highly coloured uniforms, a rigid hierarchy based on birth not competence — contrasted with the Boers' knowledge of the local terrain and their use of sustained and highly effective guerrilla warfare. It was in this context that hardy little New Zealand raced to the defence of the home country.

The Anglo–Boer War thus marked an important moment in New Zealand's self-identity: the very first appearance of New Zealand troops in an international conflict. And how they performed was critical to the nation's sense of itself. (Two hundred mounted riflemen were initially sent, but this was merely the beginning of what was expected to be, as always, a short war.)

The Colonial Office in London had insisted that Māori not be allowed to serve: this was, they said, 'a white man's war', and their presence would complicate difficult racial issues in Egypt and India. Nevertheless, kūpapa or loyalist Māori enlisted by using or adopting 'English names'. As Sir James Carroll, member for Eastern Maori and later acting prime minister, observed, there was 'a yearning in [Māori] hearts . . . to add whatever they can towards upholding the military glory of the Empire'.[5]

It is not too much to say the first appearance of New Zealand troops on the international stage led to a virtual orgasm of nationalist feeling: Dick Seddon read the national mood like a seer, and announced New Zealand's involvement *before* Great Britain officially declared war on the Boers. Then New Zealand's troops became involved in 'a friendly rivalry' with Australia about which nation could get their troops to South Africa first. It was a race, a rash of madness, an explosion of nationalist energy. This poem, one of many, is based on Conan Doyle's idea of Britain as 'the old Sea-Mother'.

> *The Old Sea-Land is calling, and the New Sea-Land replies:*
> *We are coming, Mother, coming. Every Man*
> *You expect to do his duty. Well, we know*
> *the good old plan,*
> *And each will do his duty if he dies.*
>
> *We are bred on farm or station, very peaceable and free,*
> *Mind the shop or mind the sheep, but we are men;*
> *We are the youngest of your children, and the*
> *furtherest from your ken,*
> *Yet a willing little nation oversea.*
>
> *Take our gold and take our produce — it*
> *was grown while that flag flew —*
> *Horses, corn in plenty, food for man and beast;*
> *We are children strong and sturdy; we will not be last or least*
> *When the old Sea-Land is calling to the New.*
>
> *Take the best we have to offer; take our*
> *sons and never fear;*
> *They shall not disgrace their forbears in the fight.*
> *We are yours, and you are Justice, you are Freedom;*
> *There is naught we think worthy, Mother dear.*[6]

Here we have it all, the clotted mixture of pride and loyalty, of assertion and subservience. Britain is called 'Mother dear', as if she were indeed a mother to a son (and just as Britain was always conceptualised as female, a *motherland*, the gender of the child that is New Zealand is always male, emphasising the peculiarly intense relationship between mother and son).

But there is also pride here. New Zealand now has plenty — 'horses, corn in plenty, food for man and beast/ we are children strong and sturdy'. And there is that interesting recognition that New Zealanders were not merely rural workers but also shop workers, town as well as country dwellers.

But the poem is essentially about maleness — they are the 'sons' of empire who are called into service. It's about the burden of masculinity and its relationship with war. A warrior tradition has its obligations, of proving fearlessness or bravery in combat through trials of strength. The downside, the remorse or emotional deadness — what we recognise today as PTSD — is overlooked in the rush to prove one's masculinity. As another anonymous poet expressed it, in a poem called 'Our Colonial Troops': 'The Empire's awake and her people are ready / To come at a moment's call/And our foes must learn that a blow to one / Is felt as a blow to all.'[7]

So the stage was set for a series of wars that would affect future generations, scything through the male population of New Zealand during the First World War and on to the Second, when my own father went away to Europe to fight. War is inseparable from New Zealand's sense of itself, its concept of masculinity, just as it was part of its maturing, and part of this maturing was coming to terms with war's terrible price.

But at the beginning of the Anglo–Boer War all was mad enthusiasm. The call went out for volunteers. So many young men rushed to enlist they had to be restricted to those already in the armed services or part-time Volunteer forces. District commanders could then pick and choose who they wanted in terms of fitness, height, age and ability to ride and shoot. This was to be the last war in which horse charges were used.

It was regarded as great good fortune to secure a place in the contingent — each of the five command areas in New Zealand could contribute twenty men only. On 14 October 1899 Napier's *Daily Telegraph* reported that along with three other men, 'Private Northe of the Hastings Rifles has been accepted for the Transvaal and . . . will join the New Zealand Contingent in Wellington at once.'[8] Such was the heated competition that a Captain J. Gethin Hughes, honorary member of the Napier Guards, had been told no commission was available for him and he 'immediately wired back that he would be glad to serve in the ranks'.

Further down in the same issue of the newspaper it was reported that the Steele-Payne family of bell-ringers and musicians used the intermission at that night's concert at the Theatre Royal in Napier to announce 'the official declaration of war between Britain and the Transvaal', at which point everyone stood and sang the National Anthem ('God Save the Queen') 'with spirit and enthusiasm'.

Naturally, acceptance into the New Zealand contingent for South Africa had to be celebrated and captured in photography, but as in all photographs of men sent off to war there is a barely visible but still perceptible shadow attached. Would they come back? In a group photo, their 'sacrifice' is even captured officially: they are 'Members of the Hastings Rifles, Volunteers to the Transvaal War, October 1899'. The three young men, their faces as yet unformed by life's harsh experiences, look slightly taken aback as they pose in their fresh, slightly too crisp uniforms. Sidney Northe, whose name has been incorrectly spelt 'North', appears especially thin-shouldered and stiff, as if aware of, or at least uncertain about, the weight of importance invested in him.

Our next photo is the beating of the big drum as the Volunteers march through Napier's streets on their way to the port. The heady march into war has to be seen as a form of psychological displacement, because how else would you get people gladly marching off towards an uncertain and violent future in which a good number will be killed? You need the heightened madness of cheering and applause to ease humans off to what may well be a final farewell.

The farewell from Wellington on 21 October 1899 was a climax of colonial patriotism. The town was so crowded that not a single hotel room could be found. Crowds estimated at fifty thousand, made up 'of all classes', lined the streets; bands played, mothers wept. But the *Hawke's Bay Herald* on the same day printed a small item which may have been overlooked except by an anxious mother: 'Dr Chapple has given each member of the contingent a box of opium and quinine pills'. This was a more sobering reality.

SIDNEY NORTHE FOUND HIMSELF CARRIED along in this tidal wave of emotion. He was a twenty-eight-year-old carpenter, five feet nine inches in height, a crack shot with the Volunteer force of the Hastings Rifles, of which his father, William Henry Northe, was colour sergeant.

He was very much his father's son (and grandson of Barrack Sergeant John Northe). He was a private in the same Volunteer unit as his father, always a slightly equivocal position. Does a son grow more independent sharing his father's space, or regress into a more infantile one, with buried hurts and antagonisms?

W. H. Northe was a formidable man. Napier's *Daily Telegraph* of 15 July 1884 carried a sample of his forthrightness in its coverage of his clash with the Hawke's Bay grandee, William (later Sir William) Russell. Russell was head of the Conservative Party, and the clash took place during an electoral meeting. The following day 'An Orangeman' wrote a letter to the newspaper saying he had been afraid to ask questions '*for fear that [Russell] might treat me in the same overbearing and aristocratical manner as he attempted to evade the legitimate questions of Mr Northe. See him [Russell] on the Hastings stage, with contempt and scorn in his every feature, his massive body rocking to and fro, exclaiming with passionate vehemence, "How dare you, Mr Northe, question W.R. Russell? Did I not give you employment . . . and by that act did I not buy you and the rest of you who did work for me? What right have you to think for yourselves?"*'

W. H. Northe *did* think for himself. The newspaper reported his reply: 'You were in Parliament a long time: did you ever advocate anything more important than a parcel posts of beetroot sugar?'

But there is an element of ambiguity here, given that William Henry and his wife were also guests at two of the most fashionable Hawke's Bay weddings of the period, one of which was the wedding of William Russell's daughter. How did a highly vocal 'working man' — a carpenter no less — end up under the marquee on the lawn of Fernhill, sipping French champagne alongside the members of a self-appointed squattocracy with names like Beamish, Carlyon and McLean? (The Northes gave a present of 'silver teaspoons', which sat alongside the more magnificent gifts of diamonds from family friends and antique salt cellars from the future King George V). The bride wore a gown by Worth of Paris and 'a magnificent spray of diamonds in her hair'.

Sitting beside William Henry Northe at the wedding is his wife, Elizabeth, who is sister to Matilda, who is married to John McVay, the mayor of Napier and a highly successful saddler. Is this the reason for W. H. Northe's unlikely elevation into the company of Hawke's Bay gentry? Perhaps. As we shall see, the manufacture of his son Sidney Northe into a local hero was helped along by the fact he was 'the nephew of the mayor'. (The mayor and his wife had 'no issue', so it is very likely they saw Sidney as their adopted son.)

ABOVE

Sidney Northe was one of the first Volunteers from Hawke's Bay.

LEFT

Rampant nationalism and Māori motifs.

BELOW

Sidney sent his Queen's chocolate box to a woman named 'Em'. She was not there when he returned to Napier.

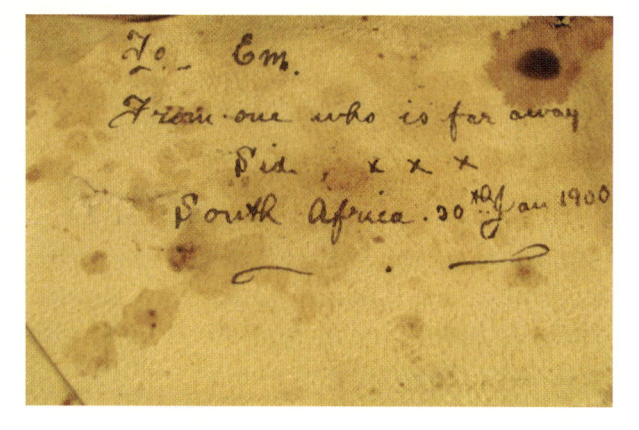

Who was Sidney Northe? What kind of man was he?

Our local hero is first seen in the public record as Master S. Northe, a boy soprano, singing at a Grand Templar event. He later sings in the choir at the Hastings Presbyterian church, where his father is superintendent of the Sunday School. Could anything be more respectable? Sidney is also intelligent. At the age of twelve he is the top male pupil in Standard Five at Hastings District School and is awarded a prize by Captain Russell. Then he emerges as a crack shot in competitions among Rifle Volunteers. This excellence at shooting begins to define Sidney Northe — he becomes, at age twenty, the second-best shot in the North Island in 1891 — until we come across a surprising fracture. In 1895, at twenty-four years of age, he is adjudged bankrupt.

The cause of the bankruptcy can be traced back to a morally ambiguous incident. We have to go right to the bottom of the South Island, to Otago, to get a report in the *North Otago Times* dated 22 January 1895 (meaning it had been sent by telegraph): 'An important case was decided at the Napier Magistrate's Court, when Police-Constable Gordon obtained judgment against S. Northe for £100 damages, with costs, for injuries inflicted through a collision while a servant of the defendant's was driving [a buggy] without a light on the wrong side of the road.'

The silence in Hawke's Bay newspapers was broken by an outraged letter in the *Hawke's Bay Herald* — by the anonymous 'Viator' ('messenger' in Latin) of Hastings — headed 'Driving without Lights'. The writer applauded the awarding of 'substantial damages to a constable who is deservedly respected, and who has been maimed owing to the parsimony or carelessness of a man who drove without side-lights; and it vindicates that constable's character from the false and cowardly aspersion cast upon it by the defendant'. This 'coward' was Sidney Northe, who had asserted that the constable was drunk. The magistrate threw out this defence as 'trumpery' and 'a cruel insinuation'.[9]

Sidney Northe declared himself bankrupt after the case, but in an appeal for discharge from bankruptcy in November 1895, Constable Gordon claimed that Sidney Northe 'absolutely refused to work, objecting to earning money to pay a man whom he had maimed for life'. Sidney Northe's counsel 'took exception to these reckless statements': Constable Gordon was on the wrong side of the road, 'not in a proper condition to be in charge of a horse' and was 'riding furiously'.[10]

The judge decided against Sidney Northe again: '[T]he bankrupt was a young man, quite capable of earning his living and paying something towards his debts.' Sidney 'ought to do something', and the judge ordered him to pay £45 to Constable Gordon, plus costs of the case.

What kind of person is it who refuses to work, as alleged, because his money will go to a man he (or his servant?) effectively crippled? And how, in any event, does a young carpenter have a servant? It appears not only disagreeable but also dishonourable, one of those little insights which does much to dent the later assumption of the glamorous armour of 'local hero'. In court Sidney is reduced to being simply 'the bankrupt'. But everyone in Napier knew who he was. The newspaper's editor took advantage of an old trick: while 'Viator's' letter does not specify Sidney's identity, only several inches away is an advertisement for the coal and wood firm of his up-and-coming thruster of an uncle — Robert Northe. The name is there for all to see.

Four years later Sidney Northe is no longer bankrupt and has won a ballot for one of the most hotly contested pieces of land following the break-up of the big estates: he wins the possibility of owning a not inconsiderable 623 acres in the Ngapaeruru block in Wairarapa. Did he ever take it up? Was it all a speculative venture, a wheeze by which he obtained the right to land, then onsold the right to ownership? We shall see soon enough that Sidney Northe's conception of himself was as a free agent who did whatever he wanted.

So here we have a conundrum: on one hand, the local hero, the patriot, the one who goes off to war accompanied by poems and song, the beat of big drums and the echo of crowd applause; and on the other a rather more ambiguous individual with a tougher kernel of self-interest.

WHILE HE WAS FIGHTING IN South Africa Sidney Northe became a media sensation. This may be overstating the case, but his very ordinary letters home to his mother were seized upon by the press and printed in both Wellington and Hawke's Bay newspapers under such headlines as 'WITH THE FIRST CONTINGENT. A Letter from Trooper Northe'. It's hard to say how these essentially private letters were leaked to the press, but a mayor in a small town is more likely to be in touch with a journalist than a private citizen like Sidney's mother. (Did she share the letters with her sister, the mayor's wife?) Another way of saying this is: in any war on-the-ground information is priceless, and Sidney Northe's unselfconscious letters provided just the dash of up-to-date, grunt reality that is nectar to a newspaper editor.

The war had in any case been providing sensational news. The New Zealand troops had been performing well, even superlatively well. 'The distinguishing feature of the skirmish on Monday [15 January 1900] was the pluck and indomitable courage of Captain Madocks and the New Zealanders,' reported the *Cape Times* on 15 January 1900. The troops had fixed bayonets and charged down a hill just when British troops were wavering. Two New Zealanders and forty Boers were killed. The following day, General French, leader of the British, 'addressed the men in very complimentary terms, telling them their conduct merited the highest praise'.[11] The Boers, who were trained in guerrilla warfare, were confronting soldiers who had also been trained in guerrilla warfare against Kīngitanga forces. Both were colonial forces hardened by combat on the ground and used to difficult conditions.

Sidney's first letter, published in both Wellington's *Evening Post* on 7 February 1900 and Napier's *Daily Telegraph* on 15 February, opens with a classic line of Kiwi understatement: '*We have had some rough times lately.*' His contingent had been '*putting in 44 hours' hard work in a blazing sun and with very little sleep*'. The men were fighting in desert-like conditions. They and their horses often moved on long marches at night as a way to evade the heat. Two squadrons of cavalry and two guns had advanced into the desert near Stensberg to locate the Boers and had come under heavy fire. Only one horse was killed and one artilleryman wounded, but back at camp they were aroused at daybreak by the firing of big guns. (This was the Long Tom Gun, a cannon with a much deeper range than anything the British had.)

This went on until nightfall and resumed the next afternoon. Sidney wrote: '*We are quite used to getting up early and usually start out at about 2.30 or 3 o'clock* [at night], *and have to get up at 1 oclock to feed and saddle the horses. We have had as much as seventeen hours in the saddle at once, and in a hot country like this it counts up . . . I have never done harder work in my life than now, but am in good health and rather enjoy it . . . We are camped in the middle of the great Karoo desert, and it is a desert — nothing to be seen for miles.*'

'*On account of the hard work we have just gone through*', Sidney and other New Zealanders were left to guard the camp. It was during this time that Sidney 'had the pleasure', as the *Evening Post* put it, 'of a short talk with General French': 'Northe was on guard of the railway line, and about 2 am the General and his staff came by, Northe ordered them to halt and give the [code word], which on that night was "Manchester".'[12]

Sidney took up the story. The general and his entourage did not know the password, '*so I blocked the way with rifle loaded and bayonet fixed*'. An orderly was sent to the camp for the necessary password '*and subsequently the General congratulated me on having done my duty. I felt a little proud of myself.*' This was celebrity news, a close-up view of a commander whose behaviour in the circumstances was gracious. '*Our General French*,' as Sidney called him, '*is a good sort and is very careful of his men, and seldom loses any in action*' — a marked contrast to British attitudes to New Zealand troops in the First World War.

When Sidney comments, '*My mare is one of the best in the contingent, and much admired. She is a good feeder, takes things quietly, and looks very well,*' it is possible he is commenting on a horse his wealthy uncle had given him. John McVay's flourishing Napier saddlery business employed thirty people. Individuals could use their own horses in South Africa, for which the government paid compensation. It is hard to see how else a private who had recently been bankrupt could afford '*one of the best*' horses in the New Zealand contingent — one, moreover, which is '*much admired*'.

Sid Northe was soon to go on to fight in important battles — the relief of Kimberly, the battles of Paardeberg, Diamond Hill and Driefontein. But in this letter (and two subsequent ones) he concentrates on two familiar topics for soldiers away from home: food and letters. At this early stage of the campaign, he thought '*[t]he way the commissariat is managed is wonderful — there is never a shortage of anything. Water is brought up by train every day . . . but we pay very dear for anything we want. We go in very heavy for jam and bread, for although well enough fed by the Govt we like a change.*'

As for letters: '*We're delighted when we hear of a mail being in, and awfully disappointed if we do not get anything . . . We start to write sometimes but one never knows how long we may have, as the order is given to saddle up suddenly and in about five minutes we are riding out. Our time is terribly broken up by alarms of this sort.*'

Towards the end of the letter, Sidney ruminates on possibly staying in

South Africa after the war. '*I expect I will stay here for a bit and see what Johannesburg is like. Carpenters before the war got £1 per day, and that ought be increased after the war. Living at a pub was 30 shillings per week, washing included, so there is a good chance to get on, I think.*' The key words here go to the heart of that typical immigrant anxiety: how to 'get on', which translates as 'how do I improve my circumstances and upwardly mobilise so I never have to experience the powerlessness of poverty (or in his case bankruptcy and shame) again?' He was clear-eyed about what he wanted. The war in South Africa was providing him with mobility and an experience of another society. Would he do better here than where he came from? Sidney Northe was a first-generation New Zealander, so his loyalty was not fixed. About South Africa's complex racial situation, he made no comment.

THE FOLLOWING TWO LETTERS, both of which merited headlines of 'News from the Front' and a subheading 'A Letter from Trooper Northe', looked at the dirty business of war which naturally includes sudden death. A New Zealander named Booth, from Ōamaru, '*a quiet, decent chap*', was killed by a shell '*dropping right in among a group of horses held by two of our men*'. Other Australians '*fell into a nasty trap*', and two were killed and twelve taken prisoner. They were buried '*in a rather bare position on the side of a hill*'. There is a feeling in the letter that the war is intensifying into unremittingly hard combat.

Sidney had not seen anything of the Queen's chocolate (tinned boxes of chocolate ostensibly sent to troops by Queen Victoria), but when it arrived he had an idea for making money: '*I intend to buy all I can . . . it will be very valuable, as only a limited number of tins of . . . are being made.*' He was a man with an eye on the main chance, one might say. Or was this how he made sense of the jumpy, erratic, life-and-death nature of military life?

His final letter was published on 7 April 1900 in the *Daily Telegraph*, following the Relief of Kimberly. By now the letters are all about combat and war. Fatalities have risen — '*we lost about 50 killed and wounded*' — and he has joined a march which began at dusk and went on all night. '*We have gone as much as 24 to thirty hours over a burning sand, and, my word, it is hot.*' He joined the rest of the army of about 23,000 men, '*and such a large lot of men and wagons I have never hoped to see*'.

It was in fact the largest British mounted division in history. But he was under orders '*to go away at three o'clock tomorrow morning. We do not know where, but expect to march on either Bloemfontein — the Boer capital — or Mafeking, which is still besieged. If you do not hear of me for a few weeks, do not be anxious, as it is seldom we get time to write, and once in the enemy's country there will be no chance of post or receiving letters. We have not had a mail for about three weeks now, and do not know anything of the outside world.*'

There were no further published letters in the Napier or Wellington papers. Why not? Was he finding it difficult to conceptualise how to tell the story of his war? Or did he find writing letters to his mother and the nation at the same time too much of a juggling act? There are cadences in his last letter that sound as if mediated for a public readership: '*We have relieved [Kimberly] now, and my word the people are glad.*' He had gone to South Africa as a 'crusader for honour', as the *Hawke's Bay Herald* of 21 October 1899 called it, but the realities of a bitter guerrilla warfare in a desert environment had yet to take shape.

War distorts human nature as much as it ennobles. And the guerrilla war as fought by the Boers and the British became increasingly ugly. Food dried up as the men went deeper into enemy territory. The horses began to suffer from the heat and the absence of fodder; increasingly, they were shot, even eaten. Three hundred and fifty thousand horses from the 'British side' died in Southern Africa. We do not know what happened to Sidney's splendid steed, but we can assume it died in the heat. Very few horses came home.

In June 1900, however, Sidney was offered what seemed an out. The troops had limped into Pretoria 'dirty, ragged, badly mounted and short of just about everything'.[13] The authorities thought the Boers were in such retreat that the war was all but over and the New Zealand troops could soon return home. However, the imperial authorities required military police to keep order among the conquered Boers in Pretoria. They were to be known as the Transvaal Constabulary. If soldiers did not want to return home, they could take a three-month contract as mounted policemen, getting paid two and a half times the amount they had as soldiers. (That is, ten shillings a day, but paid in golden krugers.)

The city was divided into sections, and the constables would patrol on horseback for four hours at a time. 'Owing to the nature of the duties ... only the most reliable and steady men should be recommended ... A knowledge of the Dutch language [is] a great advantage but not compulsory'.[14] It would be rough work. No beds were supplied and the men would be on constant rotation, sleeping on the floor with only a blanket. The golden krugers also tended to vanish in betting — gambling was an occupational hazard.

In practice, the work of patrolling conquered Boer territory broke down under the constant need for vigilance against guerrilla attacks. The mounted police were needed in field operations and duty on blockhouse lines. They weren't used as 'protection' of the settled population, as envisaged, but 'rather as part of the army involved in sweeping the country'.[15] Lord Kitchener's 'scorched-earth policy' came into effect. Initially it meant burning down houses that were obviously used for combat. Gradually it became more general. Crops were destroyed; women and children moved into what at first were termed 'refugee camps'. It was only slowly that the word changed, as words have a habit of doing, into a harder definition: they became 'concentration camps'. It had become an unremittingly ugly war.

It fell to New Zealand soldiers to implement this policy because Kitchener wished to maintain the high reputation of British regiments. There was not much to write home about here. Or not much you could put into letters to your mother. This was probably not what Sidney Northe thought he had signed up for. Soon enough Trooper Northe was on his way home.

THE *MOANA*, CARRYING THE TROOPS back to New Zealand, did not dock in Wellington until 6 p.m. on 12 December 1900. A vast crowd had been waiting on the wharf 'for most of the afternoon'. The Garrison Band played 'the moving strains of "Home, Sweet Home"' as the boat came closer, and 'rounds of hearty cheering' from the crowd were returned by the 'boys in khaki' and other passengers.

The soldiers disembarked to a goods shed, filled immediately by 'throngs' of people, but the official party — the mayor of Wellington and others — could not make themselves heard over a 'running fire of cheering'. The men, after being welcomed fulsomely, were told the government had arranged for them to have free use of the telegraph service to 'communicate with friends and family'.

They then marched in formation, led by the band, to the perhaps rightly named Empire Hotel. Here, after toasts to the Queen, an 'excellent dinner' was served, then at half-past eight the men marched in formation to an event at the Opera House. Thousands of people lined the streets and 'the scene was one of the greatest enthusiasm and excitement'. It was hard to move through the crowd 'and some found it hard to get away from the embraces of excited women'.[16]

The troopers entered the dress circle just as the first act of *Tess* was finishing. They were played into their seats to the tune of 'Soldiers of the Queen' by the Garrison Band — this was then taken up by the orchestra, and finally the spectators sang, giving way, after the men were seated, to the National Anthem. At this point everyone rose to their feet and roared out the old tune. A member of the company then sang a specially composed song, 'For their Queen and Union Jack', after which the entire cast came forward in a tableau and called for cheers for 'our boys who have returned'. Nothing could have been be sweeter. And naturally enough the historic occasion was registered in a photograph, taken looking back from the stage at the entire opera house filled with soldiers. Trooper Sidney Northe is one of them.

What did Trooper Northe think as he was feasted, applauded, loved and adored? Was it all unreal, or was it a banquet of unparalleled magnificence? Could he at long last relax, or was his mind already thousands of miles away, in South Africa? Did he have a relationship back there? A darling? The 'Em' to whom he sent a note from South Africa, along with kisses, does not feature again — she may have been married or engaged in his absence. But it is impossible not to feel the flow of approval which came from the New Zealand public. It was as if the roar of the crowd which accompanied the *Waiwera* as it left for South Africa was picked up by the same crowd when the *Moana* returned, specially chartered so the men could be home by Christmas. They had been away just over a year.

But by then Trooper Northe had made a decision: he would slip the noose of New Zealand and return to what appeared to be richer pickings. He had hardened, too. That jejeune, narrow-shouldered youth sitting shyly before the camera in 1899 has been replaced by a man who displays the almost unconscious loucheness of a military cavalier. The hat is worn with panache, and he appears as someone other, someone made different by experience. He is already, although he is back 'home', somewhere else. Like all returned soldiers, a part of him never comes home.

'A most hearty reception was accorded to Troopers Catherall and Northe on their arrival in Hastings last night by the express train. Soon after six o'clock the approach to the railway stations began to be crowded,' the *Daily Telegraph*'s Hastings correspondent reported, on 15 December 1900, 'and when the Town Band marched into position opposite the station, followed by the Church Lads' Brigade, . . . the Hastings Rifles Volunteers, . . . the Fire Brigade . . . and the HB Mounted Rifles, under Captain A. H. Russell, a very pretty picture was presented. The town was gay with flags and bunting, and the evening being a bright one, the effect was particularly striking and appropriate.'

The two returning troopers, Catherall and Northe, were welcomed by the mayor, then by Captain Russell (the local MP) and Major Chicken from Napier.[17] They were escorted to a special vehicle fitted out for the occasion, followed by a landau — a ceremonial carriage — in which Catherall's wife and her party followed to a point just opposite the post office where 'amidst cheers from the large crowd assembled there, the Mayor ascended the vehicle in which Troopers Northe and Catherall were sitting'.

Did the town seem familiar or just smaller than they remembered? Now they had been to bigger cities, did Hastings seem a version of 'Hicksville' (Hastings' original name)? Or was it a lovely, familiar setting to which they were thrilled to return?

The mayor noted that the boys had been gone a long fourteen months. Just as in future wars, everyone had made the fundamental mistake of thinking the fighting would be over quickly, only 'to find that they had to encounter trial and trouble and danger hardly reckoned on. They had shown that they were possessed of grit and courage and that they were worthy sons of the great British Empire.' His words, the *Telegraph* reported, were followed by three cheers given 'most lustily'.

The next speaker was particularly interesting and insightful. This was Captain Andrew Russell, who would go on to be one of the great New Zealand generals of the First World War. He was a leader notable for his skilful strategy amid the carnage and for his concern and care for his men. He was committed to conserving life instead of senselessly sending New Zealand or 'colonial' men forward to be slaughtered.[18]

Russell spoke of the 'two Hastings lads who had been to South Africa to fight for Queen and country and be a credit to their native land . . . Hardly anyone had been prepared for the universal chorus of praise which had come from the Commander-in-chief down to every officer, but almost from every newspaper in England and the world, about the manner in which the colonial contingents had conducted themselves, and they had more than cause to be proud of them. And especially of the boys who left Hastings, who would be heroes here for the rest of their lives. (Loud and prolonged cheering.)' The last sentence has a particularly poignant ring, as every hero knows. Legends do not often last longer than a decade. Memory is short. Life can be brutally long.

Troopers Catherall and Northe then moved in a triumphant procession up Heretaunga Street to Avenue Road, where Catherall lived, and Sidney Northe was taken to the home of a third trooper, Maddison.[19] 'Each of the men, at the end of their journey, returned brief but hearty thanks for their reception.'

This, however, was but the beginning of a roundelay of receptions. The Hastings Fire Brigade entertained Troopers Catherall and Northe 'at a social', and both men were given valuable jewellery: 'the ladies provided Trooper Northe with a set of gold studs and sleeve links'. At the Hastings Presbyterian church, Trooper Northe was 'presented with a gold chain with greenstone pendant', lauded to the skies and told about 'the value of the Northe family to the church.'[20] And at the end-of-year prizegiving for Hastings District School the chairman of the school committee commented that 'he was sure every boy and girl must feel proud of Troopers Catherall and Northe, who were both educated at their school'.

They had become that dangerously ambiguous thing: role models. But all along Sid Northe had made it very plain he was not going to stay. The *Evening Post* report of the Wellington welcome ended with a short paragraph: 'Trooper Sydney [sic] Northe . . . was so enamoured of South Africa that he purposes returning as soon as he is discharged from service, and taking a younger brother with him. Both are carpenters by trade.'[21]

The return home for Sidney Northe was really in the nature of a farewell visit. Such visits tend to be bitter-sweet.

THERE WAS, OF COURSE, no reportage of Trooper Northe's departure back to South Africa — no bands, no farewelling crowds. It would have been a much more modest, private farewell in Wellington, with his parents (who had shifted to Petone) now separated from their wider Northe and

ABOVE

The fly-speckled memorial card to Sidney Northe.

RIGHT

The memorial on Napier's Marine Parade for the forgotten sons of the Empire.

Northey families back in Hawke's Bay. We do not know how Sid Northe moved from Transvaal and the Orange Free State to Rhodesia, but it was in Salisbury that his brief life ended.

He was struck down, at thirty, not as heroes ought to be, by sword or gunfire, but by a virulent typhoid bacillus: water contaminated by faecal particles is the most common source. He had been working as a carpenter at the Natal Government Asylum in Matisberg, and on completion of the job in December 1901 he travelled to Salisbury and there he fell ill and died.

The terrible news was sent back by telegraph, and appeared in newspapers from Otago to Auckland and Hawke's Bay. It had not been long since Captain Russell had said that Sidney and his compatriots would be heroes all their lives. The short paragraph in the *Otago Witness* was headed 'DEATH FROM ENTERIC' and dated 9 April 1902 (the *Auckland Star* headed its article 'DEATH OF A NEW ZEALANDER'). 'Napier Wednesday. The Mayor received a telegram this evening stating that his nephew — Sydney [sic] Northe — had died in South Africa on February 16, of enteric fever. Deceased was a member of the First New Zealand Contingent, and returned to the colony but went again to South Africa.'[22]

For Mayor McVay it was a sad moment: Sidney had become a favoured son. William and Elizabeth Northe, Sidney's bereft parents, sent out an elaborate photographic montage, thanking the many people who had contacted them to console them in their loss. A pinhole shows where the card has been pinned to a wall — and kept there — during many a summer as a reminder of one who had no grave or other marker in New Zealand. It is covered in fly dirt.

Sid Northe was accompanied in his final moments by mates. Two of the montages' poignant photographs show a funeral cortege leaving the Salisbury Hospital — a large group of serious-looking men in summer straw boaters is halted by the funeral cart — and the same people, now hatless in respect for their friend, gathered around the grave. One has a hand on his brow in what looks like a moment of private distress. It may have been the heat, but it gives the final scene an added layering of emotion.

The poem accompanying a dandyish photograph of Sidney with a waxed moustache reads:

An oft told tale! O, Death, thou gloomy phantom,
Another triumph thou hast borne away;
A voice to which these walls so lately listened,
Thy power has stilled, its tones are hushed today.
(composed by P. Given)

In keeping with the nascent nationalism of the period, the card was decorated with New Zealand ferns.

ZIMBABWE, AS RHODESIA WAS RENAMED after independence, is today a failed state. Its inflation is ruinous. I have no idea where the cemetery in Harare (one-time Salisbury) is, what its state is, or whether there was, in fact, ever a headstone erected for Sidney Theodore Northe.

It is probably fitting that the best memorial to him — and to all the other Hawke's Bay troopers from the South African campaign — is situated in the most prominent position on the Parade in Napier. It's an outstanding piece of military memorabilia, showing, atop a marble plinth, a rough rider with the characteristic slouch hat with one side pinned back. Here he stands, his head lowered in mourning, holding his rifle, always on guard.

This memorial was created in 1906 when memory was still fresh — and it is here that Sidney Northe is finally commemorated. It is perhaps a slight adjustment of the truth that the word 'died' after his name infers he died, gloriously, in battle. But there he — or at least his name — lies, on marble, theoretically forever.

'Show me a hero and I will write you a tragedy', wrote F. Scott Fitzgerald.[23]

Charles Hill
Barrister at Law
Auckland
New Zealand

Dear Heroix

OPPOSITE

A letter from Elizabeth Ereaux to her brother Sergeant John Northe, 1847: 'She was the main wage earner, "head of the household" and a small-business owner on whom her husband depended.'

We last glimpsed Sergeant John Northe as he wrote about his first-born son, John James, swimming ashore from the *Star of the South* shipwreck. Since he and his Australian wife, Nancy, are the core of this story, it seems almost ill-mannered to have left them standing at the door, awaiting a proper introduction.

WHAT MAKES IT WORSE IS that I am going to make them wait a little longer — after all, they have been dead almost a century and a half — while I introduce Elizabeth Ereaux, Sergeant John Northe's live-wire younger sister. It is she who contextualises Sergeant John's predicament.

And it was this: how to survive in the maelstrom of a free-market economy when you have no capital, when all you have is your labour, your street smarts, your ability to negotiate your way through want in nineteenth-century Britain. You could say this was — and is — the predicament of every immigrant.

Elizabeth Ereaux was a migrant in her own way, though she never left Britain. Her migration was to the city — in fact, to the ur-city of the nineteenth century: London. How did a 'five feet nothing' (as she described herself), unskilled woman navigate her way from a small mining town in a depleted part of Britain to the most cosmopolitan city in the world? How did she survive, let alone flourish? Her gossipy, bustling little frigates of letters offer insights into how an individual, and a woman what's more, could master the trick of survival in the world's largest metropolis.

This is the opening of an undated letter that Elizabeth Ereaux sent to Sergeant John Northe in answer to his November 1847 letter telling his sister he was leaving Australia and setting off to New Zealand: '*My dear Brother and Sister . . . I had begun to think that something had happened to you or you had forgotten me . . . I was rather surprised to find you were going to remove to New Zealand but hope it is to your advantage for it does not matter much where we are as long as we can live and do well, and that is all we must expect these very bad times.*'

Her reference to 'very bad' times takes us to the heart of the situation. It was 'the hungry forties', the years of the Irish famine and escalating poverty and hunger in Britain. Many people survived by doing the most drastic thing you could, short of death. This was to leave the country you were born in. You went into permanent exile. 'Exile is strangely compelling to think about but terrible to experience,' the historian of Orientalism, Edward Said, has written. 'It is the unhealable rift forced between a human being and a native place, between the self and its true home: its essential sadness can never be surmounted.'[1]

Between 1815 and 1930, twelve million people left Britain, never to return. Seven million Irish did the same. This led to what historian James Belich has called 'the Anglophone settler explosion' that changed the history of the world.[2] My ancestor Sergeant John Northe was just one tiny atom within this population flood, as are the ancestors of practically every Pākehā family in Aotearoa New Zealand. They were driven by want, and they were prepared to accept the catharsis of exile — 'the crippling sorrow of estrangement' — in the hope of a better life.[3]

What was the life that Elizabeth Ereaux and her brother Sergeant John Northe were in such a hurry to leave? 'The original Faustian pact of the industrial age,' Naomi Klein has written, '[was] that the heaviest risks would be outsourced, offloaded, onto the other — the periphery abroad and inside our own nations.'[4]

Elizabeth and John Northey, their brother Samuel and sister Maria were born in Chacewater, in Cornwall, on the cusp of the nineteenth century and as the industrial revolution roared into action. Chacewater was a tin and copper mining town in this most isolated of British counties, best described as 'a bony ridge . . . probing out into the Atlantic Ocean . . . swept by ocean winds'. It was an unforgiving part of Cornwall, characterised by 'a series of wind-swept rolling plateau surfaces cut in granites and slates'.[5] The thing about extractive industries like tin and copper mining, Naomi Klein writes, 'is that they are so inherently dirty and toxic that they require sacrificial people and places: people whose lungs and bodies can be sacrificed in . . . mines, people whose lands and water can be sacrificed to open-pit mining'.[6] Chacewater was one such place.

'A rather ramshackle collection of squatters' cottages, small holdings and industrial buildings around the tin-stream workings . . . Chacewater had something of a rough frontier character.'[7]

The town was largely created in the early nineteenth century, a miniature boom town of the kind that springs up everywhere an extractive industry is situated. It had the lawlessness of such transient places, too. It was not beautiful; in fact, it was ugly. And when the bottom fell out of the Cornish tin and copper market in the 1820s, it suffered in the way all boom towns do when their key commodities sink in value: the community around it went into crisis.

Sergeant John Northe and his brother, Samuel, had begun life as miners — they were among the people whose lungs and bodies were 'sacrificed' doing 'dirty, toxic' work. Both men made a decision which changed the course of their lives. (As did their sisters. None of them stayed in Chacewater.) Yet if the word 'miner' conjures up labour of the most unskilled sort, this is to misinterpret the nature of traditional tin mining in Cornwall. There was a degree of agency involved, with the work being essentially let out on a contract basis. Some miners were part-owners of the mine, auctioneering off work and proceeds to other miners who had to assess what value the tin or copper seam had and make a bid. In its most basic form, it provided a small business model, with an emphasis on individual enterprise — something we have seen played out in the life of Sergeant John Northe's son, Robert Northe. I believe this level of individualism had a long-term influence on the way Sergeant Northe and his family explored their options.

Born into what seemed the very bottom of the industrial slag heap, Sergeant Northe and his family weren't inert and crushed. The work was dirty, the work was hard, and when the price of tin and copper in Cornwall collapsed, work itself vanished. But these people were active agents in transforming their lives. Mining was a skill that was highly mobile, anyway. The tin miners of Cornwall fanned out around the world.

John Northe was baptised in 11 January 1799. Elizabeth Northey was baptised on 13 June 1802. (Again we see a random difference in the surname.) This meant John Northe was sixteen and Elizabeth was thirteen when the Napoleonic Wars ended. This produced another problem: the labour market in Britain became flooded with soldiers looking for work. There was none. Unemployment rose and rose, and so did desperation and poverty. And crime. John's younger brother, Samuel, baptised in 1800, was found guilty of housebreaking in 1824.

Such was the terror of revolution that relatively minor crimes were regarded as unofficial declarations of anarchy. Samuel was tried at the Devon Lent Assizes and sentenced to death. Yet if there was an abject fear of oncoming revolution among the wealthy classes, this was also the time of humanitarianism. (The abolition of slavery was enacted in Britain in 1833.) A version of this was that a man found guilty of housebreaking was not hanged from the neck until dead but sentenced to the existential hell of transportation.

If exile can be regarded as a fundamental estrangement, enforced exile 'for the term of your natural life' deepens the sense of loss to the point of vindictiveness. Twenty-four-year-old Samuel Northey boarded the convict ship *Mangles* on 13 July 1824, bound for the Antipodes. He was five foot five, with hazel-grey eyes, black hair and freckles. His body had already been written on — he had two broad slashes on his body, scars from powder of a gun by his right eye, and S and N (Sam Northey?) tattooed inside his left arm. Already he has been deprived of language, and from here on out we have only his brother and sister to speak of him (and for his name to echo down the family tree and find a home in John James Northey's darkly handsome son, who will die at Chunuk Bair on Gallipoli).

IF THIS WERE A NOVEL, the difference between the two brothers, Samuel Northey and John Northe, would seem a perfect counterpoint: one a defiant law breaker who never escapes the system but becomes more deeply entrenched in criminality; the other working within the system capably and steadily, never doing anything wrong, marrying and founding a family of which I am a distant part. But this is not a novel, it is a tracery of what happened, of the way people in the same family can react in completely different ways to the same pressures.

Whether being a young boy at the time of the stirring victories of the Duke of Wellington predisposed John Northe towards the army I do not know. Because if being a miner was hard work, so too was being a private in the British Army. It was the traditional refuge of the working class in times of stress. Wellington, a great general but also a reactionary, famously called the lower ranks of the British Army 'the scum of the earth'. Yet the army also provided limited mobility, a roof over your head and food to eat in times of need. The pay was poor, but a soldier could still save so long as he did not drink.

A letter from John Northe, who did not drink, shows another view of British Army life. (I found this letter floating on the internet; its possessor had no idea who John Northe was.) Letters were important binding agents for people like the Northes, compressing a loosely knit family into a tight focus. The letters also functioned as financial bulletins, offering information on where might be a good place for others to try to make a living.

John had just returned from Nova Scotia in Canada, and he hints in this letter that he was creaming it, albeit on a very small scale.

'Gyth 29 January 1834

'My dear Cousins,

'... We arrived in England on the 4th December and discharged all our *company a few days afterwards except myself who they would not part with, which answers my purpose well for as I have now 14 years service and if I live to stay 7 years more I shall then be entitled to 1/10d day pension . . . it appears to me everything is very dull about England at this present time and no likelihood of it getting better. My duty at present is very easy and dear cousins I am happy to inform you that I am very comfortable. I don't know of any thing else that I have to say at present, but remain your ever affectionate and loving cousin, John Northe, Serjeant, Royal Staff Corps.*'[8]

We can contrast Sergeant John's gladsome letter with some other letters (also found on the internet) from his Northey cousins. The Northeys were an extended family, thick on the ground in Chacewater, running the gamut from wealthy and 'independent', meaning landed with sufficient income not to work, through to those who had fallen by the wayside and were listed as 'paupers'. One such person was Elizabeth Walsey, née Northey. In 1854 she wrote to her brothers William and Francis Northey, who were in South Carolina working as miners. Another brother was mining in Cuba. It was effectively a begging letter. She begins it with a customary curtsey to '*the blessing of the Almighty*' and the hope they were in '*the enjoyment of good health*'. She was living in a family house with her single youngest child: '*my other two dear children left England for Australia a few weeks since*'. There is no mention of a husband. '*I was glad you had not forgotten you had an only sister left,*' she wrote.

This leads to a segue in which she laments, '*Dear Brothers, my getting on is very slight I asure yo for I am obliged to work to mine for a bit of bread so you must need think that is bad enough.*' Women and children worked either breaking rocks or sorting through the detritus brought up from the mine, or even within the mine itself. There is a clear feeling here that Elizabeth Walsey has slipped right down the rungs. Indeed, she feels it keenly herself. Hence: '*Dear Brothers, I hope your circumstances is better than mine and I hope you will not take it in offensive light in my asking of you if it is in your favour to assist me with a trifle of money to enable me to rebuild the end of our Old House for it is nearly down.*' This shows a degree of cleverness; she is not asking money for herself but rather for rebuilding the stone family house, the end part of which has tumbled down and is open to the winds of the North Atlantic — just before winter. If the house cannot be repaired, '*I see nothing but the Union before us*' — that is, the workhouse.

She does not press her case, but returns to a piece of subtle emotional blackmail: '... *dear Brothers we that is left should be very glad to see you. Depend upon it, if you have any wish to see the Old House you must come home while it is dry weather. From your ever affectionate sister Elizabeth Walsey.*'

The letter was sent to the Coppersville Post Office, Union District, South Carolina. We do not do know whether she received a reply.

THIS BEGGING LETTER IS IN stark contrast to the brisk and even ebullient letters from her cousin, Elizabeth Ereaux, a bustling businesswoman whose words convey a lively sense of personality. (In many ways these people remind me of Dickens' characters, lively, poignant, tragic, and both patriotic and sentimental. The arc of their lives could be just as dramatic: either survive and flourish or diminish and end up in the hulks or the workhouse.)

Elizabeth Ereaux's better grasp of written language and grammar naturally conveys authority and energy. (John and his sister were probably taught writing and reading at a Methodist charity school set up to teach children to read. Its point was that they could read and understand the Bible. All of their letters invoke God in the form of a ritualistic greeting.) But in her letters there is also something as ineffable as a life force. She was what might be called a bit of a goer. Already by 1848, at the age of forty-six, she has been married once and widowed. She had then married a much younger French Huguenot, resident of Jersey, having passed herself off as at least a decade younger. John Ereaux was a school teacher, good-looking if feckless. Remarkably for a penniless migrant from an impoverished periphery, she is listed as 'head of household' and the household is made up of six people in the 1851 census. She also has servants. How did this happen?

What few biographical scraps we know of Elizabeth Ereaux are expanded and enriched by the somewhat unruly seas of language which move so moltenly through her letters. These letters are like windows into her personality. We may know very little of the historical detail of her life — who in particular taught her reading and writing, for example; when she left for London; the name and occupation of her first husband; even her later life and the year of her death — but we feel her speedy pulse through these Cockney-esque epistles, brimming with vigour and vulgarity.

Our opening letter from Elizabeth Ereaux was sent probably as far as it was possible to send a letter in the nineteenth century — from London to New Zealand. There is information on the back of the letter — that is, the blank page in which the letter was wrapped, like a packet (hence the other name for letters at the time, 'a packet', which Elizabeth herself uses in her 1848 letter). The letter is addressed to her brother, '*John Northey, Barrack Sirjeant [sic], Auckland, New Zealand*'. It does not bear a stamp, although stamps had been in existence since 1840. It has been franked three times: first in London in June 1848; then, after the six-month boat voyage, twice — first in Auckland on 16 January 1849, then, after the letter was forwarded by an unknown, slightly exuberant hand (and using red ink) to 'Rufsell' (Russell) in the Bay of Islands, where it was stamped on 27 January 1849. It had taken eleven days to get by ship from Auckland to Russell.

The first notable aspect of her letter is the curious address at the top: '*139 half Cheapside London*'. This immediately establishes Elizabeth Ereaux as that proud thing, a Londoner. In the nineteenth century there was as centrifugal a push in migration to London, as much as there was a centripetal push out to the rest of the world. London within a British context was immensely magnetic and, with the introduction of the railways, relatively easy to access. It also grew at a staggering rate, from one million people in 1800 to 6.5 million people a century later.

This did not mean it was easy to find work there or a place to live. London was a vast honeycomb of a city, rackety, dense, smoky and putrid. It was full of beggars, street dwellers, prostitutes and men, women and children who made a living off the pickings of the rest of humanity. It was also the home of monarchs, aristocrats and a wealthy mercantile class. The nineteenth century saw the development not only of civic spaces of imperial splendor like Trafalgar Square but also of utilitarian wonders like the underground railway. Most sewerage, however, went straight into the Thames, and when London wasn't overcast with soot from coal fires — it was impossible to keep white clothes clean — it was stinking from raw sewage. (Parliament regularly had to stop sitting because the fumes from the Thames were so toxic.) Nevertheless, London was exciting, tumultuous, and in a ceaseless cycle of rapid change.

Elizabeth Ereaux found her own small niche as that most English of institutions — a boarding-house keeper. This was an ambiguous title, as large houses became almost rookeries of apartments, with small areas broken down into flats and sub-let. It is notable, however, that in her 1852 letter Elizabeth refers to her 'house', although the fact she had seven boarders implies a relatively small space — perhaps the floor of a house, hence 'the half'. It was an achievement of sorts that a migrant from Cornwall could find any sort of niche in the great wen, even if it was only with a 'half' address.

Cheapside was a major thoroughfare of shops in a primarily commercial district — the City of London. (Charles Dickens Jnr called Cheapside 'the busiest thoroughfare in the world'.)[9] It was just behind the magnificent cathedral of St Paul's and further away was the Bank of England. All around were the smaller Wren churches of exquisite beauty, including St Mary Le Bow, the sound of whose bells defined a Cockney. It had once been an address of historical importance (and was still sufficiently processional for Queen Victoria to be driven along it in one of her triumphant Jubilee outings), but by the time Elizabeth Ereaux was resident there Cheapside's status was fading. It was now rivalled by the elegantly Georgian Regent Street in the West End.

The 1851 census lists Elizabeth Ereaux's address as being in 'the North West District of the City of London within the Parish of St Vedast, Foster Lane, Middlesex Farringdon'. What would this have looked like? It's hard to tell today, as the past vanished in the Blitz. In fact, to walk along Cheapside today, or to look at it on Google Earth, is to feel how abruptly the past can be screened off from the present. All the buildings, or nearly all, are post-war or even later. There is nothing to suggest that this was a street of remarkable history. All now seems bland and 'international' — that is, it could be any street anywhere in the world. (A melancholy thought.) The closest you can get to a feel of the past is a single plane tree at the corner of Wood Street and Cheapside, and a single two-storey building at 152 Cheapside. The tree is remarkable and was already 600 years old when Elizabeth Ereaux lived in the street. She would have seen it every day as she bustled about. The small building at number 152 reminds us that Cheapside was taken up with lower, more domestic buildings. The street was originally a lot wider, too — it started life as a market street for medieval London.

But our question is: how did Elizabeth Ereaux come to live there? Why a boarding house there, rather than anywhere else in city? I often wondered about this until I read online that The Cross Keys at the corner of Wood Street and Cheapside marked the end of provincial coach routes into London. It was a terminal — an ideal place for a friendly, personable provincial like Elizabeth Ereaux to set up what was effectively a small hotel. (Dickens himself had arrived at Cross Keys from Kent when he first came to London in 1815 and he has his character Pip do likewise in *Great Expectations*, commenting, 'I was scared by the immensity of London, [and] I think I might have had some faint doubts whether it was not rather ugly, crooked, narrow, and dirty.') To offer friendly lodgings in such a place gave Elizabeth Ereaux's 'hotel' a complete logic.

It is hard to work out the level of affluence or poverty in which Elizabeth Ereaux lived in 1848. Charles Booth's map of poverty and affluence in London, made nearly half a century later, portrayed Cheapside and the Parish of St Vedast as 'Poor', with 'an income of 18 shillings to 21 shillings per week for a moderate family'.[10] But this was half a century later, when the area's downward trajectory had accelerated. It's of significance that in *Pride & Prejudice*, published in 1813, Cheapside features as a place of residence for Elizabeth Bennet's much-loved Uncle Gardiner, a warehouse owner. The snobbish Darcy, still denying he is in love with the 'low-born' Elizabeth, mocks the address.[11]

In the 1852 census, Elizabeth Ereaux is not merely listed as the 'head of the house' (for reasons her letter discloses), but she also has seven guests. They include her seventeen-year-old niece, Juliet Ereaux, who possibly doubled as 'help', and three lodgers: Phillip Pellier from Jersey, a married man aged fifty-five who worked as a traveller; a fellow Jerseyman and traveller, John Le Boutillon, forty and unmarried; and an Irishman, Thomas B. Murphy, unmarried from Dublin. This gives some sense of the chain migration from the periphery (Jersey and Ireland) to the centre; possibly the Jerseymen were friends of Elizabeth's husband. There were three other guests on the night of the census: Mary Grove, aged forty, unmarried, from Stafford Walsall; Mary Harrod, also aged forty, unmarried, from London; and a widow, Elizabeth Chippendale, aged sixty-eight, from Essex — she is possibly 'the Old Lady' mentioned in Elizabeth's 1852 letter. She refers in the same letter to '*some of the gentlemen*', which suggests she had long-term lodgers close enough to count as acquaintances. '*I am surrounded with kind friends in the summer, they always laugh at me and tease me to death when they see me a little low . . .*'

LEFT

Elizabeth Ereaux in watercolour does not look like the 'cat in the tripe shop' that she saw herself as.

CENTRE

In 2017 you can still find pockets of the charm of nineteenth-century Cheapside, a Georgian area graced with Wren steeples.

BELOW

Letters were cross-written to save on paper and postage.

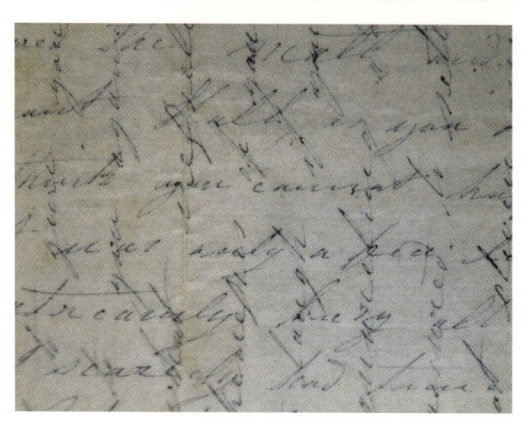

WE KNOW ELIZABETH EREAUX TODAY from a tiny watercolour, one of four she sent out to her brother John in 1852 — she described them as *'likenesses of your two brothers and sisters'* (that is, the two sisters, Elizabeth and Maria, and their husbands). Only this one survived. It is unsigned, and appears to show someone who is unhealthy, even sick. It is in distinct contrast to her letters, which are full of vitality and humour. She wears what is perhaps a blue silk dress, with a locket and some mourning hair jewellery, wide lace cuffs and collars. Photography was in its infancy in the mid-1840s, and painting watercolour miniatures was still regarded as a working job. This one may have been done in payment by a lodger or been commissioned when Elizabeth had some funds.

We have two letters from her. One is undated but is clearly from 1848 from its franking. The second letter is dated 28 February 1852 and is partially cross-written. This means she wrote down the page as is usual. Then she turned the letter sideways at a right angle and carefully wrote across the existing writing, creating a kind of plaid of prose. It was an economy measure and it required careful disentangling when reading. She described her own handwriting as *'a scrawl so badly written you will never be able to make it out but I cannot do better'*.

The two letters are survivors from an ongoing correspondence, mentioned intertextually. Sergeant John wrote to his sisters, and Elizabeth and Maria both wrote to him, as did Maria's unnamed but concupiscent husband. *('It is a great pleasure to see Maria and her husband so happy as they are. He was here this morning to see if I was writing to you or else he would have written by this packet.')* The letters are affectionate, sentimental, with occasional flights of fancy as well as moments of seriousness when Elizabeth attempts to answer her brother's sober queries about political conditions in Britain. (If Sergeant Northe was ill at ease with writing, he was obviously a good reader, as Elizabeth refers to sending him quality broadsheet newspapers like *The Times*.) The correspondence makes it clear that the two siblings, John and Elizabeth, had a close, affectionate relationship; there are frequent references to *'my Dear Brother'* (always capitalised) and to the sending of endearments: *'They both send kindest love to you all and lots of kisses to the Dear Children,'* she says to her sister and brother-in-law and their children. She had a completely confident sense of the formatting of letter writing, how to greet, farewell, and fill the contents with lively personal information.

This has interesting relevance to the other women letter writers in this book. Writing letters is often regarded as a 'gendered activity'. As the American essayist Siobhan Phillips has commented, 'Letter writers are allowed a sensation of power over the narrative of their lives.'[12] In its own way, a letter is a personal kingdom (or rather queendom) over which the female writer reigns as author. This sense of power was unusual in the nineteenth century, when church and state-enforced gender roles emphasised the subordination of women. Women did not have the vote in Britain until the twentieth century, but they could vividly recreate their sense of reality, and their priorities, within the personal schema of a handwritten letter.

Perhaps if Elizabeth had written to another woman she might have left off occasional self-denigrating descriptions of herself as, for example, 'a giddy old woman' — as if aware of 'performing' in front of the mirror of her brother's masculinist regard. She also refers several times to her childlessness, as if emphasising her failure to fulfil gender expectations and hence hinting at self-diminishment. But there is enough in the rest of the letters to point to a very healthy ego: she may describe herself as a 'delicate plant' but she also has a vibrancy that points in the opposite direction.

The two surviving letters illustrate her energy and *joie de vivre*. She was the main wage earner, 'the head of the household' and a small-business owner on whom her husband depended. She was no fool. This leads us into the heart of the first letter, which concerns the difficult economy of the 1840s and the extremely tense political situation in Europe. Revolutions had erupted throughout the capitals of Europe in 1848, and it appeared for a time that Britain, too, might succumb to an armed uprising against the antiquated, undemocratic established order. For someone like Elizabeth, a boarding-house keeper, this would have seemed frightening: it would bring disorder and interfere with business. The circumference of her world was small and limited to the essentials of survival. She had already told her brother she was surprised to hear he was going to New Zealand, but approved so long as he could '*live and do well and that is all we can expect in these very bad times for I can assure you my dear Brother that everything in England and in fact every other country is dreadfully bad in consequence of the Chartists' meetings which have taken place of late. France and Ireland are in a most dreadful state at present. Nothing but fighting and bloodshed. And God knows how everything will end.'*

The reference to events in France allows us to guess the probable date of this letter. In February 1848 the French monarchy was expelled for the final time. There had been a series of poor harvests, deepening poverty, as well as financial scandals and bank failures. Alexis De Tocqueville wrote, 'We are sleeping on a volcano ... a wind of revolution blows, the storm is on the horizon.'[13]

The storm exploded in June 1848 in Paris, and in July there was a brief and violent nationalist uprising in Ireland. The unrest in Europe bled back to Britain. *'We have sent you several papers giving an account of all the riots here which we hope you have received,'* Elizabeth writes. She uses the term 'riots' loosely, as the Chartist gatherings were tumultuous assemblies rather than riots (although riots and bloodshed had occurred elsewhere in Britain). The Chartists wished to work within the parliamentary system, democratising it rather than overthrowing the whole system, but had begun to stage mass demonstrations in London during March. The appalling excesses of the French Revolution, especially the period of The Terror, were a constant reference point for what could happen if a revolution got out of control.

The reactionary Duke of Wellington was called out of retirement to 'defend London'. Special constables were sworn in. Queen Victoria was sent to the Isle of Wight for her safety. In the end, however, the Charter was sent to the Houses of Parliament not in the hands of an unruly mob but in three cabs — the very image of British civic order. Perhaps as a warning shot, though, all the lights were smashed on the way to Buckingham Palace.

The effect of the uneasiness and unrest on a London businesswoman whose business lay in tourism and travel was clear: *'It has made trade so bad there is nothing to be done. We have done worse this summer than ever before since we have been in business. But must hope for better times ... We will write again by next Packet and my Husband will give you a better account* [of the unrest] *than I can.'*

All this implies a frequent and up-to-date communication: *'Though absent ever dear, for I am sure you are to me,'* she writes. Elizabeth now backs out of the letter with some fond allusions to all the children her brother has — and how she, by contrast, has none. *'My Dear John I think it's quite time to stop now and not have any more children, for if you go on this way you will indeed be obliged to make Parcels of them and send them* to those that have none, for you certainly will be overstocked, bless their little hearts.' (John and Nancy Northe in fact went on to have another five children in New Zealand.) She continues: '*How I wish I could see them, give them my kindest love and kiss them and your dear wife for us. And accept the same yourself from your ever affectionate Brother and Sister. John and Elizabeth Ereaux.*'

THE SECOND LETTER, CROSS-WRITTEN, is much longer, and is dated 28 February 1852. By now the doldrums of 1848 have faded and Elizabeth is more bullish. The 1851 Great Exhibition has been a huge success — the Crystal Palace had more than six million visits in one year — and London has been flooded with visitors from around the world. She begins: '*I was so extremely busy all last summer that I scarcely had time to breath [sic], I was just like a cat in a tripe shop, didn't know what to do first, and then my Dear Brother I have had a great deal to contend with.*'

It is a slightly breathless introduction to a great drama: '*This dear unfortunate husband of mine, he was twice during the summer taken with delirium tremors and at last was raving mad. They were obliged to put him into the Asylum which put me to a very great extra expense and, although he was not with me, still it gave me a very great deal of trouble. Perhaps it was well I was so busy for I had not so much time for fretting but I could not help it at times — thank God he is all right in his mind again but goes just the same as ever.*'

He is still drinking, in other words. He has also lost his looks. '*It is astounding what an altered man he is, he is not a bit like he was, I mean in the face, quite changed.*' A raving alcoholic on the premises made it 'impossible for me to manage my business', so Elizabeth reports that he has been packed off to live with his father in Jersey, possibly with Elizabeth contributing to his upkeep. She had already had to stump up fees for him to stay in a private asylum, rather than the notorious London institution known as Bedlam. For a middle-aged woman living on her own, as well as carrying a business, it was a great strain. '*It is very sad for us all but we must all submit to the will of God for no doubt it is for some all wise purpose, so you see my Dear Brother, although I have no family I am not without my trials nor can we expect to be on this side of the Grave.*'

Yet if this suggests a woman responding in a typically stoical Christian way, she bounces back in the very next sentence: '*One thing I manage to keep up my spirits as they* [her paying guests] *all tell me in a most surprising manner, and the more business the better. I am plying here, there and everywhere — as the servants say, there is Missus again, she is here, there and everywhere but I am afraid I shall tire you with all this rubbish.*' She tails off here, as if aware of her brother watching her antics with a colder eye. At the same time, she has managed to tell him that she has a thriving business, has servants and a lively, even overactive life. She is '*a cat in a tripe shop*' — in other words, so full of possibilities she hardly knows where to turn. Indeed, her business is doing so well that '*. . . all winter I have been busy having my house painted and papered and all manner of new arrangements*' in readiness for another bumper summer of guests.

She has forwarded several newspapers on the 'eighth wonder of the world', the Great Exhibition, and runs on: '*My Dear Brother you tell me that I write in good spirits but I know you will be glad to know that I can do so under all my trying circumstances. I am rather a delicate plant to play with and I feel that if I were to sit down and give way to grief my business would go to rack and ruin and that would not do.*' This lightness of manner is both defensive and placatory. A powerful woman created awkwardness among men: it was better she present an almost foolish façade behind which a relatively cool intelligence operated. Or was she just 'a silly woman'? Friendly laughter and teasing from her paying guests, she asserts, is '*a much better remedy than Holloway pills*'.

At this point in the letter she refers to a decidedly more vulgar subject. '*My Dear Brother, you say you think that me and the Sidney merchant would make it all right if anything happened to my Dear John, but I am afraid there is no such good luck in store for me; one thing I know he* [the Sidney merchant] *is very fond of me and told the old lady and some of the gentlemen in the house that he would give anything for such a wife, and that if she could wear gold she should have it, and I suppose by this time he could well afford it for he must be up to his neck in it by this time and he was incredibly rich before.*'

In other words, if she has the good luck for her current husband to die, she has another — stupendously rich — suitor in the wings. (There is no contextual information on who the 'Sidney merchant' was. Was he a returned convict sitting on a fortune in gold, a kind of Magwitch? Was he staying there through some kind of acquaintance with Sergeant John's contacts in Australia? Or was it purely coincidental? We do not know. But the reference to wearing gold points to gold mining as a possible source of wealth.) There is something decidedly vulgar about the sentiments in this part of the letter: brother and sister talking about Elizabeth 'making it alright' with a rich man while her husband is still alive.

Still, Elizabeth is wised up enough to knock that pipe dream on the head: '*I know I have been teased enough about him since, but I can assure you my Dear John that if I were single tomorrow I should not think of taking another husband. I have had two already and that ought to be enough for any woman. There are several of them waiting they tell me in joke, but I tell them they will all be disappointed.*'

She actually prefers to be, effectively, a single woman. She has had enough trials with two husbands already. But this is not an acceptable view in the nineteenth century, so she apologises for what she feels is her feminine chatter. '*I am afraid you will call me a giddy old woman for writing all this rubbish* [she was not yet fifty; the average life expectancy for women at the time was fifty-six] *but as I am no politician and I can tell you nothing upon that subject there is no particular news to tell you. I wish to give you something to read though,*' she says by way of explaining her depiction of her tiny corner of the world.

Although she refers, by rote almost, to the Almighty, she is essentially materialist in outlook. '*My Dear John, what a pity you left Bathurst just at a time all the gold mines were discovered. You might have made your fortune but I hope if Brother Sam does much in that way he will remember you and your family, indeed a little would be very acceptable in this part of the world.*'

By 1850 Samuel Northey had been given his freedom. Many convicts obtained this much more quickly, but recidivism kept him clawed back within the system. His presence in the letter, without any sense of moral underlining, implies he is completely accepted in the family and still fondly regarded: '*Brother Sam*'.

She swiftly moves on to Sergeant John's daughter, who she talks about sentimentally ('*the Dear little thing*'), and to whom she plans to send a box of dolls. As if caught up in the excitement of the technological innovations on show at the Great Exhibition, she writes: '*How I wish I could fly a craft and have a game of romps with them but I have nothing to play with but my parrot and my cat; the parrot is quite a companion, she talks so nicely.*

I have taught her to call the names of the children.' And yet she is also invoking the stereotypical expectations of a nineteenth-century English spinster, often seen as a figure of fun, someone to be ruthlessly mocked. Possibly, she just didn't care.

Now the letter is almost at an end, she returns to a theme evident in the earlier letter, too: how Sergeant John and Nancy must stop having so many children. This is delivered on the level of ribald comedy. In the first letter she simply says, '*My Dear John, I think it's quite time to stop now and not have any more children*', but in 1852 she uses a more sexually explicit metaphor, telling John that Nancy '*must not allow you to wind up the clock any more for it is quite time to stop when you have six of them*'.

A boarding-house keeper, and a twice married woman, could hardly be innocent of the facts of life. Indeed, she would have had to be sharp-eyed on that account as part of her job. Elizabeth's vitality and Dickensian vulgarity seem part and parcel of her character, as well as a thin underlining of melancholy: she was, after all, a woman on her own, without the comfort of children or a partner. The paying guests were not friends, not really. Beneath the surface agitation of the letter there is a sense that her life is hard or, perhaps more realistically, the tension in her life is constant. She cannot risk sinking into the lumpen proletariat outside her door — a dark river, like the Thames, clawing the weak and the drunk away. She has to remain ever vigilant, and this is the thin connecting wire of energy that runs throughout this letter.

But now the performance of her prose is at an end. It is time to say farewell. She backs out in a shower of kisses and affection towards relatives she has never met nor ever will. Migration in the nineteenth century, especially for poorer people, was permanent. Letters had to carry all the information otherwise gained from casual conversation, from glances into a silent face, all the signals and pleasure of our eyes just resting on the face of someone we love. But that does not stop her asking John to kiss his wife '*many times for me . . . and kiss all the Dear children for me and accept a thousand for yourself and believe me my Dear Brother and Sister, your ever affectionate and well wishing Sister*'. And since John Ereaux has vanished from her life, she signs it in the singular, possibly even with a sense of pride and relief, '*Elizabeth Ereaux*'.

WHAT HAPPENED TO ELIZABETH after this? She appears at a better London address, at 89 Guildford Street, Saint Pancras, Marylebone, in 1861, still head of the household. She had six male boarders and lived alongside solicitors and gilders and silversmiths. The boarders, too, had better jobs. One was a merchant, one a contractor for the government, one a commercial clerk. They were all young men. She also had a live-in servant. But after this date it is impossible to find any evidence of Elizabeth Ereaux's later life. No later letters survive. Did she remarry and hence change her surname?

Her 1852 letter with its giddy comment about several suitors in the wings, plus 'the Sidney merchant' who would dress her in gold, are possibilities to be set beside the watercolour, which shows a middle-aged woman no longer in the pink. An Elizabeth Northey appears with her christening date in a much later census as a retired 'domestic servant' living back in Cornwall. The words 'boarding house keeper' have been struck out. Did she slide down the scales, revert to her maiden name and creep home to a world she thought she had left behind? There were so many Northeys by the name of Elizabeth there is no certainty it is her. Whatever her future, there is no death certificate for an Elizabeth Ereaux. She vanishes into the murk of history.

Why did these two letters survive? It is clear that many more were sent. Was it due to happenstance: some letters were placed in an obscure location and only 'afterwards', usually following the death of the writer, did they become valuable sentimentally? The same goes for the four watercolour portraits, of which only one survived. What happened to the others? We have no answer.[14]

My purpose here has been not to give a blow-by-blow account of what are really two mundane letters, but to give some sense of the strong personality of Elizabeth Ereaux. I was a nascent writer when I first read copies of these letters, carefully typed out by my Great-uncle Percy Northe, the family historian. At thirteen or fourteen, reading them affected me strongly. Elizabeth's words gave me a vivid sense of her personality. Her portrait hung on the wall in my grandmother's bedroom, not too far from the french doors which allowed a watery, wavering light to play over her face, as if animating it. If I looked into her pinched face, with its curiously angled eyes, I seemed to hear her words: '*So you see my Dear Brother, I am not without trials and cannot expect to be on this side of the grave although*

I have no family.' But she also described herself as '*a cat in a tripe shop.*' The vividness of the image spoke to me. I liked her sense of self-irony and robust energy.

Her childlessness also appealed to my imagination. I am not sure if I knew at the age of about fourteen that I would never marry and have children (a family tree I constructed at the time put 'm.' by my and my brother's names in preparation for our marriage, fitting in and continuing the family tree by having children). But Elizabeth's bravura, against the odds, impressed me.

Her letter was very much an energised kingdom of which she took charge, and she occupied all the space within. I felt close to her in spirit — such is the nature of letters, a kind of quiet whispering in the ear which seems to replace the awkwardness of speech. I was also searching for ancestors who spoke back to me. Of all those I found from that time, she came closest to answering back.

One strange thing is that I somehow believed her name was 'Heroix'. I cannot now think where this came from. The letters are clearly signed Elizabeth, and the name Heroix is never once mentioned. But it might have been a trick my brother played on me; sometimes he took pleasure in leading me astray. I was very gullible. And I seem to recall him telling me that 'Heroix' was a name that arose from the Napoleonic Wars and was the feminine version, in Latin or Greek, of 'Hero'. It seemed infinitely possible amid the wide-ocean span of my ignorance.

Thinking the portrait was of someone called 'Heroix Northey' set me off on a long journey of diary writing. All through my adolescence and into early adulthood I kept a diary addressed, nominally, to 'Dear Heroix'. It was all in the form of one long confessional letter. Elizabeth was someone I felt I could tell secrets to, or, maybe more truthfully, she enabled me to erect a kind of facsimile self which protectively allowed my real, unknown, deeply contradictory character to grow. Everybody needs a mask in childhood, a horribly painful and naked state of being. Heroix was mine.

I have often thought these endless diary entries were the beginning of my apprenticeship in becoming a writer. They were like the lengths a swimmer does in a swimming pool, endless laps during which you improve your strength and endurance and — you hope — style. These few lively epistles from Elizabeth Ereaux sent me off onto a lifelong study of self, of using words to express feelings and to fashion perceptions. For that I am grateful.

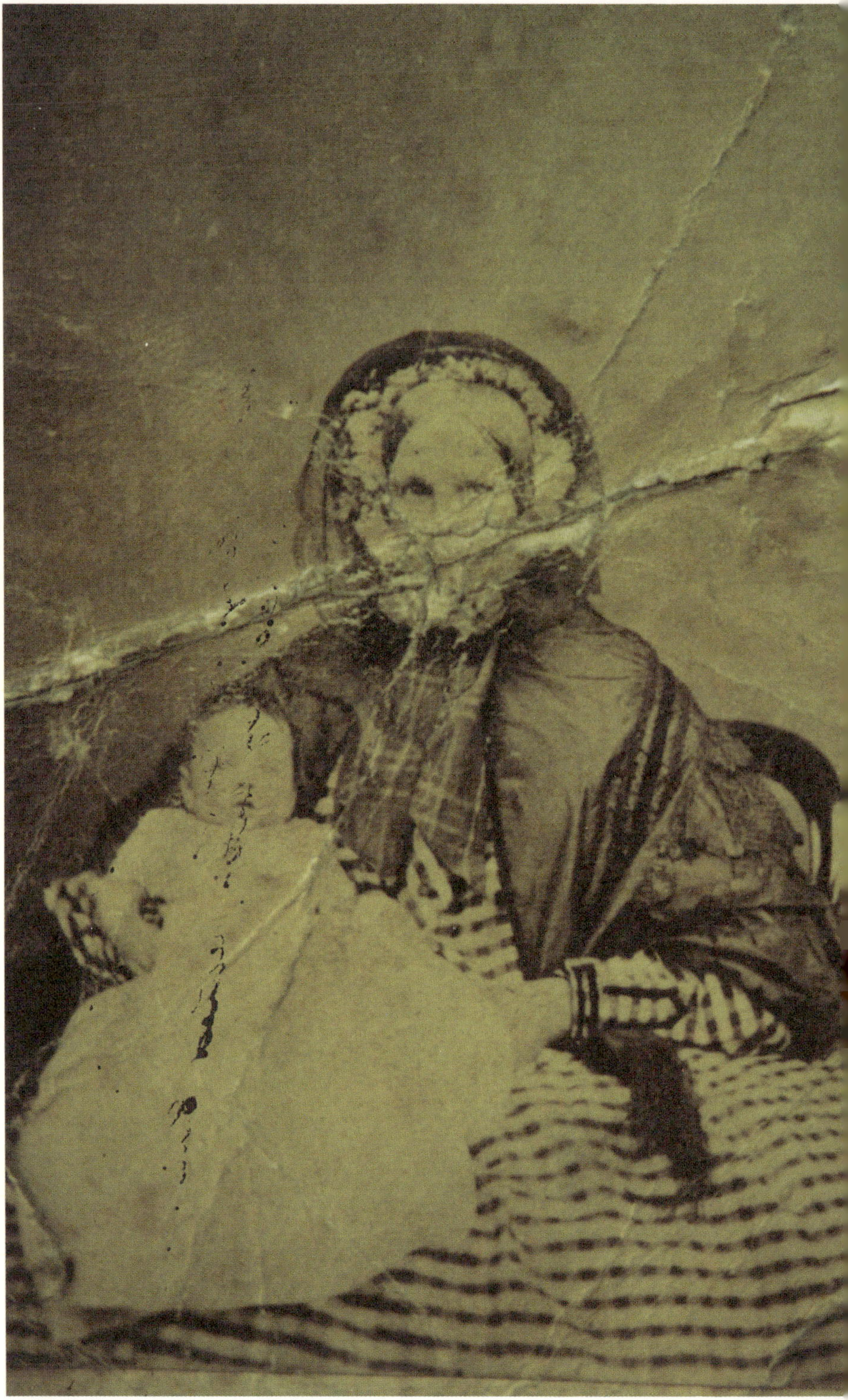

Silence Like a Bruise

OPPOSITE

Nancy Northe and her baby, Emily, in 1876: 'Written language has traditionally been the right of the property-owning classes; it was their own code.'

What can you say, or rather, how do you speak for people who cannot access written language? For me, the ability to write became part of who I am. You might almost say I wrote myself into being. I used written language and words to work out who I was and where I wanted to go.

TO BE STRIPPED OF LANGUAGE is a terrifying concept to me. Not to be able to write would be a kind of death. I take pride in possessing the plumage of language and like lingering over unusual and esoteric words. How do I then possess the humility to approach those members of my family who did not possess this trick? How do you tell their stories when they left not a single sentence expressing their own point of view?

Let's take Samuel Northey, for example. We know so little about him: we know what he looked like, or rather we know how he was described, mostly as a way to identify him should he escape. We know the details of his imprisonment — death commuted to exile for 'the term of his natural life'. We know about the hulk in Portsmouth in which he lingered for forty days awaiting transportation: the *York*, a warship from the Napoleonic wars which had seen service in Madeira and the West Indies, had then been dismasted and made into a stench-filled water-borne prison for five hundred men in Portsmouth Harbour.

And we know about the ship in which he was transported to Australia. The *Mangles* was a small schooner, 121 feet in length and built of teak, with 190 males and no females on board. The voyage took 106 days; eighty-one members of the 40th Regiment acted as guards. There were rumours of a mutiny outside Tenerife but these turned out to be false. Three men died on the voyage. The ship arrived in Sydney Cove on 27 October 1824, and Samuel Northey Mangles (as the authorities called him) was immediately forwarded to Bathurst.

From then on he would be identified by the ship in which he was transported, as if it were his nose, or the colour of his eyes, or his tribe. As for his thoughts, or his role in the rumoured mutiny or anything else, there is just a blunt, painful silence. Silence wrapped so tight that it forms a gag.

A convict does not have thoughts. If he does they are not worth anything. Besides, if thought is not written down as opinion, it escapes into the air like vapour and vanishes.

Here is what we know. He arrived at Sydney Cove and was taken to Cockatoo Island, then moved to Bathurst 'for distribution'. In 1828 he was assigned to a Mr Balcomb of Bathurst as a bullock driver. That same year he was sent into a deeper exile, to Wellington Valley, New South Wales, which was a place to fear. There were only males here, and it constituted virtual imprisonment by geography. The road to the settlement was 'one of the longest and most difficult overland routes in the colony', and Wellington

Valley was 'a sort of inland Norfolk Island'.[1] To attempt to escape was often fatal: men would wander lost in a harsh landscape, or would be scooped up by Aboriginals, who stripped them of the rags they were wearing before delivering them back to the prison settlement.

What happened for Samuel Northey to be sent into the deeper exile of Wellington Valley? Inmates here were denied all the things that ameliorate a convict's lot, such as 'better employment, the possible patronage of a generous master, the associations and networks formed with other prisoners and civilians and the company of women ... Nearly all had at some time been disciplined by a superintendent or magistrate for theft, insolence, drunkenness, gambling or being absent from muster.'[2] It was a place of despair. We don't know specifically what Samuel had done to warrant being sent there, but it was the beginning of a pattern: for every step forward there was a step backwards.

He got his ticket of leave (a document a convict had to carry, signifying he was no longer imprisoned but was free to work on condition he turned up to monthly musters) on 28 March 1835, but by 22 July 1840 it was cancelled when he was found to be 'absent from muster'. A month later he was charged with forgery by the Bathurst Bench — he had been 'illegally at large'. Three months later he was 'apprehended after absconding'.[3]

Sergeant John Northe arrived in Bathurst with the army in 1838. Did Samuel Northey go walkabout in an attempt to see a family member? It seems a human enough motive. He got a second ticket of leave on 25 April 1846 after a petition was sent to Governor FitzRoy. (Was this John Northe's work?) Finally, on 3 September 1850, he was granted a conditional pardon: he was free but could not leave the open prison that was Australia. The official record of his body — he was still regarded as a form of human livestock — registers his rough existence inside the prison system.

In addition to the tattooing and scars he had when he first arrived, there were now '[t]wo powder marks under the inner corner of his right eye, near inner corner of the right eyebrow' — more tattooing — and under his left jaw there were five crosses. These tattoos are like signs of his tribal identity — *convict*. That is how he 'speaks'.[4] There was a scar on the heel of his left hand, and another on the top of the middle finger of his left hand. (His conditional pardon lists these characteristics, in case the pardon needs to be withdrawn: he can still be identified.)

Twenty-five years into his term was very late for a convict to get a conditional pardon, and it reflects his recidivism — he couldn't keep out of trouble. He finally did so on 15 March 1860 when he died in Wellington, New South Wales (360 kilometres inland from Sydney), apparently without a common-law wife or children. I do not know where he is buried.

One document, however, gives us a flavour of his life. A handwritten document sent as a letter, titled *Journal from Memory of a Journey by Land from Wellington Valley to Port Macquarie Performed by Overseer Oliver and five men with Govt Stock from the 3rd of February to 27 May 1831*, records a geographical misadventure, an example of how these immigrants had no real knowledge of the land they set out intrepidly to cross, driving 113 cattle (100 oxen, seven pack bullocks, six pack horses) before them. 'Sam Northey Mangles' was part of the prison party, possibly chosen because of his skill with oxen. Ahead of them lay the kind of disaster that Patrick White might have written about.

The surveyor of the convict settlement had given the overseer, Alex Oliver, directions to head due north-east when the party left Wellington Valley, but this led them into a maze of landscape that was almost biblical in its extremity. February, of course, is high summer in Australia. They wandered, lost, the animals slowly dying of exhaustion and thirst. In the end they had to eat seven of the animals to survive. Others were abandoned as the party took ten days to cross a mountain range — '*the most barren I ever saw*' wrote the overseer, in this document which is essentially a long letter of apology and exculpation. Three pack horses '*[d]ied on the Barren Mountains*'. One bullock '*[f]ell down a precipice*'. '*Both Horses and Cattle were almost reduced to a State of Starvation; Three of the Horses being Old, and totally unable to withstand the fatigue died.*' But on the other side of the mountains was a river, '*the most beautiful I ever saw*', coursing through '*fine and delightful Country*'. It must have seemed like paradise to the gaunt, thirsty and probably freaked-out men.

But Oliver then decided to right their course by going in a south-easterly direction, which led them into '*a thick Scrub by which I was soon entirely surrounded*'. They could find no way out so just had to keep going forward. They had to then abandon '*[n]ine Head of Cattle through absolute fatigue and starvation*' — there was no feed in the scrub and '*three of the Pack Bullocks . . . laid down quite unable to proceed any further*'. There is such despair in that simple sentence. Once again, however, the men reached '*a fine and fertile valley profuse with pastorage of the finest quality and a fine*

Stream of Water... Had we not come to this Valley at this time, the Whole of the Cattle must have inevitably have Perished.'

From here Oliver set out to find an escape, leaving the cattle behind. After a fortnight he knew it was hopeless. He made a decision to abandon the cattle in this valley — *'knowing that the Cattle could not get away'* (he underlined this in his letter) — and to *'proceed with the Men to Port McQuarrie'*. If this sounds simple, his final paragraph underlines how even this was trial by landscape: *'During the latter part of our Journey our Provisions became entirely exhausted, in Consequence of which, and to keep ourselves from a State of Starvation we were necessitated at intervals to kill [Seven] of the smaller and Inferior Cattle.'*[5]

They arrived at Port Macquarie after three harrowing months in the wilderness. They had lost the entire herd of cattle. It was a disaster.

What did Samuel Northey Mangles make of this experience? One of the striking features of this long litany of misfortune is that the party of convicts and overseers seem to occupy a psychological *terra nullius*. Not a single Aboriginal is sighted, spoken to, or offers any directions or help. Or was it that their presence was invisible or discounted?

The narrative is as much a psychological account of being profoundly lost as a recitation of an actual journey. Oliver never speaks of his companions. The entire narrative is delivered in the first person as if he were alone and the six men were non-beings — humans who, strictly speaking, did not exist.

There's a sense of parallel, disconnected realities when Captain Smythe of the 39th Commandant at Port Macquarie, writing to the Colonial Secretary about the disaster, ends his report on some runaway convicts who have been returned to the prison system — they were *'on the road in parties of twos and threes, some are said to have died on the way from fatigue... the state of the unfortunate wretches [who reach us is that they] are invariably stripped soon after leaving Moreton Bay, in other respects The Natives are said to be kind to them until they reach Trial Bay.'*[6]

How to relate this non-being to the cheerful 'Brother Sam' of Elizabeth's chirpy letters, a man who might be lucky enough to discover gold? Significantly Elizabeth's letter was written in 1852, by which time 'Brother Sam' was two years into his freedom. It implies they were in contact somehow, either through Sergeant John meeting his brother in person or Sergeant John being in touch with people who knew of 'Brother Sam'.

There is a feeling of being up to date with news about him, possibly through the 'Sidney merchant' Elizabeth mentions, who could well have been a convict made good. (In the 1846 census the population of New South Wales was approximately 118,000. From 1780–1840, around 80,000 convicts were sent to the colony and so the chances of the 'Sidney merchant' being an ex-convict were high.) Perhaps there were underground connections of feeling and thoughts. But without written language, which has an obsidian-like way of persisting through time, we do not know. There is only an obdurate, even resentful silence. Silence like a bruise.

THIS CONNECTS US WITH ANOTHER actor in our drama: Nancy Northe, born Anne Sophia O'Donnell, who married Sergeant John Northe in 1838 in Bathurst. From this union came every member of the Northe and Northey families in New Zealand.

Nancy O'Donnell was born in 1819 in New South Wales, and for a long time I believed she was the author of the four letters written in Napier between April 1869 and August 1871 signed 'John and Ann Northe'. (Nancy and Ann seemed to be interchangeable names.) The letters, collected by the family historian Percy Northe, who collated a family tree in the 1950s, are full of information on pregnancy: *'Mrs W. Northe is expecting an increase in the family every day and Mrs Ben Johnson is talking about it.'*[7] This is more usually the province of women.

It was only when I got John Northe's will from Archives New Zealand that I discovered a vital piece of evidence: a sharp, even emphatic cross placed where Nancy should have signed the document.[8] The cross is fascinating, almost a haiku in the way the nib seems to have dug savagely into the paper. Beside it is written 'her mark'. Nancy was illiterate — she could not even sign her name, though this was something many illiterate people trained themselves to do in the nineteenth century. This makes her even more of an enigma. Who was the mark otherwise known as Nancy or Ann Northe?

Not even her name is straightforward. I am calling her Nancy Northe, but her name has a curious fluidity. Her birth certificate of 21 March 1819 lists her as Anne Sophia, but by her baptism on 6 June 1819 she is Nancy, which is probably the name she was called within the family. The letters are signed 'John and Ann Northe' — the name used on her death certificate.

Her headstone in Napier cemetery, shattered by the 1931 earthquake, has yet another version — 'Ann Northey'.

I'll call her Nancy, because this seems to fit her demotic Irish background. Nancy was the daughter of Hugh O'Donnell, an Irishman from County Sligo. He was also illiterate. His surname had a parallel instability to his daughter's Christian name, moving constantly between O'Donnell and O'Donald. The two names sound approximately the same, and a literate person was often left to choose which variant to write down. Hugh was a Catholic, working as a labourer until he went into the British Army. He had come to Australia in February 1810 on the *Anne II* as part of the 73rd Royal Highland Black Watch Regiment, and he acted as a guard on the ship which carried 197 convicts. Also on board were the missionary Samuel Marsden and the very first missionaries to New Zealand, William Hall and Thomas King. The boat also carried Ruatara, nephew of Te Puhi, under whose auspices the first Christian missions were established in Aotearoa New Zealand. This link gives some context for the O'Donnells as an early Australian colonial family.[9]

There was a thin but all-important membrane between convicts and the people who kept them imprisoned in the essentially open-prison state of New South Wales. Hugh, as a free man, was rewarded with 100 acres in Liberty Plains, Parramatta, which he seems to have been slow to develop. (This was after his discharge from the army.) In 1828 only 20 acres were cleared and he had seven cattle. Two convict servants worked in his house, which would seem to point to a modicum of comfort.

Despite her father being described as 'a devout Catholic', Nancy O'Donnell was brought up Protestant. Her mother, Mary Lakeman, was a Devonshire lass who managed to bring up every one of her children as Protestant. Nancy herself was always identified as Protestant in official documents. In the 1828 census she was listed as being P (Protestant) and BC (born in the colony). Her death certificate lists her as being Protestant. Hugh chose to be buried completely separately from his Protestant family in the Catholic cemetery at Parramatta. Where your bones lie, or rather under which faith, was important.

The brief romance of Nancy O'Donnell and John Northe is startling. He arrived in Australia on 1 September 1838, and had married her two months later. He may well have decided that at age thirty-nine time was running out; he would marry the first suitable woman who came along. (The British

Army permitted six members per hundred of 'other ranks' the opportunity of marrying. It was a kind of ballot. Up until then it was taken for granted that single soldiers would use prostitutes for sexual pleasure. Perhaps Sergeant Northe's number had at long last come up on the ballot and he hastened to make good on the opportunity.)

Nancy was nineteen. Although she had a malformed hand and was plain, she would have been regarded as good child-bearing stock: her mother had suffered through a marathon ten births. Nancy would also go on to have ten children, the last of whom was born when she was forty-five.

Nancy O'Donnell also came from an army family, so by marrying Sergeant Northe she had married 'in'. One of her sisters, Elizabeth, also married an army man, a sergeant like John Northe: Francis McSorley, colour sergeant in the 57th Regiment. John and Nancy's wedding took place in the handsome sandstone Presbyterian church of St Andrew's, Parramatta, on 17 November 1838. Nancy's sister Mary, a housemaid who worked at Government House, and her husband-to-be, a footman named Robert Green, both acted as witnesses.[10]

But what was Nancy like? Here is a family story, for what it's worth. Governor Darling's wife is out in her carriage. The horse is startled and bolts. Nancy somehow manages to grab hold of the reins and bring the out-of-control horse to a halt. The Governor's wife's life is saved. Apocryphal or not? When? Where is the newspaper report? Where was Nancy that she managed to control the bolting horse? Was she inside the carriage? Still, the image of a young woman capable of subduing a runaway horse is apt for one who is going to mother a brood of sons and a brace of daughters and keep them in order. She needed to be strong.

Here is another story. She used her malformed hand to clip her children painfully when they attended church. It was how she got them to keep quiet. One might say she was very much a sergeant's wife.

COMPARED WITH THE ABUNDANCE OF names and identities by which we know Anne Sophia/Nancy/Ann, there are very few photographs. This is by no means unusual. To go into a photographic studio was a significant and relatively costly undertaking. It is fitting to Nancy Northe's modest place in the world that the earliest photo we have of her is a tin-type, a budget form of photograph, tiny in circumference even if sharp in its

ABOVE

A tin-type photograph of Nancy.

LEFT

Nancy, also known as Ann, was illiterate. She signed legal documents with an emphatic cross — her 'mark'.

BELOW

Nancy's headstone was shattered in the Napier earthquake.

portrayal of detail. She looks out at the world over the photographer's shoulder, her eyes slightly averted to the left; her hair is combed back in a severe mid-Victorian style (unusually, she does not wear a hat). But she has dressed up for the photograph. She has a soft scarf and some flowers around her neck, and she wears what looks like a large locket. Her granddaughter Grace Northe is so like her that Nancy O'Donnell seems to have established a strong genetic brand. She looks formidable. She is not pretty. Possibly she is even a battle-axe. But that is presuming a little too much, because the immobility required of early photography demanded a set expression.

The image is a cut-price one and if you turn it sideways you get a sheen of use, of endurance through time. It is the only image we have of Nancy O'Donnell as a relatively young woman — and I always feel we need photographs of our ancestors as young people starting out so we can get some sense of them as adventurers. Mostly we end up with the rather deadening images of aged respectables draped — or is it entombed? — in black tassels and fringes and feather and jet. All sense of adventure and hot promise has gone.

I do not know where the tin-type was taken. It bears no identifying marks. She left her family behind in Australia forever aged twenty-eight. It may well be at this fracture point that she had the modest portrait done, to send back to her favourite sister Mary in Parramatta.[11]

The second portrait, shown at the start of this chapter, is fascinating. A large crease runs right across the face, seeming to delete her personality. She wears an elaborate outfit, with its lovely mid-Victorian combination of busy checks, plaids, flounces, tassels and veils. Nancy looks richly dressed, like a lady in a fashionable bonnet. But there is, I am theorising, a reason for this.

The life of the wife of a sergeant was by no means easy. Earlier she would have had to live in communal barracks, which lacked privacy and would not have sheltered her from everyday male brutality. The wife of a sergeant was also expected to do the duty of a lady's maid to the wife of an officer. It was her job, for example, to wash and clean and tend to the elaborate business of a Victorian lady's dress, at a time when dress and clothing still displayed the differences in rank. (You could tell at a glance at a person's clothing where someone belonged — higher than you or lower — and you reacted accordingly.)

I believe Nancy is wearing the clothing of an officer's lady in this photograph. The lady may have travelled on from Napier to somewhere else. Or she may have tired of the fashion, or it had gone out of style. But this woman has handed down, in my theory, a complete and rather magnificent set of borrowed plumes for Nancy Northe to wear on a very special day — a visit to the photographic studio in Napier in 1864.

We know the date of the photograph because her last child is sitting on her lap. This is Emily, who was to die of diphtheria on 23 October 1875, aged eleven years, nine months. Diphtheria, associated with overcrowding and substandard living conditions, was brought to Napier by a ship and spread about the town with startling speed. The year 1875 was a very bad one for Nancy Northe anyway. Her husband, who had been ill for some years, died; then her adult daughter Maria died in childbirth, and she lost her two youngest children, Josiah, aged eighteen, and Emily to diphtheria. As the former missionary and Napier resident William Colenso commented on 2 May 1876 in a letter to an acquaintance '*Two more of the Northes [dead, they are an] unfortunate family.*'[12]

Nancy Northe lived for another fifteen years, and died in July 1890 from cancer. Colenso, writing again to his typographer friend Coupland Harding and casting around for something to pad out a letter, noted in passing an event in the life of the small town — the death of 'old Mrs Northe'.[13]

It is not much to say about someone's life — she had died. The dramas of her life went unexpressed, as they did for most colonial women, doubly so because she was illiterate. The novelist Hilary Mantel has commented, in relation to her own great-grandmother, 'I suppose that when a woman had 10 children, she ceases to have a biography.'[14] What she means here, I think, is that the ceaseless production, weaning, educating, dressing, washing, reprimanding, loving, feeding — let alone the physical effort and mess of cyclical births — deleted or washed away or wore down whatever was individual within the person: the mothering to a degree consumed the human.

Those two slim family stories offer some sense of the poles of Nancy's personality: the young woman who could control a bolting horse (whether true or apocryphal, it must have somehow suited her personality) and the old bint using the blade of her deformed nail to pinch her children so that they sat stock still and silent. As to what lay between — silence.

ABOVE

John's Northe's lodge medal.

LEFT

Sergeant John Northe, 'trustworthy, intelligent and sober', past Grand Noble in the Manchester Unity, patriarch.

BELOW

Napier Hill Barracks. Note the whare barracks in the foreground.

THIS BRINGS US TO SERGEANT John Northe, who has threaded through this story elusively. It appears it was he who wrote the four letters discussed below. But first a word about handwriting. Learning to handwrite was once considered one of the building blocks of growing up. You learnt to handwrite on your way to learning how to express yourself in words. You began with written words as a sculptor begins with a block of wood or marble. But first you had to learn how to form those strange symbols called letters, each one meaning something different. (The relationship of a letter to 'the letter' is obvious and direct.)

I was educated in the middle 1950s, and I have a vivid recall of the arduous steps through which you learnt to hold a pen. It was not at all easy. First of all there was a long and seemingly endless exercise in which you drew a continuous circle over and over on large sheets of cheap 'butcher's paper', so your fingers learnt to form the shapes that were letters. You used either crayon or pencil to do this. You did this for so long your fingers ached. New muscles were being educated: just as in the gym, a lot of exercise goes into defining a new muscle.

My first pen was a dip-in pen, an item dating back to the quill (a moulted flight feather of a bird, its rib sharpened to a point) of the sixteenth century. By 1956, when I was six years old, my pen was large, plastic and blue, with a stick-in nib; our school desks were furnished with an inkwell in the top right-hand corner, into which you dipped the nib. I had started using ink, a compound made of carbon black as well as waxes. This was an exciting development, a step away from the painfully inarticulate state of infancy.

But progress was extremely slow — the nib had a propensity to catch on paper and splatter ink everywhere. 'You had blotted your copybook', made a mess of things, a saying that also applied to how you conducted your life. It took a long time to control your fingers, to get muscle fluency.

By the 1950s handwriting was regarded as an essential life-tool. Letters were not only the means by which people corresponded with banks, employers, insurance companies and so on, but also those strange beasts — love letters. Words were everywhere and everything, and to be incapable of handwriting was to be severely disadvantaged.

Everybody had a unique signature. This was as individual as a thumbprint and served the same purpose: to individualise and warrant that you were the particular individual carrying that name and hence sending a letter. During adolescence, it was not unusual to spend many delightful hours modelling different ways of signing your name. This was akin to trying on different personalities. It took a while for a signature to gel with your sense of self. A signature was utterly unique to you and it was meant to message the kind of person you were (modest or showy, stylish or shy). You also tried to have a few quirks or flourishes in your signature to make it difficult to reproduce.

My ancestor, John Northe, had handwriting that is pure copybook, almost arduously formed, very correct and legible. But his spelling was erratic. When it got to the 'correct costume' of words, he showed great uncertainty — almost, I would say, a form of fright. That is because highly literate people were frightening to the marginally illiterate, much in the way a native French speaker is fearsome to an English person mumbling out uncertain French. There is a sense of a reprimand in the glance.

Written language has traditionally been the right of the property-owning classes; it was their own code, if you will. It reproved outsiders by requiring them to reproduce the correct use of spelling and language. It was a kind of fundamental test. Fiction writers have always been able to evade this scrutiny by using language in an imaginative way. But for most people, hesitant about entering the brightly lit room of an empty page, this scrutiny was so offputting their spelling went to pieces, their knowledge of grammar tripped them up, and they felt they were making fools of themselves in public. So writing has always been a form of coded social control. John Northe's faltering letters with their uncertain grammar are interesting because, like those of Charles Days, they come from a section of society from whom, historically, we rarely hear.

His sister Elizabeth had said, axiomatically, when Sergeant Northe departed for New Zealand in 1848, '*it does not matter where we are so long as we can live and do well*'. On 19 June 1871, in carefully shaped, evenly spaced copperplate handwriting, he seemed to echo the same sentiments when he wrote to his daughter Eleanor and son-in-law Samuel Evinson (an ex-colour sergeant, so more marrying in) in far-away Gisborne, '*I have got all the Boys about me now. I have given them all a good Trade which is as good as a little fortune to them with care. William, I am glad to say . . . have got a nice little place of his own; Robert as* [sic] *got a piece ground near William and his* [sic] *putting up a 4 room cottage on it, Frederick I make no doubt as soon as he get out of his time . . . is making great progress in the Saddling Trade. Josiah we can't say much about as yet, I have bound him to a first rate Master Builder named Renouf for 4 years and he is to have 12/- per week first year, 15/- 2nd year and 20/- 3rd year and 30/- 4th. He is the makings of a big man, please God give him his health.*' (As we have just seen, Josiah was soon to be cut down by diphtheria.) '*John* [John James], *he has a first rate trade but as far as I can learn he has had some good chances and have let them slip. He is jobbing about now with one Chas. Day.*'

Sergeant Northe, patriarch, had shaped his sons' futures. He had not come so far without hoping the next generation would do better. He had set his sons up with potentially 'little fortunes' if they tended their work with care. He has apprenticed them to various trades — carpenter, printer, saddler, builder, shipwright — and he spoke as the patriarch who has given them these chances. His daughter Dolly '*keep herself pretty buisy at her Sewing Machine. When not at home she is at Mr Newton's Store working at his Machine — 3/- per diem.*' His son John (James) was also '*talking about taking down [the Stable] and take it to the Spit to make a Work Shop of it*' — the beginning of John James Northey's flourishing shipwright business on Westshore. All is activity and bustling enterprise in 1871, the start of the post-land war boom.

The letters illuminate the urge of all migrants: to improve their living conditions generation by generation in order to escape the constriction and horrors of poverty. At seventy-two, Sergeant Northe must have been proud that he had worked most of his life for one shilling a day and his youngest son aged fourteen was already earning just under double that, while his daughter Dolly earned three times this amount.

These letters display their author's pride in earning good money, potentially leading to the acquisition of capital — the one thing that allows for self-reliance and empowerment and independence in a free-market economy which has no 'protective net' to catch those who fall by the wayside. There's nothing unusual in this, and in its own way it's to be highly commended. It is a classic migrant strategy. It is one thing to set off into the unknown with the safety belt of capital. How much more risky to set off into an unknown world with only your labour, wits and street-smarts to guide you.

BUT HOLD ON. Sergeant Northe was *not* on his own. He travelled in the caravan of the imperial army to Napier via Auckland, Russell and, before that, New South Wales, Nova Scotia, Corfu. He was one tiny cog in a global empire. He was not an entrepreneur; he was an administrator of sorts within a vast bureaucratic unit. (As late at 1868 he was issuing notices which appeared in the local paper about the sale of unwanted barrack bedding.) The very paper on which these letters were written makes this clear.

Each letter was written on pale blue notepaper headed by the royal coat of arms. The paper is glazed and was probably purloined by Sergeant Northe, who might have regarded it as one of the perks of the job. The coat of arms, however, awards a kind of unwitting grandiosity to the letters' simple, semi-literate utterances. It also points to an adherence to the pieties of monarchy and a belief in a deferential and hierarchical social order (even if in one of the letters he is cynical about some of the men higher up the pecking order than himself). While he is writing, in his imagination he is the king and he is surrounded by magic beasts like unicorns and roaring lions.

By this time he had been in the army for more than forty years. One could almost say he was institutionalised, and his writing has an earnest sort of look, one that normally goes with a tongue tucked by the front lip as the forehead frowns with the effort of guiding a pen. A photograph of Sergeant John Northe shows his workman's hands — miner's hands indeed, used to force, to carry, perhaps even to punch. A pen to him is as awkward and unnatural as a ruff or a feather on a velvet cap.

John Northe had joined the British Army at Plymouth on 3 May 1820 as a private in the Royal Staff Corps, and 188 days later he became a corporal. He was twenty-one and he showed promise. The Royal Staff Corps was in charge of short-term engineering works (road and canal building), and it is possible that his former life as a miner gave him an advantage. The Royal Staff Corps answered to the Quartermaster General, who was in charge of supplies for the army: this was a shadowplay for John Northe's future.

Life within the army, however, was brutal and demanding. Flogging was common (even though slaves could no longer be flogged) and all the men lived communally. They were paid a shilling a day — the 'King's Shilling' — but more than a third was taken out to pay for food: three-quarters of a pound (340 grams) of boiled meat a day and one pound (453 grams) of bread. The attraction of this in times of starvation is obvious. The men had to look after their own uniforms, and keep them washed and clean.

He was a corporal for six long years, then became a sergeant on

Christmas Day 1826 — surely a day of celebration. He remained a sergeant for eleven years and twenty-nine days. In one sense he could go no further. It wasn't until the disasters of the Crimean War of 1853 revealed the idiocy of an officer class based on the simple purchase of commissions that this changed. Up until then, no matter how good you were as a soldier, you always remained 'non-commissioned' unless you paid to become an officer. You could not escape your class. Even so, within these stultifying parameters Sergeant Northe had done well: by 29 January 1834 he wrote to his cousins, as we have seen, that he had returned to England from Halifax in Nova Scotia and *'all our company'* was discharged *'a few days afterwards except myself who they would not part with'*.

He had scored for himself what amounted to a cushy office job. *'My duty at this present time is very easy and dear cousins I am happy to inform you I am very comfortable.'* Which was as well as *'everything is very dull about England at this time and no likelihood of it getting better'*. (The year 1834 was marked by the passing of the savage new Poor Law. This created the workhouse, a place so horrible that only the truly destitute could face entering it. The legislation led to widespread social unrest. During the Chartist riots of 1839–1848, workhouses were often singled out for attack and burnt to the ground.)

This also gives some context to the degree to which John Northe was *'very comfortable'*. His new desk job *'answers my purpose well for as I have now 14 years service and if I live to stay 7 years more I shall then be entitled to 1/10d pension'*. This amounted to a beggar's banquet of 10 shillings a week. Nevertheless it was substantially more than a labourer's wage.

He was discharged by the Quartermaster General on 5 February 1838 with praise, and forwarded to the Barracks Department in New South Wales. More travelling. *'Sergeant John Northe's conduct as a soldier has been Sober and trustworthy, an intelligent Non Commissioned Officer and in every respect a good and deserving soldier.'*

A month after his discharge, on 14 March 1838, he was admitted as a Chelsea Hospital Out-Pensioner, which gave him a very small pension of ninepence a day, which was raised to two shillings and one pence in 1870. (A Chelsea Hospital Out-Pensioner was an honorific pension for a long-serving 'other rank' soldier who was overseas.) But he continued to be employed by the army until at least 1868, by which time he was sixty-nine years old. It is unclear when he retired.

He had arrived in Napier in February 1858 as a barrack sergeant, loosely attached to the 65th Regiment. A barrack sergeant position was traditionally a reward for a soldier who had been in the service for a long time, who was capable and responsible. His domain, as he aged, was an indoor and administrative one, a reward for a lifetime of conscientious service and — in a world in which alcoholism was endemic — sobriety. However, his position seems to have had a degree of ambiguity about it. His daughter Eleanor described him as a 'paymaster sergeant for the 65th Regiment', while his death notice in Auckland's *Southern Cross* newspaper elevated him to a 'Barrack Master'.[15] He is not listed in the records of the 65th Regiment soldiers who stayed in New Zealand.

It is hard to get a sense of the human within this straitjacketed existence. He was moved like a piece of human chess around the globe wherever British power needed to assert itself or protect British interests. He arrived in Napier as two powerful iwi were about to fight one another and the few Pākehā in the region panicked. Yet outside this confined context we can still get a more supple sense of the man whose aspirations reached beyond his ability, or inability, to write grammatically correct English.

NOWHERE MORE IS THIS SO than in his enthusiasm for and active participation in the Oddfellows Manchester Unity. The Oddfellows was a 'friendly society', a non-profit mutual society owned by its members. In its own way it was a form of health and employment insurance for working men, arranged on a democratic principle (not unlike, in fact, the Cornish mines). It deployed, however, the mystical iconography of magic, monarchy and the Freemasons. There were costumes, signs, passwords, grips, oaths of secrecy and ceremonies. Various honorary certificates, medals and inscriptions were given to PNG (Past Nobel Grand) John Northe, who was an active and enthusiastic member. These were carefully kept and handed down by the family. (A walking stick, his medals from the Oddfellows, two framed commendations, his Oddfellow seal, all the official documents from the army, his discharge papers, his silver watch: by these few things we know him.)

In my grandmother's sitting room hung a heavily framed silk certificate dated 29 November 1847, and given to PNG John Northe when he left the Loyal Kinkora Lodge, No. 4195, in Bathurst. He was a 'worthy and respected

Member, a zealous and efficient supporter . . . your character appears to us equally admirable and we hope your example . . . Will create a spirit of emulation . . .' He would find fellow brothers 'wherever the sun rises on the Empire'. From Halifax in Canada, a medal reads: 'A mark of respect to Past Secretary J. Northe for introducing 11 Members in 4 succeeding Lodge Nights 1831'. He had initiative, enterprise and, it would seem, a degree of charisma.

Perhaps we see him at his most complete when he did what he had never been able to do before: buy land.[16] In Napier he decided he would put down roots. On 5 February 1858, within days of the troops arriving in Napier, he bought a large plot (W119) in the Napier Hill Cemetery. The very size of this plot — essentially three berths wide — was an expression of patriarchal intent: its purchase declared 'Here will lie my family, in all its glory and multitudinous; here will lie my bones and hereafter the bones of all my family'. The purchase so soon after arriving in the town also reveals a sense of relief that he was, at long last, no longer being shuttled around. He was fifty-nine years old, a father of grown men and young women. He would not die for another seventeen years. But by getting in so early, the partially literate barrack sergeant ended up surrounded in death by the town's wealthy and those who considered themselves a cut above him as colonial gentry.

Another land purchase, however, was not so fortunate. On 20 October 1858 he bought three sections in Main Street in the Onepoto Gully, a steep track that led up to the barracks on the very top of the Napier Hill. The purchase suggests a kind of conservatism, a lack of risk. Or was it just that this was the territory he knew? The land was a Crown grant and had been subdivided on the very first plan for Napier drawn up in 1855. Owners of other sections included officers and an army surgeon. Yet others were essentially speculative, and owned by absent land speculators, people like Takamoana Karaitiana, rangatira of Ngāti Kahungunu, and 'Lord' Henry Russell, a sheepocrat. Wellington speculators also owned sections. At the time the land must have looked like a good investment, near as it was to the barracks. (Hospital Hill was then called Barrack Hill.)

Sergeant Northe paid the relatively high price of ten guineas for each of the sections at 9, 10 and 11 Main Street, which his sons Hugh Frederick and Josiah occupied the following year. (A year later he sold off section 11, described in the advertisement as 'that very desirable piece of land

... surrounded by a substantial wooden fence and under crop. A well has been sunk which provides a constant supply of water.') In 1860 he spent a further £30 on a section at 13 Main Street, and built a tiny wooden cottage on the site. This is where he lived for the rest of his life with Nancy and his daughters. The receipts, which still exist — and which were as important as a teaching diploma or a university degree is now — were signed by John Alexander Smith, a trader, who was selling the land for various people including William Colenso, the ex-missionary who dabbled in buying and selling land. On pay of ten shillings a week, Sergeant John Northe had somehow managed to salt away £60 for the land.

Colenso, writing to a friend in 1870, referred disparagingly to these purchases, saying he was only 'too glad' to sell the sections at a relatively high price 'as that part of our "city"(!) is the very fag end, and must be (I fear) for years to come'.[17] He was right. Onepoto Gully was a chilly valley. It was far from the sea, from what might be called the 'dress circle' of Napier. It looked instead into an interior landscape of swampland but it was, at least, oriented towards the port and inner harbour. Yet it was very much the back end of Napier.

In 1870 Colenso had noted there were only three residents 'in all that end of the Island!'[18] After the barracks ceased to exist in the 1880s (by which stage they had become immigration barracks), Main Street lost its purpose. It went into a steep decline, ending up housing a woollen mill and the poorer workers in Napier.

But my point is John Northe was not an inert atom shifted around by historical forces, deposited in Napier like a piece of driftwood. (He along with others of the town's bourgeoisie also bought shares in Napier's first Building Society.) As with his role in Manchester Unity, or setting up his sons in apprenticeships, or the buying of land, he was advocating for himself to better his place in the world. We are reminded of the entrepreneurial miners of Cornwall, who auctioned off work and provided a model of contract work and personal advocacy.

After he died in 1875, two of the surplus sections were sold, and Nancy continued to live in the cottage at 13 Main Street. The £30 purchase had risen in value to £400 by 1882, so it was not an entirely bad investment.

LET'S SET SERGEANT JOHN NORTHE more tightly in the complex colonial world of Pākehā and Māori. What did it mean that he worked for the British Army? Did this mean he took part in confiscations and fought against Kingite Māori? On 20 April 1869 Sergeant John Northe had written to his daughter Eleanor and son-in-law Samuel Evinson, who lived near Matawhero, '*Dear Son & daughter . . . No doubt you have heard of all the goings on here with the Hou-hous and the great Slaughter they have made again, and it would appear no one can stop them.*'

The note of urgency and alarm is very real. The letter seems to be saying that 'no one' can stop the 'Hou-hous' reaching Napier, where another 'great Slaughter' might happen.[19] Fear was visceral for these migrants living in a landscape which could not help but be deeply 'other'. And surprise attacks in the dead of night or at dawn were especially frightening.

An attack by Te Kooti Arikirangi on Mōhaka between 9 and 12 April 1869 had left sixty-two dead, both Māori and Pākehā. Mōhaka was only 88 kilometres away — within striking distance of Napier. At the time Te Kooti had appeared to be heading in a completely different direction, up to Waikato or Tauranga, where indeed food was being prepared for his arrival. Instead he quietly turned back inland, and in the early hours of Saturday, 10 April he and his Tūhoe followers began the slaughter by killing thirty-one Māori men, women and children. This was revenge against Māori supporters of the Crown, called Queenites (supporters of Queen Victoria) or kūpapa (friendlies or, more derogatively, collaborators). Te Kooti and his followers also killed a young Pākehā family by the name of Lanvin and a farmer named Cooper.

The Edwardian historian and gatherer of oral history James Cowan was later to write, 'Mrs. Lavin was lying on the ground, shot dead. Her husband lay by her side with his left arm under her as if he had been protecting her when he was killed; his revolver was in his outstretched right hand. The Lavin children, according to the veteran Armed Constabulary scout Ben Biddle, who was one of the first to find the bodies, had been killed by being thrown up in the air and caught on the points of the Hauhaus' bayonets, just as the Sepoys cruelly impaled white children in the Indian Mutiny. "The little ones' bodies were all over bayonet-wounds," said Biddle.'[20]

The last detail is questionable. Facts become propaganda in a heightened atmosphere of war, and killing children can be guaranteed to motivate anger and a desire for revenge. Cowan deploys a classic image from the Indian Mutiny which draws on an arsenal of what might be best termed 'white fright'. Historian Judith Binney points out the attacks were essentially utu or reciprocity, and that Lanvin's children 'were not mutilated', though she offers no evidence for this.[21]

Te Kooti's real focus was the two local pā which were allied to the Crown (kūpapa). These were Te Huiki and Hiruharama, both of which held much-needed ammunition and guns. Te Kooti negotiated for a 'peaceful' entry into Te Huki after a day of siege, but a Ngāti Pahauwera warrior fired on him when he entered, and 'the surrender turned into slaughter'.[22] Twenty-six people, mainly women and children, were killed by Te Kooti and his party.

On Monday, 12 April word of the slaughter reached Napier after one of the kūpapa Māori rode a horse to the town's limits, then walked and ran as far as Petane before collapsing in exhaustion and fright. The news of the guerrilla attack led to panic. 'During the Monday night — commencing at midnight — the bulk of the women and children resident in [outlying districts] flocked to town,' the *Hawke's Bay Herald* reported on 16 April. 'The writer left Napier about midnight and on his way to Greenmeadows, could not have encountered fewer than twenty carts bound for Napier, laden with timid women and tender children, many of them infants who had been taken from their warm beds into the dank, unwholesome atmosphere of the night.' The *Herald* writer defined the rush to the fort as 'a stampede'. (Possibly this is the night Polly Northe remembered, when she was piggybacked up the hill by one of her 'uncles' in a panicked attempt to get inside the fort before the attack began.)

Sergeant John Northe, now aged seventy, took a sardonic view of the army command and its ability to retaliate: '*Col. Whitmoor can't do anything and now they have got another old Wash Woman, Col Lambert an old Drom Boys,*' he wrote with disdain in the letter.[23] He felt nothing could be done, partly because of the inept command on the colonial side: '*. . . they had the milita [sic] and Volunteers out, a part of them is home again but will have to go out on Sunday, William and Robt have been out and will have to go again on Sunday, we have sent you a news paper so you will be able to see how things is going on —*'

John is referring to his sons William Henry and Robert (my great-grandfather) going 'out' on active service. They were both members of the Napier Rifle Volunteers, one of two 'volunteer' companies in Napier, created on 28 May 1858 as part of a self-defence corps. A Pākehā volunteer had to present himself at the place of parade and do 168 hours' (minimum) service per annum. He was to keep his arms clean and effective. The NCOs, unusually, were elected by the men, and the dress for the Rifle Volunteers was dandyish: a scarlet serge (Garibaldi) jacket with coloured braid facings; trousers of blue serge, with a red band down the outside seams; a blue cloth forage cap with a French peak, and a coloured band with the initials or number of the corps placed at the front. There is evidence, however, that the Napier Volunteers presented a piebald appearance when called up: these were hard times financially, and many men would not have been able to afford a full uniform.

It is probably no surprise that two of Sergeant John Northe's four sons would answer the call. William Henry Northe, aged twenty-eight, was a sharp shooter and one of Hawke's Bay's crack shots. He had already seen action. In October 1866, 180 Volunteers, accompanied by 200 kūpapa Māori, had encircled and attacked a pā site at Ōmarunui, 13 kilometres from Napier. This was after it appeared Pai Mārire from outside Hawke's Bay were attempting to set up a cell near Napier. (This too had been preceded by wild rumours of an attack on Napier by stealth. The Napier Volunteers were called up out of their beds and walked in a forced march by night out to Ōmarunui.) Pākehā and kūpapa Māori fought alongside one another but in completely separate companies.

Twenty-three Pai Mārire followers were killed in the ensuing battle, which appears to have been more of a rout than an actual fight. (Two kūpapa and one Pākehā also died.) It is disputed to this day what the real intentions of these Pai Mārire intruders into Ngāti Kahungunu territory were. The Waitangi Tribunal's assessment of the battle of Ōmarunui, published in 2004, asserts that the Pai Mārire prophets, rather than coming to attack and sack Napier, were in fact coming to lay down their arms before Minister of Native Affairs Donald McLean — but they insisted on his physical presence, which he did not understand. Misunderstandings and distrust built on each other, exacerbated by the difficulties of a diffuse philosophical language on the part of the Pai Mārire.[24] Kūpapa or coastal Māori chiefs were implicated in the attack for their own tribal reasons; and an over-anxious settler militia was headed by a leader (Whitmore) who was angered by the theft of his sheep, for which he blamed Pai Mārire.

There is even a line of argument that it was all part of McLean's evil

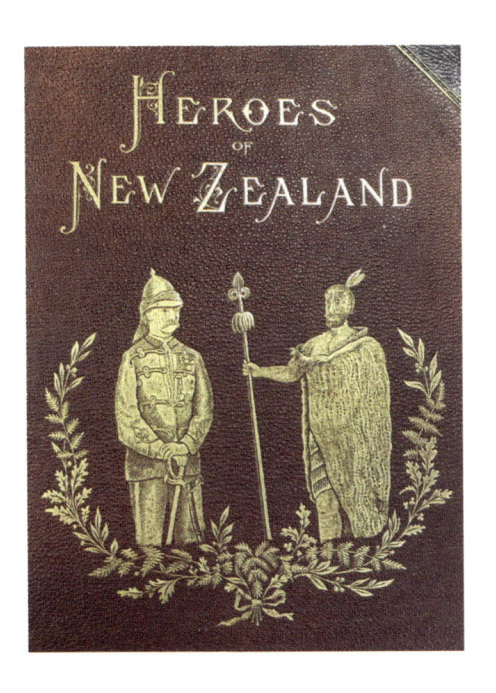

LEFT
'A Short Biography of Colonists Who Distinguished Themselves Upholding Her Majesty's Supremacy in These Islands'.

BELOW
Māori prisoners about to be exiled to the Chatham Islands without trial. It is rumoured that Te Kooti was among them.

plan to steal Māori land, and that Pākehā militia were just donning military uniform as 'settlers [who] could always hope to use the law, particularly the Native Lands Act, to secure their landed interests, [but] they were equally ready to don their uniforms as local militia, take to the field against Pai Mārire, and seize their land under the New Zealand Settlements Act 1863. In one way or another, the settlers would solve their problem of frontier security and advance their land interests.'[25]

All of this is infinitely possible in a theoretical sense, but it absents from the picture the psychological reality of the situation for Pākehā. The sacrificial killing of the Reverend Völkner, his beheading and the drinking of his blood by Pai Mārire in Ōpōtiki in 1865 had whipped up anxieties to an unprecedented level. It was a hysterical environment, and the actions of Pai Mārire in coming to Hawke's Bay and then diffusely answering queries about their intent were alarmingly naive in this context.[26]

When anxiety is high, a situation too easily gets out of control. And while the Waitangi Tribunal's 'Mohaka ki Ahuriri Report' goes out of its way to absolve the Pai Mārire of any aggressive intent, the group's belief that they could appear in Hawke's Bay without carrying the dark and bloodstained history of their apocalyptic religion is not credible. But then, of course, how does credibility relate to an apocalyptic religion in which people feel they can walk into bullets and be somehow magically untouched? Is it possible to communicate in this situation?

History is context. To take away the psychological context is to present a one-sided interpretation. But then I'm a descendent of one of the men who fought at Ōmarunui and perhaps I'd be expected to intuit how this incursion would be seen from my ancestors' point of view — a perspective entirely lacking in the Waitangi Tribunal historical assessment. (The battle led to lamentable consequences: the Pai Mārire captured were sent away without trial to the Chatham Islands, and there was widespread confiscation of land of those iwi implicated in, or blamed for, the conflict. Ironically some of these exiles became recruits for Te Kooti when he later set out to avenge his imprisonment, leading to the attacks on Mōhaka.)

William Henry and Robert Northe also took part in the Mōhaka incident. I was surprised to read that my great-grandfather Robert was in the Volunteers, let alone that he risked seeing action in Mōhaka in 1869. At this date he would have been the randy, directionless age of nineteen, possibly just out of his apprenticeship with Robert Holt, builder, although his obituary says that he started out training to be a printer. One senses the carefulness and patience of this craft would have been anathema to the faintly swashbuckling Robert. He did not continue with the Volunteers after 1869 — perhaps he decided it was just not his style. But in terms of whether Robert Northe ever saw action, the force of landscape in New Zealand intervened. By the time troops 'rushed' to the spot, it was too late. The very mobility of Te Kooti meant he had slipped the noose and vanished.[27]

An aspect of this muddle and misadventure was a fall in the esteem in which the British Army's officers were held. They were now seen as blundering, inept and foolish. When a sergeant writes about a superior officer as '*an old Wash Woman*' it is an indication of a loss of faith. This view, interestingly, was echoed in the *Hawke's Bay Herald,* which reported a state of dithering about how best to counteract the threat to the north. The troops were kept close to Napier while they awaited supplementary Volunteer troops from Hastings. Then the command made the mistake of marching the men up to Mōhaka, via steep hills and deep valleys, instead of fast-forwarding troops in one of the two ships in port.

On Tuesday, 13 April 1869 Colonel Lambert — the 'old Drom Boy' of whom John Northe spoke with so much disdain — started out for Mōhaka with the Napier Volunteers but had got no further than Tongoio, about 25 kilometres from Napier, when he received a dispatch saying Te Kooti had vanished. The Volunteer troops were sent back to Petane, while Colonel Lambert pressed on 'for what might be called the front'. From Petane the troops were force-marched back to other side of Napier, which they found deserted because of the panic. 'Next day they were dismissed to their homes, from which they should never have been taken.'[28]

Meanwhile, up at Mōhaka, Lambert and other military leaders talked about how they should pursue Te Kooti though it was 'utterly fruitless'. (Cowan described Lambert as 'extraordinarily lacking in military enterprise'.)[29] They had got there too late and it had taken too long to deploy all their forces. Local Māori, wanting utu for the slaughter of their women and children, were desperate to pursue and capture Te Kooti. But Lambert prevaricated and lost the initiative. Te Kooti withdrew in triumph with one hundred pack horses loaded with plunder.

It all risked being a farce. As the *Hawke's Bay Herald* commented the following day, 20 April, the day John Northe wrote his letter: 'Our force is scattered here, there, and everywhere but where they ought to be . . . [and it all ends] in nothing, absolutely nothing.' The *Herald* noted gloomily, 'An Exodus of the population will probably set in. The Abrupt withdrawal of men of all classes from their daily occupations, the consequent deprivation of all comfort, cessation of business, and alarm to their families, is more than most people can stand; and already many look out for what they cannot obtain here — a place of rest.' It did not bode well for a small and isolated outpost like Napier.

William Henry Northe was awarded a Military Medal for his service at both Mōhaka and Ōmarunui. What action did he see at Mōhaka? It's hard to believe he would get a medal for marching up a road, then turning around and marching back again. I believe he was one of the twelve Rifle Volunteers who went up to Mōhaka in a lifeboat. He was, after all, one of the best shots in Napier. The boat was loaded with sixty rounds of ammunition. 'On arriving off the mouth of the river, the crew watched the attack on Hiruharama pa and saw the explosion of the gunpowder at Te Huke pa which was on fire,' Cowan wrote.

The boat prepared to land so the Volunteers could rescue any fugitives. But unknown to them the blockhouse was filled with Te Kooti's followers, who began to fire on the boat as it came to land. From a cliff top further gunshots pursued the boat, so it had to pull out of range. Gunshots were fired back over the stern but 'the party decided to return to Napier'.[30] It was not an especially glorious episode.

As if both accepting and dismissing this, the retired sergeant moved on in his letter to talk of more mundane matters: how his family was settling down and trying to scrape together a living in colonial Napier. '*We received a letter a short time since from a Mr Bagnall Dolly's admirer, he begs permission to become one of the family that he had spoken to you on the Subject and you had no objection . . . Now of course we know nothing about him, but from what John* [John James Northey] *say of him it would appear he is a respectable young man, a good trade and from a respectable family' . . . So we don't See there can be any objections — only that they must not be in a hurry.*' That is, Dolly must not be pregnant, which would necessitate a speedy wedding.

As it was, Mr Bagnall faded away. I tried to find out more about him in *Harding's Almanac* but he is nowhere to be seen. Perhaps he was one of those people who joined the 'exodus' away from the tiny and economically fragile polis.

WHAT DID SERGEANT JOHN NORTHE look like? His enrolment papers tell us he was five feet nine inches (1.75 metres) tall, three inches above average height at the time; that his hair was black and his eyes were grey. But in a portrait taken by the notable photographer Samuel Carnell (who specialised in images of Māori rangatira) John Northe is already an old man. In the quick of his condition he had probably been handsome; even as an old man he has residual good looks. But *who was he?*

One of the complicated aspects of working out who actually wrote the four letters signed 'John and Ann Northe' is that Sergeant Northe is referred to in both the first and third person in the letters: in June 1871, in the middle of winter, he writes about '*my being so unwell and the cold weather nipping up I have no heart to do anything*'. But in the first lines of the letter we read that everyone is well '*except poor father he is very unwell*'. Later in August the letter says, again, all are well, '*except poor Father, he is very unwell, the cold weather cuts him up*'.

Is it possible the letters were partially dictated by Nancy and written by John? The same hand, sober and copybook neat, wrote all the letters. (John Northe's will is written and signed by him in the same stately hand.) The letters establish that by his early seventies his health was beginning to give out. He had already lived nearly thirty years longer than the average age for a man in the nineteenth century. As an ex-miner and soldier he had had a tough life. He had crisscrossed the world on several occasions, and at a time when ocean voyaging was demanding and often perilous.

By 1870 John Northe had only five more years to live. Perhaps awareness of his advancing years was the nudge to get a photo taken. He is cast as a *pater familias*, almost self-consciously proud. His military cap sits beside him on the table, although no identifiable badge seems to adorn it. He holds in his large thick-fingered hand a handsome walking stick which still survives, with its killer-whalebone head and Australian cedar stem. This would have had practical uses — to fend off the wild dogs that roamed the Napier streets, and as a weapon if push came to shove. It had elements of panache; it nodded back to the swagger sticks of the officer class to which he aspired.

John Northe appears distinguished, and the silk topcoat he is wearing is perhaps borrowed — photographers kept flash clothing for their clients so they could appear better dressed than was usual. But it is also possible that Dolly ran up the frockcoat as well as the waistcoat for her father. The two pieces of clothing belong together. They add to the impression of him as an 'elder'. The photo also exists as a rather gaudily hand-tinted version, and this may have assumed the gravitas of a family icon on a wall after John Northe died. (It's interesting that so many of his possessions were kept, compared with those of later Northe generations. There was a real sense of him as the founding patriarch.)

In a way John Northe is the most enigmatic personality in this book. We know little of his relations with his brood of sons and daughters, except that he selected two of his sons to have property. (They become the first members of the Northe family to own any property at all in New Zealand.) Other contextual information we can work out from his letters. It is through his drive and determination (or desperation) to leave the old world that so many people like me find ourselves placed — rooted, one could say — in a world far away from our genetic root stock. He was part of one of the great tidal movements in history in that sense. At the same time there is an inherent conservatism which runs like a stain or a ribbon through the family personality: he stepped out into the new world, but under the protection of one of the most conservative and constricting bodies imaginable — the British imperial army.

To John Northe we could apportion an enduring conservatism but also a strong work ethic, as well as an element of intuition and cunning. He ended up in what could be considered a 'cushy' job: by his middle to late career we find him indoors, in the relatively powerful position of apportioning food, drink and living quarters, but also in the deeply ambiguous position of being between a caretaker and a landlord's representative. This ambiguity, this uncertainty about where exactly the family belonged, echoes down the family tree, with its ghostly impulse of deference sitting alongside something much tougher and livelier, more entrepreneurial.

Edward Said's notion of exile as 'an . . . essential sadness [that] can never be surmounted' is not apparent in John Northe's prosaic letters.[31] His view of the world was entirely practical and pragmatic. He probably had no concept of letter writing as a way of expressing the innermost essence of his soul. He may have even despised that sort of introspection. But its absence from overt expression in his letters does not mean a melancholy sense of loss did not exist. He would never see his sisters again. By 1869 his brother Sam was already dead. His homeland — his 'true home' — was as if dead to him, except in memory.

ANOTHER WAY OF SEEING THIS, however, is that Napier — Mataruahou — has a ghostly likeness to parts of Cornwall. It, too, is on an extremity, far away from the centre. It is coastal and it has a primal relationship to the sea. Perhaps there was some kind of echo of place that answered to him when he finally got here. William Colenso, a fellow Cornishman, also selected Napier Hill as tūrangawaewae and final resting place. He said the sea gods of the Cornish world echoed those of the tangata whenua. Perhaps by going so far John Northe had, in a sense, come home — to a new place.

'We carry the genes and culture of our ancestors,' writes Hilary Mantel, 'and what we think about them shapes what we think about ourselves and how we make sense of our time and place.'[32] Meaning in a family emerges in a cascade of generations, both in what joins and what separates. Who am I today — Elizabeth Ereaux, London survivalist and '*cat in a tripe shop*'? Sam Northey, exile and lost in the wilderness? John Northe, a trustworthy soldier who, on arriving in a place, turns around and buys a burial plot? Or Nancy O'Donnell, the girl who leapt on a runaway horse and signed a cross on paper as if with a scimitar while someone else wrote her 'mark'?

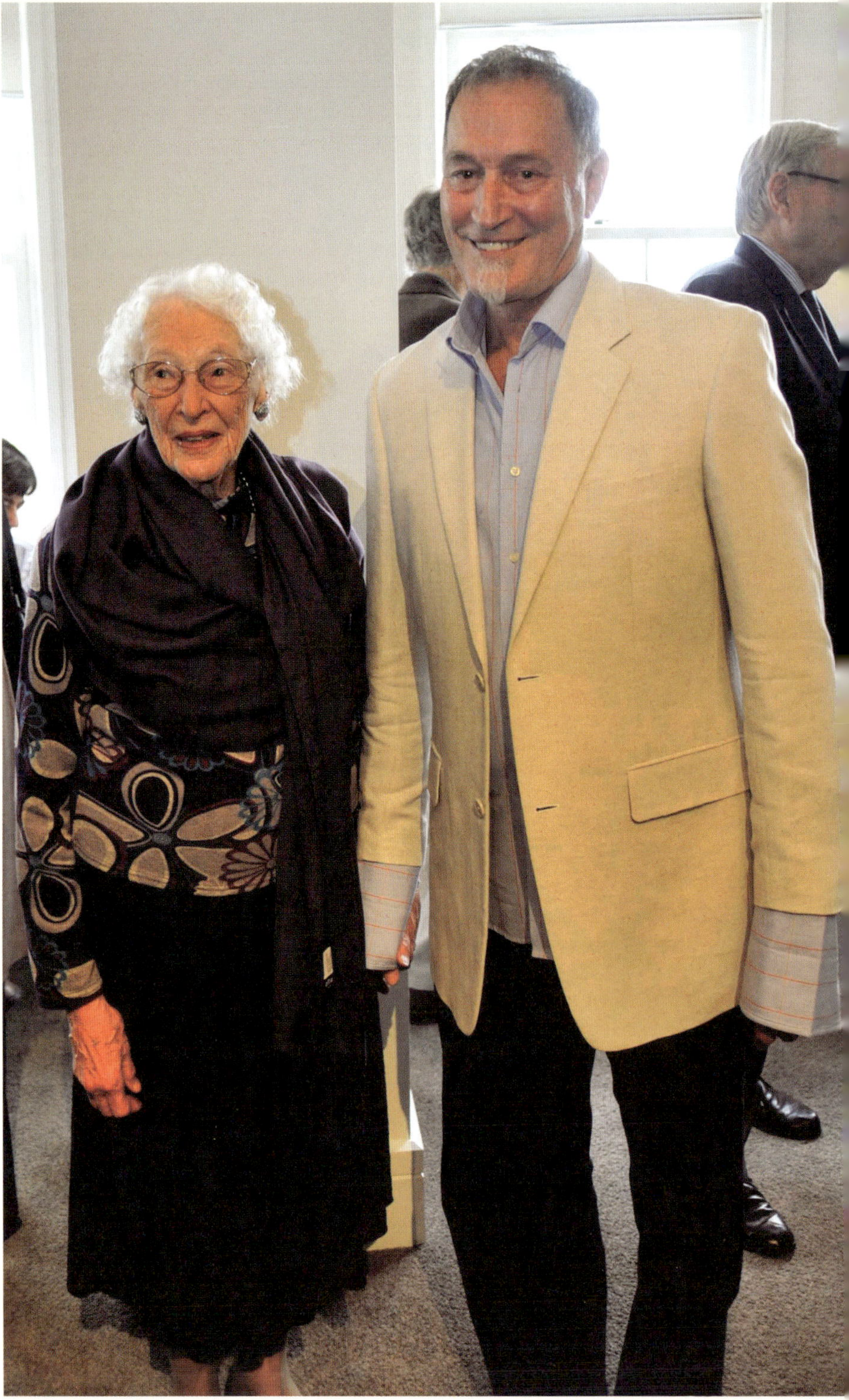

The Failure of Language

OPPOSITE

Bess and Peter Wells in 2011: 'I have looked at the evidence — I have lived the evidence you could say — and these are my thoughts.'

My cellphone rings. It's Anabel, the nurse at Princess Alexandra Retirement Village. Her tone is careful. There's a faint underlay of weariness, too. Since her job is looking after the elderly and smoothing their path towards death, it's no wonder her voice has a compressed quality.

'IT'S BESSIE.'

What else could it be? I enter strange space, feel an almost delicious apprehension that Bess could be near death; it's followed quickly by a sense of fright. Is she going to vanish from my life?

Bess versus Bessie. Bess is my preferred name: it's classy, infers a connection with 'Good Queen Bess'; it was also what her family called her. Bessie is what the name plate says on her studio door. (A name plate that can be easily removed and replaced with another name, from a similar era: Hilda. Mollie. Thelma. Maggie.)

'I'm afraid Bessie is starting to behave inappropriately.'

I can't remember if these were the exact words. Nurses, people in public life, have to be so careful of terminology. But the basic tenet was — trouble ahead.

A sense of panic overtakes me.

'What's she been doing?'

'She took her clothes off in the lounge downstairs.'

I feel appalled. Deeply appalled. I also feel pity. Most of all I feel mortification. Shame.

This is what comes from pretending she is Bess rather than Bessie. Bessie is who she really is. 'Bess the Mess', as I used to call her, only partly humorously — chagrin stuck in my craw — when I was looking after her seven years earlier and she had the episode which announced her dementia. I was trapped in her townhouse for Easter weekend, trying to answer her psychotic trajectories with reason, as if by simply reducing everything to rationality it would diminish the chaos. After three or four days I was the one who was going insane.

Then she stabilised and slowly returned to her recognisable self. I'm not so sure now if this 'recognisable self' isn't a fiction I have created. I am not sure my mother isn't in fact an entirely fictional being who I have spent my life creating. I can't explain this strangely powerful connection of a son to his mother — a homosexual son to his mother. Barthes said 'my mother is my inner law'. Proust's idea was that his mother spent her entire life preparing him for her death, readying him for that moment when he found himself 'motherless'. Alone. (This was foreshadowed by that crisis that opens *In Search of Lost Time*, where Marcel calls out for his mother while lying in bed.)[1] Barthes talks in terms of *abandonitis*.[2] It is no respecter of intellectual status, this harrowing, constant need, interwoven as it is with hate and a deep desire to escape. Shut up, Freud, we're not really interested in your tidy cul-de-sac. We're in the wide, open prairie here.

But I'm also unwaveringly aware Bessie is only herself, and I attend her and watch her, much as a zoo keeper might attend to an animal he has bonded with, come to love, whose sickness he watches with a queasy feeling in his stomach. There's complicity, a realisation that he has spent his life caring for the animal but it could not care less. The animal is demanding its own wairua, is maintaining its own obdurate independence, by deconstructing, by manifesting the deep irrationality which is sickness and death.

'What exactly has she been doing?"

I'm aware my voice is filled with an almost reverent horror. But there's also something else, a spark of hilarity, even pleasure in knowing that she is making a mess of herself. This is quickly cancelled by a deep sense of pity that she is betraying herself, her presentation of a self. Bessie, who is courteous, almost innately well mannered, who even now tries to introduce me, again and again, to other inhabitants at the home: 'This is my son, Pete.'

'You're all I've got,' she says to me at times when we're alone. I hate this. Or when I leave, and I bend down to kiss her cheek, she grabs hold of my hand and holds on tightly. 'Thank you, Pete, for all you do for me. I'm so grateful.' But when I relax and feel pleased, she adds, 'Look after yourself. You're all I've got.'

There it is, the toxic mixture of pity, love, blackmail, need.

'Poor Mum.'

'Yes, I know. I hate to see your mother like that. She would hate it.'

I recede further into shock. Deep shock. My mother. Taking her clothes off in public. Her old body. Exhibitionism.

'We got her into her room. She couldn't make sense of what she wanted to say. She thought she was constipated.'

'What are we going to do?'

This was the beginning of another stage of her deterioration. I came home and couldn't tell Douglas. I couldn't bear to put it into words. I was frightened he might laugh — not cruelly, but because it is horribly funny. Bess, the daughter of Jess, Gestapo officer of the manners police, taking her clothes off in public.

How bad was it going to get? What could I say when people asked, 'And how's your mother?' I couldn't articulate what was happening to her. All I could say was, 'Not good. She's not so good now.'

I dreamt up fantastic solutions. Sedating her. Keeping her in her room. I thought very clearly about suffocating her with a pillow. I went through how I would do it — visit her in her room as I always did. Nobody else was ever there. But I always came up against the snag: I would be observed entering her room and I would be the last person to see her alive. Besides, when I got down to it, I could not live with myself. I also knew she would fight. That incredible willpower that dominated her life, that sped her on, recklessly almost, to her one hundred and first year — she would fight against me stifling her. I could almost feel, in premonition, the slim column of her neck rising up against the pillow. She would kick, maybe even bite. (This is what she does when she starts to undress again during the drinks session a few days later. Has she become a figure of fun? Do they all shrug and laugh about her? Or is it a horrific presentiment of what is to come for them, too? Is it her 'raging against the dark'?)

'We got her into the toilet. Then she walked out with her trousers round her ankles.'

I have to laugh then. Anabel does, too. Apologetically.

'It's all you can do in the end. Laugh.'

I feel fear and horror. Most of all I feel shame. But also chagrin. I think back to Russell's death and Bess's — Bessie's — breakdowns. Both of them took up so much space in my life (I recognise this is a selfish thing to say) with their bravura crack-ups, their showy descents into madness. Then I think further and deeper into whether this undressing is not endemic to our family, like a strain of madness. What is this writing, anyway, but a form of undressing? I undress my family, I even undress myself. It is compulsive, as if my sanity, my life, depends on it. I humiliate my family by revealing flaws, secrets.

Or is it the other side, an inextricable part of the closed, closeted, highly mannered façade we sought or seek to present? Isn't this form of writing itself the presentation of a façade? I do not download my own pathetic untruths, failures, the sense of time overtaking me and rendering everything I've done trivial and senseless, worthless as a piece of space junk.

She is daily growing more and more tired. I think I recognise the look a cat has when its kidneys suddenly stop functioning. You know there is no looking back — or even forward — as the intermediate days will be taken up with the messy, sad, horrible business of preparing for death. I text a close friend: 'Bess is checking out.'

'It's a shame she can't just drift away in her sleep,' I say to Anabel over the phone.

She doesn't reply but I sense there is empathy in her silence.

But this is too tidy. We're not in a tidy zone now.

THE NEXT TIME I VISIT her she is so tired I say to her, 'You just snooze off, Mum. I'll sit here.' It is a very hot day and she has said repeatedly, 'What a beautiful day.' A variant — an especially daring variant because the words are quite difficult — might be, 'Aren't we lucky with the weather?' Or, as she said to me about her own life, almost with a shrug, as if despite everything life has dealt her — an unhappy marriage, a brilliant son who died a shameful death, the absence of the many grandchildren and great-grandchildren she had probably expected — 'I've been lucky. *Lucky*.'

I take a photo of her on my cellphone. I put it on silent and archive my mother's face, as if to record it for when she is no longer there. For days afterwards I gaze at this image in which I can see both exhaustion and a kind of immutable dignity.

THE SHAME — WHERE DOES it come from precisely? Any son would be ashamed of his mother taking her clothes off in public. But it's more than this. It's the conflict between her age and the sexual acting out (if it is in fact sexual, which is not clear). I had already seen her radiance and shameless pleasure when she scored a boyfriend at the home. He was ten or twelve years younger. Her 'toy boy', I used to call him. She was surprisingly philosophical when he abandoned her for a younger woman. Then more recently she was hit on by a man with dementia. I was never quite sure what this meant — how far it got — but the staff were on red alert to keep him away from her. (Was he the man who kissed her on the cheek when we walked in, like celebrities, to her one-hundredth birthday party? I registered it at the time as being unusual but just put it down to her popularity.) Bess as a party girl. A girl 'who likes a good time'. An appetite for life.

But it becomes 'inappropriate' as she gets so old — the mismatch between age and desire. Or is it that old people are not allowed the pleasures of sex? Or has it in fact nothing to do with sex and desire? And is the shame I feel — now this is true — because I wonder if I am infected with the same inappropriate shamelessness? One could call it desperation. In my emotionally complicated childhood and adolescence, I essentially shut down. I came out in my early twenties but my sex life, as could be expected, was chaotic. I was always searching for a monogamous relationship founded on intense, almost overpowering love — what I came later to recognise as a *folie à deux*, perhaps an echo of the love affair between Russell and me, or between Bess and me.

It wasn't until much later that this spell ended. It seemed to die a natural death, and at that time in my life I became intensely interested in sex, and sex with a wide variety of men. It is not unusual for gay men from the repressive period to experiment with sex later in their lives. This is partly because the natural evolution of desire and play was stopped by social pressure, laws forbidding it, stigma, shame. So I suddenly found myself as a man no longer possessing the charms of youth entering a sexual marketplace predicated on youth and beauty. This did not deter me. It gave me strength. And while there were humiliations aplenty (if I chose to recognise them as such), I also discovered a depth of sexual pleasure that helped me mature as a human and cast off the thrall, the frozen part, of my earlier life.

Yet the sudden eruption of Bess into a shameless sexual being (even if there was no overt sexual content in it) gave me pause for thought. Was this really what I myself was? A shameless man who had lost touch with what was appropriate? The keen pleasure I felt when I realised I could undress completely and no longer be ashamed about whatever faults my body had: this had seemed to me to be a major transition, even a key turning point in my life. I was lucky in that I had found in Douglas a partner who is loving and constant, who understood the strange malformation of my past. But I also knew the powerful allure of desire and the potential for anarchy it created.

All these complicated feelings were in my mind. The shame was about myself as much as it was about the shame of a one-hundred-year-old mother who had taken to undressing in public.

I REMEMBER A HOLIDAY AT Hicks Bay on the East Cape. It was the halcyon holiday of my childhood. I was probably nine, so we are talking 1959. We camped on the foreshore under an ancient pōhutukawa, and there was a sense of us being the only humans alive, though we were in profoundly Māori territory.

My parents had a separate tent. Russell and I shared a pup tent. My parents' separate tent was so they could have sex, I see looking back. This explains why they had slipped into an easy, happy camaraderie. Gone was that niggling resentment, that totting up in the book of plaints, regrets, insults. Had Dad forgiven Bessie? Had he made a compromise, decided that he loved her so much that he would forgive, or absolve her, of her wartime lovers? They were happy. It was as if we had different parents — adults who were companionable, friendly. Dad enjoyed building fires and camping; perhaps it took him back to the best part of his war. But what I remember, because it was so unusual, was that we swam 'in the nuddy'. Nuddy is a childish word that probably desexed the activity, giving it a slightly risqué emphasis. It was daring but lovely.

I still have an image in my head. The waves have made the golden sand as vast as a ballroom floor made of spun glass. In the glass is the sky overhead. We seem to be advancing into the sky itself, a form of heaven. And we are walking forward together, excited by the adventure of being naked — turned back into something almost biblical, a family salved of sin, existing briefly in heaven.

I WRITE TO A FRIEND, Shonagh Koea, also an author, on a weekly basis, sometimes even when we are in the same city. She and I tend to use personae at times of stress or occasionally in an outbreak of frivolity. She becomes Douglas Bader (DSO, retired) while I become June Opie. (Real people from our youth, both of whom wrote memoirs about overcoming their disabilities with courage and stamina. Our intention is lightly satirical, as is our change of gender.)

After the incident in the home, I wrote to Shonagh, and she replied: '*You have said in your letter that she has suddenly been behaving outside her character, so that is a sign of an inadvertent decline due to great age. It is not really Bess doing that, whatever it is. So you do not need to worry or be embarrassed about whatever has occurred. It is not really Bess at all. It is some primeval sense of life and survival that we all may have hidden away somewhere in the recesses of our psyches, long overlaid with good manners, deportment, cultivation and much else, possibly even pretension. It may be an ancient remnant of prehistoric life when we had to find a waterhole by knowing the scent of water on the wind, or to know that danger lurked in the darkness when we had invented fire and could raise a burning stick in the night to show a ring of predators' eyes glowing in the sudden light. It is an ancient primeval thing, like a howl echoing down a dark valley, so the end must be near, I think.*

'Douglas Bader (DSO, retired).'

Doesn't this show the beauty of a letter sent at the right moment? I opened her letter up several times to re-read her words of wisdom and comfort. I kept the letter nearby so my fingers could touch it, or my eyes glance at it, as if it were a good-luck token.

I would carry on. Isn't that what my background told me to do? To persist. This applied to my grandfather after the 1931 quake as much as to his daughter, who at almost one hundred and one had forgotten how to die.

12 MARCH 2017

A young nurse, who is always pleasant, phones me to say Bess has vomited up something like coffee grounds. This is apparently a serious sign. Bess has some sort of internal bleeding, and the nurse seems to be saying she is entering a dying process. 'Entering a dying process'. How absurd. She is dying.

Immediately I experience an outbreak of anxiety. It is hard to comprehend. Why am I feeling so anxious when I know she will have to die sooner or later, and some rational part of my mind celebrates the fact? It would be better for her to die rather than to enter a deeper state of dementia. Yet I feel an elemental panic. It is as if I was standing on a platform high up in the air and the floorboards under my feet have given way. *Abandonitis.*

I go down to visit her. She is lying on her side, asleep. She keeps murmuring, 'Oh dear, oh dear, oh dear.' Gradually she rises to consciousness, sees me sitting there, and tells me not to stay, to go home. She seems to think I have just driven down to Napier or wherever she thinks she is.

Later she says to me, 'Go, you mustn't be late for school.' I say I'm happy sitting there and she should just keep snoozing. I have brought a *New Yorker* to read and have my iPhone.

She gradually becomes more conscious and I ask her if she would like me to brush her hair. I pick up her 1930s silver brush with her initials elegantly engraved it, the silver almost black with tarnish, and I brush her hair slowly, thinking back to how I used to do this when I was an apprentice pouf. Her skull is so visible now. This seems to ease her. I make a cup of tea, put cold water in it so it doesn't scald her, and give her a chocolate biscuit. She seems to be hungry. She sits up and sips the tea. After a while she asks me where the toilet is. She makes to get up and I panic at what I might be forced to see. Lecture myself about not being so selfish. She can't get up from the bed, so I somehow wrestle her upwards from behind, my hands under her armpits, get her walker, and she manages to get into the toilet. I go and stand where I can't see her. Eventually she finishes and I help her back to the bed.

'You're a wonderful son,' she says. It is heartfelt.

We talk a little more. For the first time she acknowledges her own death. 'What will you do when I kick the bucket?'

I'm not sure quite what she is asking me. I decide to say, 'I'll be very sad, Mum. Very sad indeed.'

I want to say, You have loved me unconditionally in a way no one else will ever do and we have had an enriching friendship. You who were worried I would always be poor as a writer have supported me. You have been a bewildering, spellbinding mother. I will be all right. And I have Douglas, and he understands me, knows what and who I am, is my rock.

But I don't say that. I say something else, and I don't know why: 'Don't worry, Mum, we'll meet again when I die. We'll be together then.'

It is such a curious thing to say, because I am unsure whether I believe this. One part of me, the rational part, sees it as a ridiculous statement. Some other fairy part of my consciousness holds out a hope it is true.

'Well, let's not think about that,' she says in her pithy, down-to-earth way.

Later, settling down to snooze, she says, 'I don't know what happens.'

Finally I decided to go. I knew she didn't want me too near her. She was too sick, probably nauseous. She complained of pains in her feet. I said, 'I'm going to kiss you, but on your forehead.'

I kissed her on her forehead, right where the brain lies.

'I'll see you tomorrow,' I said.

She seemed quite cheery when I left, or at least as if she had got some consolation from my visiting her. I am not sure if this isn't an expression of vanity. Just before I left, a nurse came in, plumped up Bess's pillows in a boisterous way, called her 'darling' and said to me as we stood at the door, 'Knowing Bessie, she'll probably be right as rain tomorrow.'

I got a sense of how popular she was with the nurses. Later in the evening I composed a funeral soliloquy which included the words 'of good old pioneer stock'. I meant her peasant strength. Her ability to endure. But also something else to do with her humour, her practicality, her adaptability. Even as an old woman without power she managed to disarm by charm.

27 MARCH 2017

Bess has been shifted to 'the special care unit'. It's in response to her undressing. You need to press a buzzer in order to get in, then you enter a neutral zone where another buzzer needs to be pressed to allow you to enter the 'special care' area. This is a ring of rooms around a forecourt, the whole area fenced off so there is no possibility of escape. Everybody in the unit has advanced dementia, but they are on the whole peaceful old people who have returned to the simplicities of childhood.

This is a step beyond the hospital, which is where Bess feared to go. Anabel had taken her down there on her own, and had rung and told me, 'Bessie was peaceful and it went surprisingly well.'

Now I face the task of emptying out her studio, selecting clothes for a single room with a double-door closet. You are encouraged to bring personal items, and there is a box on the door in which you can place family photos — certificates indicating who the person once was.

I feel exhaustion at the thought of sorting through her possessions yet again.

BESS IN THE UNDERWORLD. The place she feared to go. Bess stripped down, reduced, face naked and raw. She has no make-up or earrings. She looks like a refugee in a refugee camp. When I speak to her she has to travel back a long distance to respond, and even then it is across a deep, empty space.

We sit outside in the sun. I chafe her hands and she eventually responds with her customary 'And what else?' She also asks me 'What's out there?', indicating with her head the rest of PA, from which she has been exiled.

On my way out I meet the young nurse who had told me Bessie was on the point of dying. I treat her as someone who has betrayed me. The nurses and staff outside 'special care' all ask me brightly, 'How is Bessie getting on?' I also feel they betrayed her. But the situation is more cut and dried. If she had not started behaving 'inappropriately' she would still be back in PA, in conditions which now seem to me paradisial.

Maria, the smiling matron of 'special care', says they will put a 'onesie' on Bess with a zip up the back so she cannot undo it when she wants to undress. 'It's to save her dignity,' she explains.

I wish she had died.

SOMETIMES I THINK OF HER as she used to be. I see her in motion. I see her walking along energetically, on her way somewhere. She is full of purpose. She also makes small movements with her hands, as if she is in the middle of an animated conversation. She is 'making a point'.

Packing up her room, throwing things away — I think of all the times I've done this — reducing possessions into ever smaller units. In all her drawers, behind cushions, in cupboards, endless tissues she has secreted 'for a rainy day'. I find a questionnaire from PA: 'What do you think of Princess Alexandra Retirement Village?' She has filled it in with shaky but determined handwriting, all in capitals, 'It is very boring but I suppose that is what these places are.'

Bess with her full engagement book, playing endless bridge, 'off to a show'. 'Let's have a spot.' 'You *do* pour a good G & T, Pete.'

THEY HAVE CUT HER HAIR brutally short. It hangs limp around her gaunt face. She reminds me of Marie-Antoinette on the tumbril. She is outraged but keeps to a kind of brooding silence. When we are together she doesn't say I betrayed her, but there is a kind of lost connection between us — perhaps of trust. I didn't, couldn't, protect her from entering the Underworld.

TOP

Bess on the beach while Gordon was overseas.

CENTRE

Bess and Gordon, the outwardly happy, glam couple, in the 1960s.

LEFT

Bess dressed up and about to go out during the war years on her own at Point Chevalier.

I go down to visit her. I dread the lack of privacy. I always used to take her up to her room so we could have tea together and talk in private. When I walk in, I ask, 'Isn't there a family room?' There is. It's not much more than a large cupboard and it has surplus equipment in it, but there are two armchairs. I get Mum in there and we sit down together. I close the door.

Surprisingly, she is quite focused.

'How are you, Pete?'

'How are you getting on?' I counter.

She is mellow today and we manage to make a small picnic of chat. It feels, in the circumstances, like one of those days you unexpectedly go out and find the perfect spot, and the sun comes out, and you feel relaxed as time expands all around you.

I mention various family members and she knows who they are. She maintains eye contact and is philosophical.

'You have a good time,' she says to me when I stand up to go.

(Translation: I have had a good time, why don't you?)

Then she says: 'Look after yourself, Pete.'

(I translate this as: Be wary, I can't look out for you any longer.)

Then she says, just before I go: 'You go and do whatever it is you have to do.'

11 APRIL 2017

'I'm going to die.'

Bess said this five times to the nurse this morning. They tell me this when I come in. I sit with her. She is barely conscious. She is in pain, can't get comfortable. Is nauseous. I sit beside her, and when she becomes conscious of me it is to deliver her verdict, typically plain and straightforward: 'I'm buggered.'

She doesn't even add my name. She has no time for courtesies. Time is running out.

She turns away and tries to sleep.

It's time she is on morphine but we have to wait for the doctor to come to insert the morphine drip. He is busy, and when he arrives he indicates I may not want to stay in the room. I go and sit in the main room.

I listen to the quiz the nurse aide gives to the variously damaged old people sitting in a circle. None of them is in pain or even apparently unhappy. They exist in the tranquil now-time of childhood. It's only their old bodies or rather their brains that have betrayed them. I try not to look at an old Pākehā man — he could have been a builder or a carpenter — who holds a doll in the shape of a baby. He hugs it to his chest.

'What bridge was opened in 1959?'

There is a note of good-tempered belligerence in the nurse aide's voice. She repeats the question at least four times.

BESS IS GIVEN MORPHINE.

We hold hands.

'Owww, your hands are so cold,' she says in the voice of a spoilt little girl. I weep. We keep holding hands. She sinks into a morphine sleep.

I take my hand away when I realise she is in an uncomfortable position. I hear the nurse asking the old people in the lounge if any of them can sing a song. And suddenly a woman's voice, surprisingly melodic, starts singing *Cockles and mussels alive alive oh.*

I find this very emotional. When she sings *She died of a fever / and so no one could save her / and that was the end of sweet Molly Malone,* the nurse aide says loudly, 'Oh we don't want to hear that', but the old woman's voice continues to the end: *Now her ghost wheels her barrow / through the streets broad and narrow / singing cockles and mussels / alive alive oh.*

It seems beautiful to me.

Bess is in her own world now, travelling inwards. I take one or two pictures of her. I don't know quite why I do it, or even if it isn't tasteless. But some other part of me is more basic. Storing up nuts for the coming winter.

I realise I'm exhausted. I've had two terrible nights of sleeplessness in a row. I can't explain what's happening to me. It is as if her soul is being wrenched physically from my body.

Maria, the matron, goes home, saying she will deliver a chair for me to sleep in. It doesn't arrive.

The young doctor comes by, turning the light on. He says, 'Bessie's face still has a good colour. I don't think anything will happen tonight. Of course we don't know.' (He doesn't say the word 'die', which is somehow forbidden — too naked, too real.)

I look at her face in the light and see it is still quite pink. I suddenly feel intensely grateful: I might be able to go home and lie down flat on my bed and sleep. I know her ability to last. And I cannot take another night of sleeplessness. I'm a wreck.

I arrange that they will phone me immediately if there is any change. And as I walk outside I'm aware of the intense sweetness of the living world: plants, grass, sky — all seem miraculously alive, as they seem when you're tripping. Maybe that's what I'm doing. As is she.

12 APRIL 2017

The phone goes at 3.40 a.m. 'Come immediately.'

I get up, dress and drive down there, but can't get into the building. The doors are all locked; nobody answers the phone. I drive around to the closed front door, which has printed directions to go to 'York Wing', but there is no map of where it could be.

I go to the next door, knock on it and wait.

A nurse, passing by, sees me and lets me in.

'My mother Bessie is dying.'

I get into special care where there is a nurse I have never seen before. She is on the phone.

'She's just gone.'

Do I imagine I see a flicker of guilt on her face?

I run into the room and Bess is lying there, so tiny, her mouth wide open, jaw slack. I kneel down by the side of the bed. I find I'm weeping, as if in a separate action which is not related to me. The words I say don't make sense to me. 'Oh Mum, Mum, oh Mummy.' I touch her arm. It is warm. How could I not be there at the final moment? I sit there for a long time, incapable of leaving.

Aggy is in the corridor outside. 'Phew, what's that?' one of the staff says. Aggy says, 'Do you want to see it?' The staff member says, 'Come on, Aggy, we'll go and clean you up.'

Throughout the morning various staff members come into Bess's room to say goodbye. I've draped one of her coloured scarves over her face. It seemed wrong to leave her like that, her mouth gaping open. (Later I read that you are meant to prop a cushion under the dead person's chin, so it stays closed. Why did I not have information like this? Because I never thought I would be in that situation.)

'What a noble woman!' one of the staff says to me after a hug. This pleases me, and seems to resurrect a Bess who was alive in the world. The young nurse who was so kind to Bess and to whom I was rude gives me a fierce hug. 'She was so delightful.' Anabel comes in, and I thank her for looking after Mum so well and for telling me that she was near death not so long ago, so I was better prepared.

I chide myself for not being there. It seems very cruel — I who have watched over her and guarded her to the last moment was not there when she died. I don't know what happened — why I was called only at the very last moment. But I have to accept it.

Later I tell the two women funeral directors about her being only nine days away from her one hundred and first birthday: 'She was tough, she was of pioneer stock.' The funeral director, searching for a suitable cliché, says, 'They don't make them like that anymore.'

LOOKING AT HER FACE IN the funeral parlour, I can't believe it's the last time I will ever see her — the familiar shape of her cheekbones and forehead, her neck and nose and mouth. The space she fills, very particular and unique to herself, will now forever lie vacant — be a blank. This is so obvious, but it has never occurred to me before with such precision, and I linger there as long as I can, just looking, as if to imprint her face on my mind. Accepting I will never see her again is the hardest thing. I kiss her on the brow. She is repellently chilled. Yes, she's dead.

I leave the room.

they had never taken her to Hospital
so sorry. I was too because she has
life. Beryl lives on Colombo Hill. s
books for the shop. Kathleen wan
keep it on but she cannot buy. Be
be able to. It is still a nice shop, bu
the girls are not business like. The
people pull over things & never
Beryl has two children younger tha
her girl is 20. & I think is enga
for the Bridge notes they are intere
Bery is in Hospital with a ba
Bill Popplewell & his wife in tow
sday. Sirett is in Hospital aga
think of Bill's wife's name, sh
they thought Sirett was going to d
George always gets her off
he gets panicky. You reme
it was at times, & they get on
right they would have to send f
She is much better now. She alwa
Hospital. proper food & attention
ks old & rather uncared for. I
cooked rather shabby & a bit di
ways nice. Good catholics have h
ldren & then learn no more.
said Sirett felt seeing Bill
I would go mad with a life
but then I have never been

Afterword

OPPOSITE

An eight-page letter written by Jessie to Bess in 1959: 'It was part of the *bella figura* of letter writing.'

This book is dedicated to my mother, Bessie. I did not understand that I was writing the book to commemorate her life until a few days after she died. Then I had a sense that there had been a hidden pattern behind all this writing of which I was, at the time, completely unaware. It is the final bone I lay at her feet, aware it is not a bone, or tribute, she would want.

'YOU DON'T HAVE TO TELL people that,' I can hear her say. 'You want to be proud of your family, not let other people know all those secrets about us.' But in the end they are not so much secrets about us as mistakes, u-turns, defiant gestures we all falteringly make as we seek to understand the conundrum of life. It seems to me there are many different ways of trying to make sense of what may in the end not make sense.

We're a life form granted the grace of intelligence or consciousness, which also carries its burden of being ill at ease, unhappy, greedy, lustful, all of it underlain by a search for happiness, for balance — for the grace of understanding. I don't know the way. All I know is how to be conscious and to listen and to look and to make my own conclusions, which may yet be completely invalid. But what I can say is I have looked at the evidence — lived the evidence, you might say — and these are my thoughts.

I had been through the long and exhausting experience of caring for someone who was dying. At the same time I recognised that looking after my mother answered a profound human need in me. I had cared for her as I would have cared for a child. In one sense I was just returning the love that she had lavished on me. It was her due. But I was also educated into understanding myself, my own needs, even into a closer understanding of who I was and who she was — this perfectly ordinary woman who, like all humans, once you look at them, was extraordinary in her own particular way. I seemed to see the past in her, partly because, up until she lost her connection with it, the past was so intimate with her. She lived with the past, as indeed I do now.

I saw in her the hardiness of her pioneer background. It was there in her stoicism and also in her essentially democratic point of view — to which was added, like the curlicues of the veranda of a Victorian villa, a filigree of courtesy, and her own brand of kindness and shrewd humour. She was, just as I am, a conduit of all the genetic aspects of her past, yet she was also her own individual exploration of that experience.

I had felt infinitely enriched by knowing her, just as I accepted I was to some extent crippled by her. I had tried to live with a degree of dignity, and deploy the wry sense of humour she used as a weapon against the knocks that life had delivered to her. Her sheer survival was both depleting and enriching.

When I re-read the personal parts of this book, I flinched before the cruelty of my own perceptions, as well as my complex feelings of love and hate. I wondered if I had put enough in this book to signal my deep love for her. In the end I decided that simply my proximity to her — the alertness of my looking after her — signalled what she meant to me. I was also aware, very clearly, that some people would view this as pathetic. Yet if one looks at things with a clear gaze, I see no pathos, only a kind of strength.

I asked myself, too, if it was the ultimate in disloyalty to reveal to the world the last confused moments of her life. At the same time I had to quiz myself: I am a homing pigeon to guilt because of my past. I feel at home there. Yet the fact is that many of my generation have to live with parents or partners with dementia and Alzheimer's, and there is nothing in my experience with Bess which was unique.

But after Bess died, I came to a different understanding of what lay behind her undressing. I think she had a primal sense her life was ending. She was, at the finish, like a tree about to die, dropping its leaves. She was casting off the outer wrapping, undressing as a way as saying goodbye to all that was exterior. Just as when she herself said, 'I am going to die', she was trying to determine her own role in what was happening to her. Control freak to the end, I suppose you could say.

I had tried to guard her and keep her safe and look out for her, and be her advocate. But in the end there is a space in life wherein that fails, necessarily. When you have to stand aside and let nature take its course.

It seems very cruel I was not there with her in the very final moment of her life. But that is how it worked out. It was a strange time for me, as it all happened during the lull and magic of a full moon. Then the day after she died an immense hurricane swept across Hawke's Bay, uprooting trees, lifting roofs, flooding rivers. Her death seemed part of an intensely living world.

We are all mysterious to one another, and if this book has been partly about the obsessiveness of a mother towards her child — and a child towards his mother — about how the past dwells in us as we make it into stories and the stories become us, it is also, I hope, about the enduring power of love.

WHY DID I WRITE THIS BOOK? 'White people don't know their own history,' James Baldwin has asserted, and I believe this is true for Pākehā in Aotearoa New Zealand.[1] Part of this may have to do with a sense of discomfort with the straitened circumstances of so many Pākehā migrants when they crashed into the earth of Aotearoa. There is little sense of heroism there. I would assert, however, there is a kind of quiet heroism in the endurance required in setting up a new life, beginning again in another land. But who would know if we do not know our own stories? Too many have been lost.

Michael King's understanding of the process of loss of memory is key here. The first generation had to work so hard they could not afford the luxury of looking back. Besides, there were painful things there, the curvature of the past as well as that fundamental melancholy which goes with a loss of a cultural homeland. The second generation, energised by a sense of risk and opportunity, was anxious to get on. They weren't interested in looking back. But it was the third generation who began asking questions: Who are we? Why are we here? Where did we come from? By that stage there was usually an eerie silence. The vital links had been lost.

Diaspora marked, one could say savaged, my mother's family as it did most migrant families travelling into the unknown. We are not used to seeing the Pākehā experience investigated in terms of psychological dislocation, yet my argument is that the experiences of migration, and exile, are profound, and this needs to be acknowledged. The commonality of the so-called pioneer experience has allowed us to overlook the extremity of its condition.

I believe the new migrants were subject to unexpressed anxiety — grief at losing their past, the landscapes that had nurtured them, their kinsfolk, everything that was familiar to them. All this had been ripped away. Their exile was voluntary in one sense, but implacable economic and population factors were so extreme they had few other options. And it was these migrants who — to give them a little aura of heroism — stepped out into space.

But then they bumped down into a world formed almost entirely 'other' to their expectations — of language, landscape, culture. The temperatures were different, the way the land was formed was different, where the sun set in the sky was different, and certainly the indigenous people were profoundly different in their tribal structure, the way land was owned, and their cultural and sexual mores. Even their gods were different.

This shock produced an almost endless psychic strain on the migrants' nerves. They had by and large to scratch for a living at the most basic level. There was hardly any infrastructure; they had to build it themselves. Very few migrants brought capital with them. Most had to live in struggle street, often for years — sometimes forever. This combination of constant nervous tension and hard scrabbling day by day, year for year, in unfamiliar surroundings, made for a weirdly taut and strained universe.

I think if you want to put into context some of the very strange decisions made in the colonial period you need to factor in the strain of this anxiety, leading to hair-trigger responses, misdirection and even a kind of spiritual blindness: it was as if the migrants' spiritual compass was severely disturbed or misaligned. They weren't at home. They weren't comfortable in their skins. They were walking in the dark, a little like being in a never-ending McCahon painting, with stark religious warnings daubed in white brush-strokes.

British empiricism and materialism aim to filter out the deeper emotions involved in being human, but they don't stop them being experienced. The extremes of homesickness, and attempts to blot out reality with alcohol, were how this sense of dislocation was expressed — just as it was, more agonisingly and with a greater depth of deprivation, among nineteenth-century Māori. (This might have been why New Zealand was such an unhappy place at the time of the land wars: two cultures experiencing a shock of dislocation, a veritable sink of misery.)

Part of the problem for Pākehā wishing to understand our own history is that we were, until recently, too close to it to get any perspective. From the 1890s we were the dominant cultural group, so lacked self-awareness because 'everybody was the same'. This was in fact an illusion created by residential clustering and in-marriage. There was no looking out because there was not enough space to look back. This numerical dominance is changing, will lessen and then vanish as more cultures pour into New Zealand, and indeed as Māori, Polynesians and others increasingly intermarry with Pākehā. The specifics of our own cultural condition stand out more sharply the further away we get from it, and the closer we are to losing it.

One of the remarkable things about this story is how little intermingling of any sort there appears to have been between my family and Māori. There was no intermarrying at all for at least four generations of direct descent. For one hundred years we kept to our caste, carefully guarding our whiteness as if it were a precious asset, an essential aspect of who we actually were. One can say this is how racism informally works — it's a form of tacit agreement about boundaries and borders over which you do not cross. You keep to your kind, just as the Irish Protestants and Irish Catholics kept to their kind, both fiefdom, fort and prison. The prison gates were there, and in fact were so powerful they did not need a name, or even a physical presence. It was and is a psychological construct, seemingly native but actually a form of learned behaviour. Within the fort or fiefdom, it hardly needed mentioning or addressing.

In the very early 1840s, when Māori were much the stronger and larger group, Pākehā had to rely on and interact with Māori. Many of the very early migrants learnt te reo Māori simply as a survival tactic, much as new migrants now strive to speak English as quickly as possible. Perhaps the fact my ancestors came with an army meant they were part of a more self-sufficient entity, complete to itself, isolated within its own organism. There was something tightly packed about their early existence in Napier, living virtually in the same residential clustering for a century.

After the trauma of the land wars and the ensuing illegal confiscations, Māori by and large withdrew to live rurally. Geography placed us far apart, especially if we were townspeople as the Northe family essentially remained. Cities became, more or less, 'white spaces' right up to the early 1960s. The invisible gates were there and you did not walk past them — or you did so at your peril.

My brother Russell embraced the Māori world when he was a solicitor for the Maori Affairs Department in the 1980s. He learnt te reo and was an advocate for change, working closely with Treaty organisations. He was present and did work at a key hui at Waitangi in 1985 when the Treaty moved from the periphery to become the core document of Aotearoa New Zealand. He also worked with Māori in the Far North: with Tom (Tamihana) Parore, manager of Tai Tokerau Māori Affairs, for example, to end the discharge of sewage into the sea at Opononi. When Russell unobtrusively asked permission to replace a damaged plaque at Tom's marae, Te Houhanga in Dargaville, *'this he arranged without any fuss or ceremony but certainly as we saw it, with love and respect for the marae and we as the whanau belonging to the marae'*.[2] This confluence points to a different energy. At the same time you could say Russell's progress through life was assisted by white privilege. Yet there are plenty of white people with very little privilege. Nancy Eisenberg's *History of White Trash* looks at a persistent class of humans regarded as 'waste' — the poorest white people whose 'whiteness' is not enough to save them from a life of unemployment, illness, imprisonment and addiction. Race alone, or cultural privilege, do not foretell destiny.

Take the two Northe brothers: John Northe, who spent his entire life working hard within the British Army, still working when he was sixty-eight; and Samuel, whose fate as a convict expressed the extremes of white powerlessness. He became a statistic, enduring a living sentence of non-being — 'for the term of his natural life'. Both men started life as 'sacrificial beings' in an industrial wasteland, yet one harnessed the small business practices inherent in being a Cornish miner, while the other took a short cut, broke into a house and ended up with a commuted death sentence.

My great-grandfather Robert Northe's career as a successful coal and wood merchant and contractor seems to imply the genes jumped a generation and that all those skills honed in Cornwall were reactivated in him; he worked in an extractive industry, he was a contractor. Yet his older brother William Henry, attempting the same trick, went bankrupt. Human variation plays its part, even in a life underpinned by white privilege.

IF ANYTHING, MY TALE POINTS to the role of another force in New Zealand society, and one nearly always overshadowed by race: class. You could say the family slowly transformed itself over a century and a half, but once again human variation enters the picture. One branch of the Northe family accelerated, while other parts of the family were relaxed and happy to stay where they were.

The name Renouf occurs several times in this book, notably in the 'To Whom It May Concern' chapter, when Mr A. P. Renouf, JP writes a reference for Bessie in 1936. 'Mrs Renouf' also features pejoratively in Jessie Northe's letter in 'How To Write a Letter', condemned as a chatterer over the bridge table in 1958. (Mrs Renouf was also a 'Balquhidder Belle'.) In 1871, however, sixty years earlier, Josiah Northe, the youngest son of Sergeant John Northe, was fortunate enough to get an apprenticeship with 'the first rate Master Builder by the name of Renouf'. The gap seemed wide. But by 1933 the Renoufs and the Northes (or at least my grandparents Ern and Jessie) were social equals. The women played bridge together, in evening gowns. The men played snooker and crewed on the same yacht.

A parallel change in circumstance can be plotted with the rise and fall of James Rochfort, the engineer who features so fearsomely in the 1870s in 'What's in a Name?' In the 1920s, Bessie could remember peeping in a door and seeing him when she was a child. He had shrunk to a tiny little mannikin lying in a bed. Bessie lived just down the lane from Rochfort. (Ern and Jessie's house was built on a subdivision of the Rochforts' carriage drive, which was sold in 1910 to become Lawrence Road.) Mr Rochfort's second wife, impoverished by the Great Depression, would knock on the door of my grandparents' house, seeking to sell off furniture and paintings in an attempt to keep afloat. Rochfort had ended up marrying his housekeeper. Times change and people's positions in relation to one another change, too.

I could never work out whether my grandmother's obsession with social class was actually a personal tic, like colour blindness or a liking for treacle: was she a snob in a way that the landed wealthy classes themselves were not? It was possible. Perhaps her snobbery was an expression of the ambiguity of her position — a child of upper servants, she married a coal merchant, as my grandfather wrote on his wedding certificate, much to my grandmother's chagrin. (He should have written 'wood merchant'; so much cleaner and more respectable.) Or was it that she was a naturally intelligent woman, of striking looks and energy, who felt misplaced in the position to which a provincial — and colonial — society had confined her? Possibly. Class works in many ways, oppressive as well as aspirational.

Snobbery today seems the most outdated of feelings. Or perhaps we should be a bit more specific here. Snobbery about social class is démodé but really snobbery has just transferred itself to other things — to food origins, the latest technological breakthrough, youth itself. Snobbery will always exist; it is a human impulse to want to demarcate, emulate, admire — and scorn.

Besides, white privilege had its hidden costs. John James Northey's son Samuel — named after his convict great-uncle and cousin of Sidney who had gone to South Africa — went off to the First World War. He was a chemist and he joined an ambulance company. But once overseas, following the macho family tradition, he transferred to the field. He was wounded, sent to a hospital in Egypt, patched up and packed off to

Gallipoli. He fought at Chunuk Bair with the Wellington Infantry, which was reduced in one action from 805 men to eighty survivors. He was not among them. His mother, Jane, who had watched her husband die from arsenic poisoning had now lost her son. Sergeant John Northe lost two grandsons in the First World War.

Yet history also twines around us and pulls us forward. My mother's eldest sister, Jean, became a pharmacist in the 1930s. Was this the long arm of the past reaching into the present and pulling her into the future? Her father's admiration for Samuel, his chemist cousin, can only have been an encouragement for Jean in her choice of a profession, just as her training with the Red Cross allowed her on the day of the quake to stop and help people in the street, bandaging broken limbs, staunching blood, while my grandfather, having different priorities — taking on the survival of the family tribe — went off in search of food. Any family is an intricate mosaic of coincidences, connections, disconnections, random sallies forth into the unknown — and duplications. Yet all in all it makes for a story.

James Baldwin said of Americans that they are 'an incoherent people in an incoherent country', and I believe Pākehā suffer from the same incoherence; we refuse to look back at our own history and try to make sense of it.[3] Shame over illegal land confiscation and fraudulent dealings makes us want to look away. But this isn't the complete story. In one way it is a distortion. The findings of the Waitangi Tribunal have enriched, deepened, and in many cases completely changed our understanding of what our history is. I am not arguing in any way that these findings are not accurate and just. But we are foreseeably nearing a period in which financial compensation and the return of lands are concluded. A different psychological landscape becomes possible, one with a broader view.

What I am calling for is a widening of the lens to look at the complete picture of our history. Since Pākehā have been disrobed of the noble toga of 'pioneer', 'settler' and 'colonist', we have been left singularly naked, stripped of all dignity let alone identity. We are the silhouette without a face, demoted into non-beings — we are simply 'non Māori'. Yet the truth is Aotearoa New Zealand was fundamentally created, for better or for worse, by the interrelationship between Māori and Pākehā over two hundred years of contact. The understandings and misunderstandings of being together have made us who we are — tangata whenua and tangata tiriti. And even with the great faults that are endemic to our unequal system, we can still look around the world and think that what we have arrived at, imperfect as it is, is not such an entirely wretched outcome. The whole point of the Treaty settlement process was to bring us closer together, in forgiveness, acceptance and regret — and my hope is that in future a telling of stories will be wider, and more empathetic to the early European migrants who arrived in Aotearoa New Zealand, and to the journeys that brought them here. The reality is that most Māori have some Pākehā whānau, Pākehā genes: we are here whether we are wanted or not. One might as well be courteous to genealogical interconnectedness and explore the difference in journeys. It may just help us understand one another.

'Nations are built on wishful versions of their origins,' says Hilary Mantel, 'stories in which our forefathers were giants of one kind of another. This is how we live in the world: romancing.'[4] With this book I have made my Pākehā family and ancestors into stories, subjects of a romance in its traditional meaning (lives of love and death). Some stories may be true, some may be my own misunderstanding of stories, but it is an attempt at telling a story about being Pākehā in Aotearoa New Zealand through time.

'Complexity is our only safety,' said Baldwin, a homosexual Afro-American novelist who knew what he was talking about, 'and love is the only key to our maturity.'[5] What I am calling for, in a way, is some more romance, some more imaginative storytelling about the Pākehā past — an understanding of its emotional complexity — and maybe even more, for Pākehā, and Māori, to feel a little aroha.

Acknowledgements

I WOULD LIKE TO THANK the Michael King Writers Centre, which is supported by Creative New Zealand, for a summer residency in 2014 where I developed this project. I would also like to thank the family members who helped me by providing information, photographs, family stories and support. These include Lawrence Northe, who gathered together family photographs at a time when they lay scattered among many different branches of the family; Barrington Northe, who has the biggest collection of Northe family memorabilia; and Val Swailes, who kept tabs on an enormous amount of genealogical information and was always generous in her sharing of knowledge. I am especially grateful to Val's father, Percy Northe, who wrote the initial family tree in the 1950s and established lines of descent and gathered up a few crucial letters.

My cousin Suzanne Blumhardt supplied useful contextual information and memories of a grandfather I never met. Pete Bullivant was very kind in allowing me to use the remarkable photographs his uncle took on the day of the 1931 Hawke's Bay earthquake, immediately after impact. The archives at MTG Hawke's Bay provided a nest for information, and Gail Pope, at that time the archivist, often pointed me in the direction of information relating to the Northes.

I am a Northe by descent through my mother, and carry the surname as my middle name, but I have to thank the wider Northe family for allowing me to delve among the mysteries and sometimes tragedies of the wider family. All the views in the book are of course my own.

This book had a long gestation, and was carried along by my mother's life and then death, but was eased by the constant companionship, empathy and love of my partner, Douglas Lloyd Jenkins. Jane Parkin as editor was a pleasure to work with.

'The past is prologue', as Shakespeare wrote in *The Tempest*, and it is my hope that this glance back sends some glints and gleams into the future.

Image Credits

Images copyright © Peter Wells and the Northe family, except for: page 54 and 55 (top): Pete Bullivant; page 55 (bottom): Hawke's Bay Museums Trust, Ruawharo Tā-ū-rangi, photograph gifted by Mrs Jeanine McKay; page 162 (top): Hawke's Bay Museums Trust, Ruawharo Tā-ū-rangi; page 268 (centre): Archives New Zealand AAOW 22760 W3846 735/115; page 271 (bottom): Hawke's Bay Museums Trust, Ruawharo Tā-ū-rangi, 1978, from the estate of Mr C. D. Cornford; page 283 (bottom): Alexander Turnbull Library, Wellington, 1/2-118691-G.

Notes

RED LETTER DAY

1. James Belich, *Replenishing the Earth: The Settler Revolution and the Rise of the Anglo World, 1783–1939* (Oxford: Oxford University Press, 2009), 62.
2. Richard Holmes, *Footsteps: Explorations of a Romantic Biographer* (London: Vintage, 2001), 198.
3. Anthony Trollope, *Phineas Finn* (London, 1996).

OBSCURE INDIVIDUALS

1. Object #1015380, Donald McLean MS-Papers-0032-0245 1, Alexander Turnbull Library, Wellington.
2. Object #1002202, MS-Papers-0032-0245, Alexander Turnbull Library, Wellington.
3. Alice Woodhouse, *The Naming of Napier* (Napier: Hawke's Bay Art Gallery and Museum, 1970), 5.
4. Peter Wells, *Journey to a Hanging* (Auckland: Vintage, 2014), 165–67.
5. J. B. Annabel, 'Planning Napier 1850–1968', PhD thesis, Massey University, 2012, https://mro.massey.ac.nz/bitstream/handle/10179/3955/02_whole.pdf (accessed 21 July 2017).
6. *Daily Telegraph*, 31 March 1871. Halkett wrote: 'Napier is not usually considered a lively place, even by the few enthusiasts who insist upon regarding Hawke's Bay through rose-coloured spectacles . . . But though dullness reigns supreme in Napier, it does occasionally, like Mrs Dombey, "make an effort" and the effort is generally rewarded with success.'
7. Oliver Sacks, *On the Move: A Life* (London: Picador, 2015), 63.

DEAR OLIVER

1. Joan Didion, 'On Self-Respect: Joan Didion's 1961 essay from the pages of Vogue', *Vogue*, 22 October 2014, www.vogue.com/article/joan-didion-self-respect-essay-1961 (accessed 21 July 2017).
2. The direct descendants of John and Ann Northe, who arrived in New Zealand in 1847, numbered 516 in 1950, so this is a remarkable diminution.
3. Oliver Sacks, *On the Move: A Life* (London: Picador, 2015), 360.
4. Willa Cather, *Not Under Forty* (Lincoln: University of Nebraska Press, 1988).
5. Alan Downs, *The Velvet Rage: Overcoming the Pain of Growing Up Gay in a Straight Man's World* (Philadelphia: Da Capo Press, 2012).
6. Rachel Aviv, 'The Philosopher of Feelings — Martha Nussbaum's Moral Philosophies', *New Yorker*, 25 July 2015, www.newyorker.com/magazine/2016/07/25/martha-nussbaums-moral-philosophies (accessed 21 July 2017).

HOW TO READ A LETTER

1. Janet Malcolm, *The Silent Woman: Sylvia Plath and Ted Hughes* (London and Australia: Picador, 1994), 135.
2. W. E. Murphy, *The 2nd NZ Divisional Artillery* (Wellington: Historical Publications Branch, 1966), 734.
3. Ibid., 739. The official war history of the Medical Corps notes wryly that 'in May–June and July [of 1945] 695 fresh cases of VD were reported, the worst rate experienced during the entire war'. In Tony Simpson, *Ambiguity and Innocence, The New Zealand Division and the Occupation of Trieste May 1945* (Wellington: Silver Owl Press, 2013), 38.
4. Quoted in Joanna Biggs, 'Short Cuts', *London Review of Books*, 6 October 2016, 26.
5. Doug Flett, service number 23123, Lance Sergeant, 24 Infantry Battalion. Died 10 August 2006. Born 29 March 1917.
6. Bess and Gordon had come to live in Point Chevalier through a form of chain migration. Gordon had been engaged to Nora, a young woman from Thames where Gordon grew up. The engagement did not work out, but when Nora (as mentioned in the letter) and her mother came to live in Point Chevalier, near the beach, Gordon and Bess followed.
7. Murphy, *The 2nd NZ Divisonal Artillery*, 736.
8. 'Medical Man's Advice: The Ex-Soldier's Home Life', *Evening Post*, 29 October 1945. 'It is found on a man's return that his standard of values has altered. After he has lived "in big business" most jobs appear petty and trifling and not worthwhile, and with restlessness and lack of concentration added, it became difficult to stay the course.'

THE COMING OUT LETTER

1. The letter is dated 11 June 1975.
2. The letter is dated June 1976.
3. The letter is dated 31 January 1976.

4   My first piece of published fiction came out in *Islands* 5, no. 4 (Summer 1976). *Islands* was edited by Robin Dudding, and the piece was 'Five Political Memories: Made in New Zealand'.
5   'It was not until the late 1980s and 1990s that scholars recognised a need for study in the field of sexuality.' www.wikipedia.org/wiki/gender-studies (accessed 2 September 2017).
6   NZ Defence Force 2nd NZ Divisional Artillery, NZDF Personnel Archives and Medals, copy of Records for Gordon Ladner Wells Service #472930.
7   Matt Trueman, 'How Taking Flight in London Helped "Angels in America" Soar', *New York Times*, 7 May 2017, Theatre Section, AR 14.
8   A. N. Wilson, *The Victorians* (London: Random House, 2005), 21.
9   Deborah Lutz, *The Brontë Cabinet: Three Lives in Nine Objects* (New York: W. W. Norton & Co., 2015), 127.
10 Rosemary Hill, 'Preface, Unicorn', *London Review of Books*, 3 November 2016, 127.

TO WHOM IT MAY CONCERN

1   Early duplication of typed material used a purple carbon paper, pigmented with ink and coated with wax. This was the only way to copy typed material before the invention of the Xerox. The carbon paper was placed under a blank sheet and carefully aligned. It was a messy and time-consuming process.
2   I found a handwritten note among Bess's papers in which she listed the stations as 'Bluff Station & another at Te Pohue & possibly more'.
3   In Bess's note she wrote that Mr A. E. Renouf was known as 'Granny Renouf', a reference to his predilection for playing 'dame' roles in local dramatic productions, a harmless form of crossdressing.
4   Dorothy Page, 'Thompson, Marion Beatrice', first published in the *Dictionary of New Zealand Biography*, Vol. 3, 1996. Te Ara — the Encyclopedia of New Zealand, https://teara.govt.nz/en/biographies/3t31/thompson-marion-beatrice (accessed 21 July 2017).
5   Ibid.
6   Anne Tregurtha, *Remembrance of Things Past: Solway College Golden Jubilee* (Masterton: Solway College, 1966), 121.
7   A letter Bess kept from Mrs T traverses the fracture line in her marriage. On 16 April 1942, with Gordon called up, Mrs T wrote: 'I am so sorry to hear that the war has broken up your home . . . Your Father & Mother will be so glad to have you in Napier.' The letter was addressed to 'Mrs Gordon Wells, Lawrence Road, Napier'. But the envelope has been re-addressed on 12 August 1942 to '512 Point Chevalier Road, Auckland'. Bessie had returned to her flat. When Mrs T commented, 'We have been given very clearly the rules to live by in God's word', she was marking the dividing line between a teetotalling Presbyterian of high principles and a young woman who now enjoyed a drink and was about to savour her freedom.

HOW TO WRITE A LETTER

1   'How to Write a Letter', www.google.co.nz/webhp?sourceid=chrome-

instant&ion=1&espv=2&ie=UTF-8#q=how+to+write+a+letter&* (accessed 19 July 2017).
2   'A Member of the Aristocracy', *Manners and Rules of Good Society — Or Solecisms to be Avoided*, 43rd edition (London: Frederick Warne & Co. Ltd, 1922).
3   Ibid., 25.
4   I found the Sheaffer fountain pen given as a gift from her parents among Bess's possessions after her death. It was in its original presentation box and included the 'Directions for Using Self-Filling Type Swan Pens'. On the front she had written 'Bessie P Northe, Lawrence Rd' in unformed handwriting. Along the back she had written a man's name and address, 'Frank Fordham, 11 Cliff Street, Wgt.'
5   The family all had pet names. W. E. Northe, Bess's father, was always called 'Ern', but his pet name was 'Cook'. (He was cook on the *Seabird*, a yacht he had as a young man.) Jessie Northe was called 'Mrs Kutz', the derivation of which I no longer know. There is an idea it related to a film character. Jean Northe, the eldest daughter, was called 'Bill', Patti was 'Little Patti', and Bess was 'Chick' or 'Chicken', a small fluffy bird to be adored. Pet names seemed part of the texture of a close affectionate family.
6   Cousin Suzanne Blumhardt writes: 'One protection for Grandma in case of a diabetic event was that [her sister-in-law] Doris [Northe, née Northey], living next door, could see the big sash window in the kitchen from her house. If the blind on this window did not go up at the usual time each morning, Doris was to check.' It was a small and interwoven world geographically and in familial terms. Email from Suzanne Blumhardt, 26 May 2016.
7   In a letter written from Napier Hospital towards the end of her life, Jessie commented she was near the room 'where Dad died'.
8   Jessie was known as 'The Duchess' to the workmen of R. Northe & Sons. It was not a fond attribution.
9   Sectarianism was alive and well in 1950s New Zealand. When Walter Foot, Jessie's Catholic son-in-law, died of a heart attack, his and Patti's baby daughter, Geraldine, became a focus for religious tensions, though she was only six weeks old. Suzanne Blumhardt writes: 'After Walter died, Patti [his wife] travelled to Auckland with Geraldine in the company of Pat Foot [an uncle on the Catholic side] and others. I was told that Pat's mission on that trip was to persuade [Patti] to bring Geraldine up as a Catholic — hence your mother's [Bess's] hurried arrangement of the christening [in the Point Chevalier Anglican church].' It was a Protestant triumph. Bessie felt that she had been fighting for Geraldine's very soul. Suzanne noted: 'I can remember nuns coming to the house in Lyall Bay [where Walter and Patti lived] to see Geraldine soon after Walter died.' They were just as intent on recruiting Geraldine to what Bess always called, pejoratively, Roman Catholicism, inferring its foreign status as against the English church.
10 Nancy Eisenberg, *White Trash: The 400-Year Untold History of Class in America* (New York: Penguin Random House, 2016), 1.
11 Mrs Renouf was the wife of A. P. Renouf, who supplied the testimonial, and a 'Balquhidder Belle' (that is, a friend), but, as was common at the time, the women called each other by their surnames, never by their Christian names. This would have been regarded as overly familiar.

12 Karl Knausgaard, *My Struggle, Book 2: A Man in Love*, translated from the Norwegian by Don Bartlett (New York: Farrar, Strauss & Giroux, 2014), 17.

THE BUSINESS LETTER

1 Less than 15 per cent of New Zealand children went on to secondary school in 1900, so Ern was an exception, even within his family. His younger brother, Robert Percy Northe, also went to Napier Boys' High. It is possible that going to Napier Boys' High School gave Ern a wider range of professional acquaintances than his other brothers had, as well as a better general education. This may have given him a sense of the wider opportunities available. 'History of Education in New Zealand', https://en.wikipedia.org/wiki/History_of_education_in_New_Zealand (accessed 9 August 2017).

2 Information from my cousin Philippa Larkindale, followed up in an email of 26 May 2016 from her sister Suzanne Blumhardt, the eldest grandchild and the only one to remember Ern. Suzanne wrote: 'Grandpa was a qualified plumber.' Suzanne is affectionately referred to as 'Tuppence' in a letter in this chapter.

3 When sorting through her papers, I found that Bess had written down the costs of the first house. The house at 517 Point Chevalier Road was purchased on 16 December 1948 for £1016. Commission was £35. Mortgage stamp duty was £6 1s. Solicitor £20 3s. Paint £3 10s; cupboards £25; hot-water electric system £22 10s; plus £31 other set-up costs. The interest rate on £500 was 2.5 per cent, to her father, Ern. The detail is typical of Bess who was described by Janet Coombes, a Solway old girl and friend, as 'one canny customer'.

4 Dior had debuted his New Look Collection in February 1947, and its sumptuous use of material heralded the end of wartime restrictions. Its excesses became a source of popular commentary and humour.

5 Suzanne Blumhardt, in an email 26 May 2016, wrote: 'He smoked roll-your-owns of a dark and tarry brand of tobacco called Tasman Dark. It came in tall cylindrical green tins, I remember.'

6 Ibid. She wrote: 'Grandpa mowed the very steep bank in front of the house by letting the mower down on a rope . . . I remember Mum being worried about him doing the lawns when he was so ill.' By this time Ern was in his late seventies.

7 Ibid. 'Part of his insistence on still riding a bike,' Suzanne writes, 'was so that he could stop and talk to people he saw on the way. You couldn't do that in a car, he said. Besides this attachment to old ways, he had very conservative taste in clothes and always wore navy blue socks of a certain type which became increasingly difficult to find, and navy ties with white spots.' Another reason he did not buy a car was that feared he would 'never see his wife again', as she would be out playing bridge all day and night. It is possible the indulgent widow I knew was the reaction of a wife kept on a tight leash all her life by her budget-conscious husband.

POLLY

1 It was probably a point of pride that Ern Northe, Polly's son, had enough money for his wife, Jessie, to employ a laundress, an Irish woman, Mrs Audrey. By such

small steps do we demarcate social and economic changes. In a similar way, Ern gave Jessie a house as a gift after she had her first child, Jean. This would ensure that Jessie had her own 'pin money'. In this way Jessie also became a rentier.
2 James Belich, *Replenishing the Earth: The Settler Revolution and the Rise of the Anglo World, 1783–1939* (Oxford: Oxford University Press, 2009), 62.
3 *Daily Telegraph*, 12 January 1871.
4 By 1886 most Pākehā were born in Aotearoa New Zealand, so a tipping point had been reached. It was no longer a country dominated by foreign-born migrants, although Britain was still called 'Home', with a capital 'H' to signify its emotional importance. https://nzhistory.govt.nz/culture/history-of-new-zealand-1769-1914 (accessed 10 August 2017).
5 *Hawke's Bay Herald*, 29 January 1879.
6 *Daily Telegraph*, 2 February 1891. The Union Rowing Club's Trial Fours took place on the inner harbour, 'the weather being perfect, and the water beautifully smooth'. R. Northe's crew kept up 'a slashing pace'.
7 Belich, *Replenishing the Earth*, 553.
8 *Daily Telegraph*, 25 March 1911. A further obituary in the *Hawke's Bay Tribune* on the same date noted 'Nobody in Napier knew as much about the town.' The Harbour Board League meeting stood for a minute in silence and a wreath was 'forwarded on behalf of the League'. Polly remained unnamed and unacknowledged.
9 http://archives.govt.nz/womens-suffrage-petition (accessed 5 SEptember 2017).

WHAT'S IN A NAME?

1 Hawke's Bay Superintendent's Local Inwards Letters, 1871, 69/300-112/71/2, Archives New Zealand.
2 'Loss of the SS Star of the South', *Hawke's Bay Herald*, 28 June 1870.
3 *Daily Telegraph*, 4 April 1871.
4 *Hawke's Bay Herald*, 29 December 1871.
5 New Zealand had been broken into six separate provinces by Governor Grey in 1853, with Hawke's Bay as part of the Wellington Province. 'Although it formed a distinct geographic region bounded on the north by the 39th parallel, on the west by the ranges and on the south by the Seventy Mile Bush, it had insufficient settlers to qualify as a separate province' (*Picture of a Province* [Hawke's Bay Provincial Centennial Council, 1958, 11]). As Hawke's Bay became more populated, there was a feeling the province was contributing too much to Wellington's revenues without getting equivalent value. Effectively, Wellington loans were being raised on Hawke's Bay land, with little financial benefit to the region. In 1858, the central government of E. W. Stafford was petitioned by 317 Hawke's Bay residents, and Hawke's Bay was granted local self-government. The foundation of the province was celebrated, in typical colonial style, by two days' racing, a public dinner, and a ball. (Ibid., 13.)
6 In the 1850s it is calculated that 75 per cent of European migrants could read and write, which seems extraordinarily high. Only 17 per cent could read but not write. 'History of Education in New Zealand', https://en.wikipedia.org/wiki/History_of_education_in_New_Zealand (accessed 9 August 2017).

7   Richard Halkett Lord was a sophisticated Londoner, who commented 'that snobs are sure to abound' in a society in which 'money is admired above all' (*Daily Telegraph*, 10 March 1871). His newspaper commentaries revelled in exposing the hypocrisy and social shortcomings of both Napierites and Hawke's Bay's self-created aristocracy. In the end he was hounded out of Hawke's Bay, attacked with a whip by a solicitor at a social event.
8   *Daily Telegraph*, 12 May 1871.
9   The Maggy Northey referred to in my grandfather Ern's 1946 letter as dying in the back seat of 'Jack's' car was the wife of Jack Northey, John James's son, who carried on the shipwright business after his father's death. This business lasted until the 1960s. The present shipwright business on Westshore is a continuation, under different ownership, of John James's original enterprise.
10 Adam Gopnik, 'Are Liberals on the Wrong Side of History?', *New Yorker*, 20 March 2017, 90.
11 *Hawke's Bay Herald*, 8 July 1880.
12 Ibid.
13 *Hawke's Bay Herald*, 1 April 1880.
14 *Daily Telegraph*, 15 April 1871.
15 *Hawke's Bay Herald*, 30 June 1900. 'Harbor Board Bungling' is the heading for the letter.
16 *Hawke's Bay Herald*, 16 May 1903.
17 *Daily Telegraph*, 28 September 1894.
18 *Daily Southern Cross*, 12 February 1863.
19 Ariel Levy, 'Elizabeth Strout's Long Homecoming', *New Yorker*, 1 May 2017, www.newyorker.com/magazine/2017/05/01/elizabeth-strouts-long-homecoming (accessed 5 September 2017).
20 *Hawke's Bay Herald*, 17 May 1904.
21 Ibid.

LOCAL HERO

1   Alice St Clair Inglis, *Souvenir Album of the First New Zealand Contingent for South Africa 1899–1901* (Waipawa: 1902), 31.
2   Pai Mārire was a millennial sect with beliefs which have been reframed today as a liberationist theology. They rejected the European version of Christianity and invented a religion that was partly Old Testament and partly a composite of ancient Māori beliefs. Pai Mārire started out as peaceful but quickly became associated, in Pākehā minds, with violence. Its followers were seen as reverting to pre-colonial cannibalism, provoking intense anxiety among Pākehā migrants. In a larger sense, it was a form of resistance to colonisation.
3   Thomas Wayth Gudgeon, 'An Alphabetic List of Volunteers and Militia men who received the New Zealand Medal having been either under fire, or attached to Her Majesty's Imperial Forces, during the War of 1860–1870', in *The Defenders of New Zealand — Being a Short Biography of Colonists Who Distinguished Themselves in Upholding Her Majesty's Supremacy in These Islands* (Auckland: Henry Brett, 1886), xxiii.

4   Michael King, *Being Pakeha Now: Reflections and Recollections of a White Native* (Auckland: Penguin, 1999), 69, 70.
5   Ian McGibbon and John Crawford, *One Flag, One Queen, One Tongue: New Zealand and the South African War* (Auckland: Auckland University Press, 2003), 124.
6   The poem by G. P. W. was anonymous and one of many penned in New Zealand at this time. It appears in St Clair Inglis, *Souvenir Album*, 5.
7   Ibid.
8   The other two Hawke's Bay men called up were Sergeant G. Holroyd and Private J. Catherall, also Hastings Rifle Volunteers. They were photographed together with Sidney Northe as 'Volunteers for the Transvaal War'.
9   *Hawke's Bay Herald*, 21 January 1895.
10   *Daily Telegraph*, 13 September 1895.
11   St Clair Inglis, *Souvenir Album*, 3.
12   *Evening Post*, 7 February 1900.
13   Thomas Craig Wallace, typescript memoir 'Military Career', Alexander Turnbull Library.
14   David M. Anderson and David Killingray (eds), *Policing the Empire: Government, Authority and Control, 1830–1940* (Manchester: Manchester University Press, 1991), 168.
15   Ibid.
16   *Evening Post*, 13 December 1900.
17   Sergeant G. Holroyd, one of the original three volunteers, had remained in Sydney and came back later in a different boat. In the end he went to live in England. Catherall had had a much more troubled war than Sid Northe: he had been taken prisoner by the Boers, at Sanna's Post, taken to Pretoria, and released only when General Roberts entered the city.
18   General Sir Andrew Russell was born in Napier, educated at Sandhurst and was a member of the Hawke's Bay gentry. He led New Zealand forces in the First World War, managing a textbook evacuation of Gallipoli by night without a single loss of life. His war ended with a brilliant attack on Le Quesnoy, France, in which he managed to take the German-occupied town by surprise. After the war he was instrumental in setting up the RSA. His favourite son, John, died in Libya in 1942, and Russell continued writing fortnightly letters to him. Letter writing was how he expressed his grief, a form of long goodbye. This expresses the strange power implicit in letter writing.
19   Maddison had nothing to do with the Anglo–Boer War and his name cannot be found among the ten contingents Hawke's Bay provided. Possibly he was a member of the Hastings Rifle Volunteers and a friend.
20   *Daily Telegraph*, 29 December 1900.
21   *Evening Post*, 13 December 1900.
22   *Otago Witness*, 9 April 1902.
23   Edmund Wilson (ed.), *Notebooks of Scott Fitzgerald*, Notebook L, 1945, https://en.wikiquote.org/wiki/F._Scott_Fitzgerald (accessed 10 August 2017).

DEAR HEROIX

1. Edward Said, *Reflections on Exile and Other Essays* (Cambridge, Mass.: Harvard University Press, 2000). Quoted in James Wood, 'On Not Going Home', *London Review of Books*, 20 February 2014, 3.
2. James Belich, *Replenishing the Earth: The Settler Revolution and the Rise of the Anglo World, 1783–1939* (Oxford: Oxford University Press, 2009), 21.
3. Said, in Wood, 'On Not Going Home', 3.
4. Naomi Klein, 'Let Them Drown', *London Review of Books*, 2 June 2016, 12.
5. Rollo Arnold, *The Farthest Promised Land: English Villagers, New Zealand Immigrants of the 1870s* (Wellington: Victoria University Press, 1981), 214.
6. Klein, 'Let Them Drown'.
7. The Cornwall Industrial Settlements Initiative Report (Chacewater), http://www.historic-cornwall.org.uk/cisi/chacewater/CISI_chacewater_report%20.pdf (accessed 21 July 2017).
8. Just how small-scale Sergeant John Northe's 'prosperity' was can be seen if it is compared with Charles Dickens' wages as a law clerk in the same period. Dickens as a fifteen-year-old started on 10s 6d a week, whereas John Northe as thirty-five-year-old was earning 7s, though this 7s also included his food and his 'lodgings', i.e. the barracks he lived in. It was still a very small wage. By 1838 he also obtained an additional pension, raising his weekly wage to 10s.
9. Charles Junior Dickens, *Dickens' Dictionary of London, An Unconventional Handbook* (London: Charles Dickens & Evans, 1879), 274.
10. Charles Booth conducted and published a survey of London's poverty on a street-by-street basis. He also founded the Salvation Army. 'Charles Booth Inquiry into Life and Labour in London, 1886–1903', https://booth.lse.ac.uk/learn-more/what-was-the-inquiry (accessed 21 July 2017).
11. When Darcy was told that the Bennets' daughters had relations who lived in Cheapside, he replied, 'But it must very materially lessen their chance of marrying men of any consideration in the world.' (Jane Austen, *Pride and Prejudice* [London: Vintage, 2007], 33.)
12. Siobhan Phillips, 'Should We Feel Sad about the Demise of the Handwritten Letter?', https://aeon.co/ideas/should-you-feel-sad-about-the-demise-of-the-handwritten-letter (accessed 21 July 2017).
13. De Tocqueville, in a speech delivered on 29 January 1848, said, 'I am told there is no danger because there are no riots . . . Gentlemen, permit me to say you are mistaken.' ('Gale of Revolution in the Air', www.speeches-usa.com/Transcripts/alexis_deTocqueville-gale.html [accessed 31 August 2017].)
14. Looking through a photograph album of my cousin Lawrence Northe, I spied a Victorian photograph of a watercolour. The watercolour, similar in style and level of competence to the one of Elizabeth Ereaux, is of a young pretty woman, within an oval. I believe this to be one of the missing watercolours, possibly photographed to share around the family.

SILENCE LIKE A BRUISE

1. David Andrew Roberts, '"A Sort of Inland Norfolk Island?": Isolation, Coercion

  and Resistance on the Wellington Valley Convict Station 1823–26', *Journal of Australian Colonial History* 2, no. 1 (April 2000), 55.
2 Ibid.
3 State Archives NSW; Series; NRS 12202; Item: (4/4097), Reel 922.
4 Convict Registers of Conditional and Absolute Pardons, 1788–1870, State Archives NSW, Australia, 1850, Reel 794, A/s1818 CP 50/625.
5 NSW Colonial Secretary Letters Relating to Moreton Bay and Queensland 1822–1860, 31/04386, A2.6, 081-084.
6 NSW Colonial Secretary Letters Relating to Moreton Bay and Queensland 1822–1860, 31/04386, A2.6, 077-079.
7 Robert Percy Northe (1896–1961) was one of the three younger brothers my grandfather Ern pushed out of the family firm into white-collar work. He and his brother Gordon worked for the Guardian Assurance. (R. Northe & Sons was, incidentally, an agent for Guardian Assurance: it was a close and interconnected world.) Percy, as he was known, enlisted in the army on 8 January 1916. He won the Military Medal for 'exceptional gallantry' at La Basse-Ville in Belgium. On returning to Napier the handsome young hero became secretary to the Napier Hospital Board, a position he kept for the rest of his life. (The head of the board had been in the same unit.) In the 1950s he wrote to all existing Northe relatives, asking for information. He located the four letters from 'John and Ann Northe', plus the two letters from Elizabeth Ereaux, which form the basis for this part of the book.
8 Will of John Northe, AAOW W3864 22760, Box 735, A, Archives New Zealand. Cotterill, Solicitor of the Supreme Court of New Zealand, noted that 'this affidavit was read and explained by myself to the deponent [Ann Northe] and that the deponent appeared perfectly to understand the same and that made her mark therefore in my presence'.
9 Nancy's brother Thomas accompanied the celebrated botanist, Alan Cunningham, on an 1823 exploration in which Cunningham discovered 'the great route of communication between Bathurst and Hunter River and the Liverpool Plains'. Cunningham's accounts of these two journeys from Bathurst, 'A Specimen of the Indigenous Botany . . . between Port Jackson and Bathurst', and 'Journal of a Route from Bathurst to Liverpool Plains', were published in Barron Field (ed.), *Geographical Memoirs on New South Wales; by Various Hands* (London: John Murray, 1825); *The Australian Dictionary of Biography*, http://adb.anu.edu.au/biography/cunningham-allan-1941 (accessed 14 August 2017).
10 Form 11, No. of application 45905/51. No. 597. Vol. 75, Registrar General Office of New South Wales., State Archives & Records of the NSW Government, NRS 12937, Reels 5001-5048.
11 *Cartes de visites* of Eliza Green and Mary O'Donnell, housemaid to Governor Darling, show them stylishly dressed in a showy Australian fashion. Mary may be wearing a cast-off from Lady Darling, as her dress is both rich and exceedingly fashionable.
12 Correspondence of William Colenso, MS-Copy-Micro-0485-4, Alexander Turnbull Library. 'We have still more of sickness and death than we could wish,' Colenso wrote to his friend, the land agent Andrew Luff.

13　Correspondence of William Colenso, MS-Copy-Micro-0485-4. Her death notice in the *Daily Telegraph* on 11 July 1890 noted Nancy died after 'a painful illness'.
14　Hilary Mantel, 'Why I Became a Historical Novelist', Reith Lecture, *The Guardian*, 3 June 2017, www.theguardian.com/books/2017/jun/03/hilary-mantel-why-i-became-a-historical-novelist (accessed 21 July 2017).
15　*Daily Southern Cross*, 26 January 1875. It is possible his death notice was in an Auckland newspaper because his army acquaintances would be scattered across the North Island. There was no death notice in Hawke's Bay newspapers.
16　It's noteworthy that John Northe never voted, even though he seems to have been politically conscious and interested in contemporary affairs. In 1853 the prerequisite for voting in New Zealand was that you owned land worth £50. His individual piece of land was worth £30, though as we have seen he spent £60 on land overall.
17　William Colenso to Mantell, 24 October 1870. Correspondence of William Colenso, MS-Copy-Micro-0485-4.
18　Ibid.
19　'Hauhau' or 'Houhou' was a generic name given by Pākehā to Māori religious movements of many different kinds. Based on an opposition to British colonisation, one version was Pai Mārire which originated in Taranaki and spread to the Bay of Plenty and Gisborne before finally coming to Napier in 1866. Another version was led by Te Kooti Arikirangi who, exiled to the Chatham Islands, saw Gabriel in a vision and set up what has been described as a liberationist theology, whose followers also practised guerrilla warfare against their Pākehā and Māori enemies. This often meant surprise attacks.
20　James Cowan, *The New Zealand Wars: A History of the Maori Campaigns and the Pioneering Period: Volume II: The Hauhau Wars (1864–72)* (Chapter 31: 'Te Kooti's Attack on Mohaka'), www.nzetc.victoria.ac.nz/tm/scholarly/tei-Cow02NewZ-c31.html (accessed 21 July 2017).
21　Judith Binney, *Redemption Songs: A Life of Te Kooti Arikirangi Te Turuki* (Wellington and Auckland: Bridget Williams Books and Auckland University Press, 1995), 161.
22　Ibid.
23　An 'old Drom boy' referred to the British troops who rode dromedaries in the Middle Eastern and Indian parts of the Empire. It seems to imply old-fashioned, stuck in old ways.
24　Waitangi Tribunal, 'The Mohaka ki Ahuriri Report' (Wellington: Waitangi Tribunal, 2004), 174, https://forms.justice.govt.nz/search/Documents/WT/wt_DOC_68598011/Wai201.pdf (accessed 5 September 2017); Hinuera Deed of Settlement 2014, http://ngatihineuru.com/wp-content/uploads/2014/08/Hineuru-Deed-of-Settlement-for-initialling.DOCX.pdf (accessed 5 September 2017).
25　Ibid., 174–76.
26　The above report posits the view that McLean was an evil man and Pai Mārire innocents walking into a trap. Whether human nature is more complicated than this, I leave up to the reader.
27　The parallel to the Vietnam War is notable — there too a highly mobile indigenous force was arrayed against an army, loaded down with heavy equipment, which could move only with laborious slowness.

28 *Hawke's Bay Herald*, 20 April 1869.
29 Cowan, *The New Zealand Wars, Volume II*, Chapter 31.
30 Ibid.
31 Edward Said, *Reflections on Exile and Other Essays* (Cambridge, Mass.: Harvard University Press, 2000). Quoted in James Wood, 'On Not Going Home', *London Review of Books*, 20 February 2014, 3.
32 Mantel, 'Why I Became a Historical Novelist'.

THE FAILURE OF LANGUAGE

1 Alain de Botton, *How Proust Can Change Your Life* (New York: Vintage International, 1997), 56. Botton quotes Proust as saying: 'My mother wanted to live in order not to leave me in a state of anguish which she knew I was in without her . . . . all of our life had been simply a training, she for teaching me how to do without her the day she would leave me . . .'
2 Roland Barthes, *Mourning Diary,* translated by Richard Howard (New York: Hill & Wang, 2009), 4.

AFTERWORD

1 James Baldwin, 'Letter from a Region in My Mind', *New Yorker*, 17 November 1962, http://www.newyorker.com/magazine/1962/11/17/letter-from-a-region-in-my-mind (accessed 31 August 2017).
2 Letter sent to me in fax form, 24 September 1999, from Tom (Tamihana) Parore, QSO, manager of Tai Tokerau Māori Affairs. Ten years after Russell's death I organised a dinner to celebrate his life. Tom and his wife, Eileen, attended, and Tom spoke of his admiration for Russell as 'kind, considerate, immensely able and dedicated to improving the status of Maori as well as other New Zealanders'. He described Russell as 'a legend that will never be forgotten'. The accompanying photo shows the plaque which Russell organised for Te Houhanga marae. Almost symbolically, Russell, who would die a few years later, is missing from the photograph.
3 Ed Pavlic, 'Come On Up, Sweetheart, James Baldwin's Letters to His Brother', http://kalamu.com/neogriot/2017/08/16/history-james-baldwins-letters-to-his-brother/ (accessed 31 August 2017). In this essay, which first appeared in the *Boston Review*, Pavlic quotes Baldwin saying that beneath white America's 'conqueror image' lie 'a great many unadmitted despairs and confusions, and anguish and unadmitted crimes and failures'.
4 Hilary Mantel, 'Why I Became a Historical Novelist', Reith Lecture, *The Guardian*, 3 June 2017, www.theguardian.com/books/2017/jun/03/hilary-mantel-why-i-became-a-historical-novelist (accessed 21 July 2017).
5 Pavlic, 'Come On Up, Sweetheart'. The quotation used in this essay is actually from Baldwin's last published essay, 'To Crush the Serpent' (1987). The final line is 'And love is where you find it.'

About the Author

PETER WELLS IS A WRITER of fiction and non-fiction, and a writer/director in film. His fiction looks at a world of secrets, identity, subterfuge and illusion, frequently using the lens of a gay narrator. His first book, *Dangerous Desires*, won the Reed Fiction Award, the NZ Book Award, and PEN Best New Book in Prose in 1992. His memoir *Long Loop Home* won the 2002 Montana New Zealand Book Award for Biography, and he has won many awards for his work as a film director. He is co-founder of the Auckland Writers Festival. In 2006, Wells was made a Member of the New Zealand Order of Merit for services to literature and film. His most recent histories examined William Colenso, a resident of Napier, and Kereopa Te Rau, the Pai Mārire follower who was hanged in Napier for murdering Reverend Carl Völkner. *Dear Oliver* brings to an end this Napier trilogy.

Northe family tree

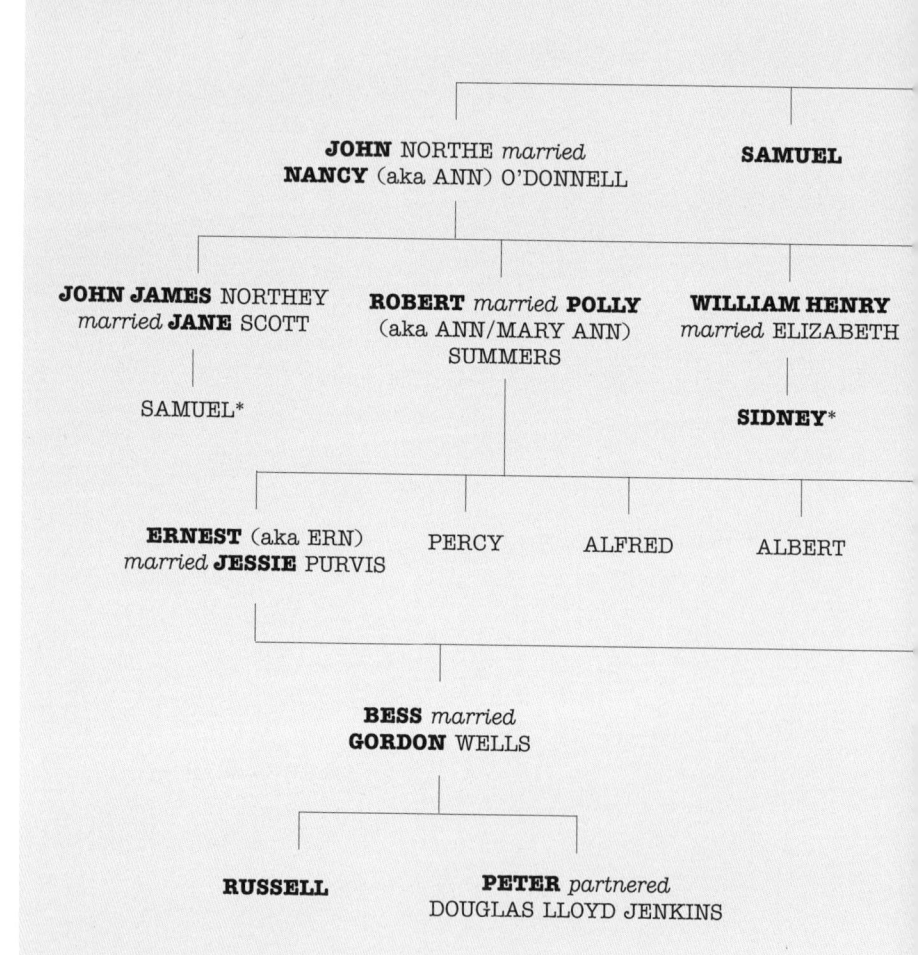

JOHN NORTHE *married* **NANCY** (aka ANN) O'DONNELL — **SAMUEL**

- **JOHN JAMES** NORTHEY *married* **JANE** SCOTT
  - SAMUEL*
- **ROBERT** *married* **POLLY** (aka ANN/MARY ANN) SUMMERS
  - **ERNEST** (aka ERN) *married* **JESSIE** PURVIS
    - **BESS** *married* **GORDON** WELLS
      - **RUSSELL**
      - **PETER** *partnered* DOUGLAS LLOYD JENKINS
  - PERCY
  - ALFRED
  - ALBERT
- **WILLIAM HENRY** *married* ELIZABETH
  - **SIDNEY***

* Not all children are listed
Names in **bold** are mentioned in this book

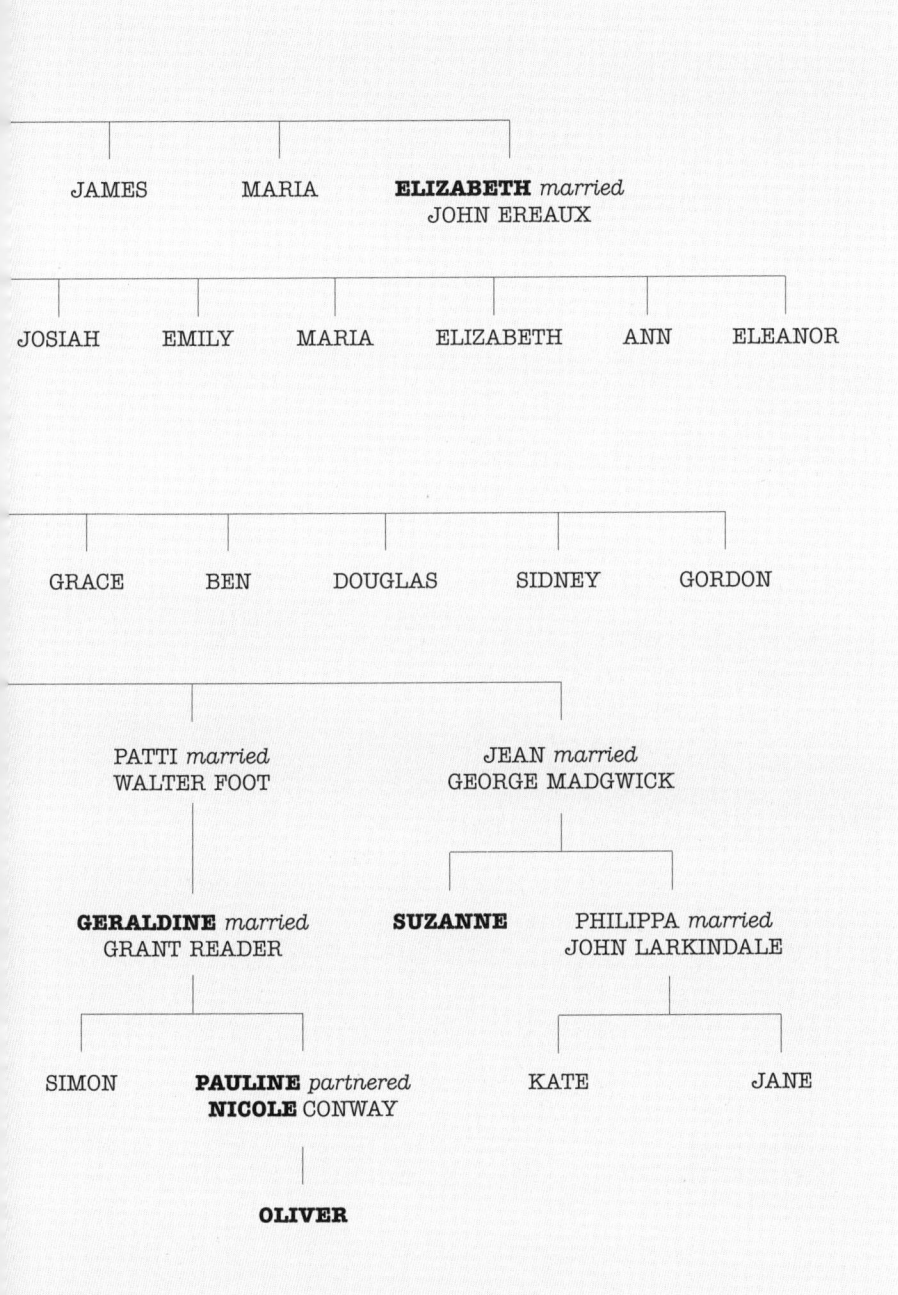

```
                    JAMES        MARIA      ELIZABETH married
                                            JOHN EREAUX

JOSIAH    EMILY    MARIA    ELIZABETH    ANN    ELEANOR


    GRACE      BEN      DOUGLAS      SIDNEY      GORDON


        PATTI married              JEAN married
        WALTER FOOT                GEORGE MADGWICK


        GERALDINE married      SUZANNE    PHILIPPA married
        GRANT READER                      JOHN LARKINDALE

SIMON    PAULINE partnered                KATE        JANE
         NICOLE CONWAY

              OLIVER
```

MASSEY
UNIVERSITY
PRESS

First published in 2018 by Massey University Press
Private Bag 102904, North Shore Mail Centre
Auckland 0745, New Zealand
www.masseypress.ac.nz

Text copyright © Peter Wells, 2018
Images copyright © as credited page 321

Cover image: Peter Wells, his mother Bess and grandmother Jessie at Auckland Airport in the late 1960s. Back cover image: A letter from Richard Mercer to Jessie Northe, written in the 1890s.

Design by Kate Barraclough

The moral right of the author has been asserted

All rights reserved. Except as provided by the Copyright Act 1994, no part of this book may be reproduced, stored in or introduced into a retrieval system or transmitted in any form or by any means (electronic, mechanical, photocopying, recording or otherwise) without the prior written permission of both the copyright owner(s) and the publisher.

A catalogue record for this book is available from the National Library of New Zealand

Printed and bound in China by 1010 Printing International Limited

ISBN: 978-0-9941473-6-3
eISBN: 978-0-9941473-7-0

The assistance of Creative New Zealand is gratefully acknowledged by the publisher

creative nz
ARTS COUNCIL OF NEW ZEALAND TOI AOTEAROA